Rethinking Dance History

From the *ballets de cours* of the seventeenth century to Matthew Bourne's *Swan Lake*, *Rethinking Dance History* invites the reader to revisit key moments in the history of western theatre dance practice. This exciting anthology of new writing considers recent approaches to the study of history in a postmodern age and offers fresh perspectives on important periods in dance history, seeking to address some of the gaps and silences that currently exist. Featuring contributions from some of the major names in dance writing and discourse, *Rethinking Dance History* covers topics as diverse as a re-evaluation of the work of Rudolf Laban, an account of the historical construction of Odissi dance, the imaginary reminiscences of a Victorian ballet girl on the music-hall stage and the 'queering' of King Louis XIV.

This fascinating anthology will prove an invaluable resource for both scholars and practitioners, and of interest to anyone who is intrigued by the rich and multi-layered history of Western dance theatre.

Alexandra Carter is a Reader in Dance Studies at Middlesex University, where she also teaches dance history and critical studies. She is a regular contributor to dance and performing arts journals, and editor of *The Routledge Dance Studies Reader* (1998).

Rethinking Dance History

A reader

Edited by
Alexandra Carter

LONDON AND NEW YORK

First published 2004
by Routledge
11 New Fetter Lane, London EC4P 4EE

Simultaneously published in the USA and Canada
by Routledge
29 West 35th Street, New York, NY 10001

Routledge is an imprint of the Taylor & Francis Group

Typeset in Bell Gothic and Perpetua by Graphicraft Limited, Hong Kong
Printed and bound in Great Britain by MPG Books Ltd, Bodmin

British Library Cataloguing in Publication Data
A catalogue record for this book is available from the British Library

Library of Congress Cataloging in Publication Data
Rethinking dance history : a reader / [edited by] Alexandra Carter.
p. cm.
Includes bibliographical references and index.
1. Dance—History. I. Carter, Alexandra.
GV1781 .R48 2004
792.8'09—dc21

2003013057

ISBN 0-415-28746-4 (hbk)
ISBN 0-415-28747-2 (pbk)

The one duty we owe to history is to rewrite it.

Oscar Wilde

Contents

Notes on Contributors

Ramsay Burt is Senior Research Fellow in Dance at De Montfort University. He has written two books, *The Male Dancer* (1995) and *Alien Bodies* (1998), and is currently working on a book about postmodern dance in Europe and the United States. With Professor Susan Foster, he is founder editor of the journal, *Discourses in Dance*.

Alexandra Carter is a Reader in Dance Studies at Middlesex University, London. She edited the *Routledge Dance Studies Reader* (1998) and writes regularly for dance and performing arts journals on history and contemporary critical debate.

Ananya Chatterjee is a dancer, choreographer, dance scholar and educator. Graduating from Temple University's Dance Department with Distinction in 1996, she joined the faculty of the University of Minnesota's Department of Theatre Arts and Dance. Ananya has published her work widely in journals such *Dance Research Journal, Asian Theatre Journal* and *Women and Performance*.

Judith Chazin-Bennahum was a Principal Soloist with the Metropolitan Opera Ballet. She received her PhD in Romance Languages at the University of New Mexico where she is now Chair of Theatre and Dance. Her books include *Dance in the Shadow of the Guillotine, The Ballets of Antony Tudor* and *The Lure of Perfection: The Culture of Fashion and Ballet 1780–1830.*

Beth Genné is Associate Professor of Dance Studies and History of Art, University of Michigan. She has contributed to a variety of journals and published her book on Ninette de Valois in 1996. She is director of film research for the Popular Balanchine project and a member of the editorial board of the Society of Dance History Scholars.

Lena Hammergren is Associate Professor and Head of Department, Theatre Studies, at Stockholm University, Sweden. She has written on twentieth-century dance and historiography, e.g. in Foster (1995) *Choreographing History*, Grau and Jordan (2000) *Europe Dancing* and in the forthcoming *Ballerinas and Barefoot Dancers: Swedish and International Dance Culture Around 1900.*

Marion Kant is a musicologist and dance historian, specialising in nineteenth- and twentieth-century dance history. She has a PhD from Humboldt University, Berlin, and has taught at universities in Berlin, London, Cambridge, Guildford and Philadelphia.

André Lepecki is Assistant Professor in the Performance Studies Department at New York University. He is a dance critic and dramaturg. He is editor of *Of the Presence of the Body: Dance as Critical Theory* (Wesleyan University Press). He is currently working on a book on 'still acts' in contemporary dance.

Alastair Macaulay is theatre critic of the *Financial Times* and dance critic of the *Times Literary Supplement*. Since 1980, he has taught dance history at BA and MA level. His books include *Margot Fonteyn* (1998) and *Matthew Bourne and his Adventures in Motion Pictures* (2000).

Larraine Nicholas is a Lecturer in Dance at the University of Surrey, Roehampton. Her doctorate from Roehampton in 1999 explored the cultural and historical context of British choreography in the years 1945–55, a period she continues to research.

Chris Roebuck trained in music and classical ballet. He began his career as a freelance musical director and choreographer and has taught both Cecchetti ballet and dance history at Suffolk College and Middlesex University. He wrote his doctoral thesis on representations of masculinity in contemporary dance.

Helen Thomas is Reader in Sociology at Goldsmiths College, University of London. Her publications include *Dance, Gender and Culture* (ed.) (1993) *Dance in the City* (ed.) (1997), *Dance, Modernity and Culture* (1995) and *The Body, Dance and Cultural Theory* (2002).

Linda J. Tomko is Associate Professor of Dance at the University of California, Riverside, and Past President of the Society of Dance History Scholars. Her book *Dancing Class* was published by Indiana University Press in 1999. With Wendy Hilton she has co-directed the Stanford Summer Workshop in Baroque Dance and its Music.

Cara Tranders was a dancer at the Empire Palace of Varieties between 1892 and 1899. Soon after writing her reveries in her diary, she was moved to the front row of the *corps de ballet* but her lack of consistent training prevented further promotion. And what did she do after she left the ballet? That, my reader, is up to your imagination.

Acknowledgements

I THANK ALL THE CONTRIBUTORS to this volume who have generously allowed their research to be published, especially when these short chapters represent only summaries of extensive research.

For information and advice, I extend my gratitude to Marianne Schultz and Anne Daye. Amy McGann offered invaluable help in my search for an appropriate visual image to capture the content of the book. I am further indebted to Lesley Main at Middlesex University for her sensitivity to my work programme.

Lastly, on behalf of dance scholars everywhere, I thank Rosie Waters who nurtured the birth of the project and Talia Rodgers and Diane Parker at Routledge for their advice and support along the way.

Permissions

Permission for reprinting the following chapters is gratefully acknowledged:

Judith Chazin-Bennahum, 'A Longing for Perfection: Neoclassic Fashion and Ballet', *Fashion Theory*, 6, 4 (December 2002). Reprinted with permission of Berg Publishers. All rights reserved.

Alastair Macaulay, 'Matthew Bourne, Dance History, and *Swan Lake*'. Excerpt from *Matthew Bourne and his Adventures in Motion Pictures* by Alastair Macaulay. Copyright © 2000 by Alastair Macaulay. Reprinted by permission of Faber and Faber, Inc., an affiliate of Farrar, Straus and Giroux, LLC.

Chapter 1

Alexandra Carter

MAKING HISTORY

A General Introduction

> Historical enquiry is not to be cut off from personal experience, nor is it to be locked into personal experience. It is fundamentally a way of relating the internal, the personal to the external, the public.
>
> (Husbands 1996: 134)

AS WITH HISTORICAL ENQUIRY ITSELF, the editing of a reader is both a personal and a public act. Choices are made about what and who to include, and in what order. These seemingly personal choices are bounded by publicly accepted concepts of a 'discipline' or subject domain, and, in this case, a recognised notion of what constitutes 'history'.

How can the field of dance history be characterised? Or, rather, so as not to let this singular question lead us in to the trap of a singular answer, what are the different interpretations of what constitutes the 'historical' study of dance? The debate about whether dance history is, or should be, a discrete discipline has been well rehearsed as part of the wider postmodern debate about the nature of knowledge and disciplinary boundaries.[1] Bryson (1997) and Koritz (1996) favour, if not the dissolution of these boundaries, at least 'a greater integration into other intellectual and institutional sites' (1996: 88).[2] As Koritz suggests, 'history does not occur naturally in disciplinary segments' (1996: 98). Almost everything we do carries a historical dimension – each step in the ballet class is imbued with centuries of tradition and change; each choreographic strategy rests on acceptance or rejection of the strategies of others, whether formed years ago or yesterday. History is, therefore, woven into all our studies. Nevertheless, it can also be approached as a discrete field in which curricula may be long and thin ('from the *ballets de cours* to the present day') or short and fat ('postmodern dance in America'). They may start with current practice as a means of engaging interest and establishing relevance, or may take a traditional stance, moving from past to present. The study of history, whether as a named field or as part of integrated or cultural studies, may be engaged with in practice in the studio, at the desk or in the field.[3] Methodological approaches may be so diverse that the notion of a special, historical perspective becomes slender indeed.[4] Like the concept of art, we may not be able to define it or characterise its boundaries, but we do tend to recognise it when we see it. And when we don't 'recognise' it, or dispute something as a fit subject or approach for 'history', therein lies the vitality of the field.

Choices about the content of a history book and how that content is organised contribute, wittingly or otherwise, to the debate about the nature of 'history', for its boundaries are unstable. Notions of what it is and how it should be studied are contested and constantly changing. Editorial choice can reinforce traditional ideas about history or extend those ideas with new topics and new approaches. The editorial impetus, therefore, arising from a simple wish to help the student of dance by providing new source material, becomes one which is neither 'neutral nor theoretically innocent' (Hutcheon 1989: 21).[5] Such a burden, however, is not borne in a vacuum, for the selection of writings presented in this reader rests upon a set of criteria. These criteria embrace the notions that:

- dance has a history which is worthy of study in order to enhance knowledge and understanding of both the past and the present;
- there are readers who are located in pedagogical contexts or 'learning' situations wherein, currently, there is a focus on the historical development of theatre dance;[6]
- there are researchers/writers who are adopting new approaches and developing new subject matter;
- there is a macro discipline of history which provides skills, methods and concepts.

Furthermore, in deference to the imperative for revealing the editorial voice, I admit that the selection of material for this book is also based on personal interest.

This book aims, therefore, to bring researchers and readers together by offering a selection of work which embraces new perspectives on key periods and people in theatre dance history; fill in some of the gaps and silences of that history and extend the traditional notion of 'theatre dance' by exploring the intersection between its varied forms and popular culture.[7] It rests upon the assumption that dance history is a recognisable field of study which is engaged with implicitly or explicitly. This field has been disrupted by changing concepts and concerns, some of which are explored in Chapter 2 in which I look at how debates in macro history impact upon dance history. In Chapter 3 Lena

Hammergren considers the selection and interpretation of source material, disrupting some of the conventional notions about the status and value of historical sources. Helen Thomas, in Chapter 4, tackles what is now the 'minor industry' of dance reconstruction, addressing issues such as the selective criteria by which works are chosen for reconstruction, the diverse and contested terminology and the notion of authenticity. Two versions of Fokine's *The Dying Swan* are used to illustrate her debate.

The contributors to this reader shift the perspectives on certain periods and people, and disturb the privileging of 'key' periods in extant historiography by exploring some gaps in the records. All of the accounts are personal, for 'all historical narratives contain an irreducible and inexpungeable element of interpretation' (White 1978: 51). They are also partial, for there is always both too much information for the historian to include yet also too little, leaving gaps in knowledge which demand inference and speculation. The historical record, claims White, 'is both too full and too sparse'. But, despite being 'personal' and partial, these historical narratives are also publicly accountable for they rest on reasoned argument supported by keenly researched and verifiable sources. As discussed in Chapter 2, history is an imaginative act but it is not an arbitrary one.

If the content of each chapter proffers new meanings, new understandings, then the organisation of that knowledge in book form similarly creates meaning (see Hutcheon in Chapter 2). It is in the structure of this book that I have trod most warily. A thematic account would have been possible, with collections of chapters grouped under headings such as 'Gender Perspectives'; 'Race, Class and National Identity'; 'Dance in its Social Context', etc. Such groupings became false, however, for each piece of writing sat happily in several categories. Structuring by genre seemed over-reductive, for it is certainly not the intention to offer even a partial history of particular genres. Eventually, I decided to organise the chapters in a traditional, chronological perspective. This was not in order to present a teleological view nor a case for 'cause and effect'. Nor was it to claim, albeit implicitly, any notion of progressive development: the idea that dance has somehow 'got better' over time. The chronological order is simply an organising strategy which offers the reader the opportunity to encounter a range of very different events across time and place. Such is the disparate nature of the contributions that the conventional periodisation of events constructed by historians is hopefully avoided.

The reader is free, therefore, to 'dip in' at any point or roam thematically. Each chapter may fit in to an existing schema of knowledge and, hopefully, nudge it askew a little. In relation to the aims of this reader, all the contributors 'bring new perspectives to bear' on their subject matter. Some do so overtly by revisiting topics which are already well documented. For example, Chris Roebuck (Chapter 5) takes the iconic figure of Louis XIV and queers his dancing image in a persuasive example of how the questions raised by recent developments in cultural theory can be potentially profitable when asked of dance practice. This marriage between one of the more recent theoretical stances on sexual identity(ies) and the earliest form of western theatre dance makes for an intriguing debate. Marion Kant (Chapter 10) revisits the even more extensively documented life of Rudolf Laban, raising questions about his possible sympathies with the creeds of racial purity and Germanic identity embedded in Nazism. Herein lies an implicit debate about the interrelationship between an artist's personal beliefs and his or her public work, and the extent to which knowledge of the former (albeit, in this case, contested) affects our understanding and appreciation of the latter. Furthermore, Kant offers the reader direct questions about the interpretation of documents and how the historian deals with interpretations which may read against the grain of conventional opinion. What happens, she asks, if we find something that does not fit in with preconceived notions, either public or private? Such is the stuff of historical debate, the 'argument without end' referred to in Chapter 2.

Other contributors 'fill in the gaps' of extant historiography in a more direct sense. Although the voices of dance makers have been heard, particularly from the beginning of the twentieth century when, as Lena Hammergren (Chapter 3) discusses, the 'early moderns' wrote their life stories, it is more rare to find sources from choreographers who speak about their actual work. In conversation with Alastair Macaulay (Chapter 14), Matthew Bourne discusses the general influences of his own formal and informal education in dance history. He speaks of the value of a knowledge of past practice which allows choreographers not to replicate (unless this is a conscious strategy) but to 'develop their own way'. In this interview, Macaulay parallels the role of the historian, for it is the interviewer who asks the questions of his/her (live) 'source' in the same way that historians do of their sources. The framing of questions, of course, also frames the responses. Furthermore, the notion of the primacy of Matthew Bourne's own words as a 'raw' source is tested under Hammergren's argument in Chapter 3.

Cara Tranders's journal (Chapter 7) also raises questions about whose 'voice' speaks in historiography, and alerts us to an almost invisible period in British dance history. Squashed and suffocated by the weight of the preceding Romantic era and the succeeding Ballets Russes, and hampered by its location in the palaces of varieties rather than the temples of high art, the ballet in late Victorian England has barely been able to breathe. Tranders's journal also raises current concerns in macro-history about the blurring of distinctions between 'fact' and 'fiction'. Writers such as White (1978) and Jenkins (1991) argue that history is an imaginative act, a view endorsed by Husbands:

> If the boundaries between history and fiction are no longer clear or distinct, if, indeed, the argument is that understanding the past is

> itself a creative act which can be rendered differently by historians, novelists and poets, then the place of the imagination in the construction of historical accounts becomes central.
>
> (Husbands 1996: 58)

Tranders's autobiography may be deemed an imaginative account and, in that sense, is 'fiction' but it is based on documented evidence. It is writing, therefore, which manipulates evidence with an overt rather than an implicit fictional drive; it takes the philosophical notion of the writing of history as an imaginative act and extends it into a consciously constructed imaginative act. It is also concerned with 'history from the inside' (Husbands 1996: 60); a speculative account of what people thought and how they behaved – a kind of historiography which gives shape, in terms of a 'story', to human experience.

Another invisible period in British dance history is that of the 1940s and 1950s. The change of policy by Ballet Rambert and their importation of the Graham-based technique, and the establishment of the London Contemporary Dance Theatre and School (also based on the aesthetic practices of American modern dance) have resulted in the mid-1960s as being perceived as the period when modern (known as contemporary) dance in Britain was born. Larraine Nicholas (Chapter 11) reminds us, however, that forms of modern/contemporary dance stretch back through the seeming desert of the 1940s and 1950s. In this period, Central European influences are manifest, fuelled by a social and political consciousness which is later resurrected in the impact of the European mainland on Britain from the 1980s. Thus, cultural influences from Europe and the United States weave their way through British modern dance history. Conversely, as Ramsay Burt argues (Chapter 9), the European experience was an important one for Katherine Dunham, who toured Europe from the late 1940s. Even though all the pioneers of modern dance had their very personal and individual ways of making work, Dunham did not, perhaps, fit in with the dominant trends as perceived by later historiographers. Once a key figure in American modern dance, Dunham's work and contribution has been neglected.[8] Also neglected, from an earlier period in American modern dance history, is the social context which facilitated the work of early modern dancers such as Isadora Duncan, Ruth St Denis and Loie Fuller. Adopting ideas from Foucault, Linda Tomko (Chapter 8) enters the debate as to whether history is, or should be, a search for 'origins' and 'causes' of change and the identification of agents for change (a traditional historiographical and pedagogical project, addressed also by Lena Hammergren in Chapter 3) or whether history operates not with linear development moved forward by key individual agents but as lateral moments in time. The characteristics of identifiable periods evolve from 'conditions of possibility' constructed by social networks and systems. Arguing that we need to explore both approaches, Tomko suggests that the social conditions of the 'separate sphere' ideology for men and women in the late nineteenth century enabled middle- and upper-class women to construct their own social networks and become custodians of culture. It was within these conditions that the practitioners of early modern dance operated, not as free-floating agents unhinged from social circumstances but as women who grasped the potential of those circumstances.

Either explicit or implicit in the above chapters is the consciousness that no dance writing today can avoid acknowledgement of the many contexts in which dance takes place; its manifestation as an activity hermetically sealed from the rest of society, so common in earlier dance historiography, is no longer tenable. For example, in Chapter 6 Judith Chazin-Bennahum traces how the fascination of late eighteenth-century western Europe with the classical aesthetics and cultural practices of antiquity was reflected in the clothes of the period. She argues how the female body was 'reborn' in the looser lines and lighter fabrics of neoclassical fashion. The influence of fashion, the literal embodiment of a contextually specific return to classicism, impacted on ballet, liberating the dancers' bodies and feet and facilitating new moves and the 'new' movement of Romanticism. When produced and performed with a regard for its history, the Romantic repertoire today bears within it a history of fashion and a cultural history of ideas. In a very different context, Beth Genné, in Chapter 12, also explores how dance embodies (and, of course, contributes to) culture. With some very focused research on dancing in the streets in musical film and video, Genné reveals not only cinematic techniques but also how both the 'dancing' and the 'streets' have changed. From the safe playgrounds of Gene Kelly to the threatening environments of Michael Jackson, the city streets are sites for dancing out the age.

For the historian, the interpretative act often requires a temporal distance from events. From a long view, those events take shape more clearly and webs of significance fall into place. André Lepecki (Chapter 15) looks back on our very recent history, venturing into the twenty-first century in order to discern these webs which 'traverse both sides of the Atlantic'. Of relevance to our understanding of history itself, Lepecki claims a trend for European modern dance practitioners at the end of the twentieth century not to subscribe to the imperative of always rupturing the past by creating the 'new', but to acknowledge the past 'as common ground, as the surface it is inevitably destined to wander on'. Thus, notions of time and history as teleological, as always 'moving forward' in progressive waves of rejecting the old and establishing the new, are disrupted.[9] This disruptive tactic is endorsed by Ananya Chatterjee (Chapter 13) who argues strongly, in the preface to tracing how the history of Odissi has been constructed, that historiography has been based on a western model which privileges modernity, with its organising concepts of development, linearity, coherence and 'truth'. Within these, she claims, are the implicit strategies of power and the control of narratives which masquerade as 'history'.

André Lepecki suggests, in the final contribution to this reader, that

> the past is not that which vanishes at every second that passes, but rather that which presents itself in the present as a forceful absence, a set of references, signs, lines of forces, all traversing the body on stage, and defining the ground on where dance (all of us) stands.

Thus, it is hoped that the contents of this reader, in presenting new research in dance history, will help us to acknowledge the common ground of past and present; expose how history is conceived, created and interpreted, and recognise our personal role as writers and readers in the public construction of the narratives of the past.

Notes

1 Adshead-Lansdale (1994) offers an overview of the challenges of new, macro history to dance and engages in sprightly debate with Richard Ralph (1995) about both methods and approaches (Adshead-Lansdale 1997).

2 See an interesting counter-argument to the notion of disciplinary integration in Dolan (1993) who disputes the integration of theatre studies into 'performance studies'.

3 See, for example, Geraldine Morris (2000) on the use of a historical approach in the teaching of ballet technique and repertoire as a way of combating the homogeneity of performance which results from the blanket adoption of contemporary technical values.

4 The highly diverse nature of approaches to 'dance history' and the context in which it is taught and studied is evident in the content of recent educational books, in curricula strategies and in the concerns of professional associations. For example, Dils and Cooper Albright's dance history reader (2001) is an example of highly diverse subject matter and methodological approaches which reflect curricula in the United States. The proceedings of the Society for Dance History Scholars similarly embraces an eclectic field. In the United Kingdom, the concept of history is arguably tighter than in the United States but, again, content may be organised in highly discrete modules covering ballet and modern dance or as a facet of broader study. Similarly, in Australia and New Zealand, curricula range from specific history courses to those where it is integrated in general dance studies, with both approaches tending to focus on the twentieth century. In Europe, dance is still developing as a discrete subject in its own right and the European Association of Dance Historians has tended to focus on pre-twentieth-century 'historical' or early dance,

though their remit is broadening. Such is the slippery nature of the concept of 'dance history' in an educational and research context.

5 Hutcheon here is discussing feminist approaches to forms of cultural representation but knowledge, too, in a wider sense can be seen as 'culturally re-presented'.

6 This is not to deny the significance of histories of diverse dance forms and functions which are now contributing to the expansion of dance studies. See, for example, Desmond (2001) who addresses dance history and sexuality in contexts such as the nightclub, the street and film as well as theatre.

7 This reader does not comprise primary sources in the way that, for example, Cohen (1992) or, to a large extent, Huxley and Witts (1996) provide.

8 See Perpener (2001) for more recent work on Dunham.

9 As a further example of this 'attitude to history' in practice, see Ramsay Burt's review of Boris Charmatz's work in *Dance Theatre Journal* (2002) 18, 2: 11–15.

Bibliography

Adshead-Lansdale, J. (1994) 'Border Tensions in the Discipline of Dance History', in *Retooling the Discipline: Research and Teaching Strategies for the 21st Century*, Proceedings of Society of Dance History Scholars Conference, Brigham Young University, Utah: SDHS.

—— (1997) 'The "Congealed Residues" of Dance History: A Response to Richard Ralph's "Dance Scholarship and Academic Fashion" – One Path to a Predetermined Enlightenment?', *Dance Chronicle*, 20, 1: 63–86.

Bryson, N. (1997) 'Cultural Studies and Dance History', in J. Desmond (ed.) *Meaning in Motion: New Cultural Studies of Dance*, Durham, NC: Duke University Press.

Cohen, S. J. (ed.) (1992) *Dance as a Theatre Art*, London: Dance Books.

Desmond, J. (ed.) (2001) *Dancing Desires: Choreographing Sexualities on and off the Stage*, Madison, Wis.: University of Wisconsin Press.

Dils, A. and Cooper Albright, A. (2001) *Moving History/Dancing Cultures: A Dance History Reader*, Middletown, Conn.: Wesleyan University Press.

Dolan, J. (1993) 'Geographies of Learning: Theater Studies, Performance and the "Performative"', *Theatre Journal*, 45, 4: 417–41.

Husbands, C. (1996) *What Is History Teaching? Language, Ideas and Meaning in Learning about the Past*, Buckingham: Open University Press.

Hutcheon, L. (1989) *The Politics of Postmodernism*, London: Routledge.

Huxley, M. and Witts, N. (eds) (1996) *The Twentieth Century Performance Reader*, London: Routledge.

Jenkins, K. (1991) *Rethinking History*, London: Routledge.

Koritz, A. (1996) 'Re/Moving Boundaries: From Dance History to Cultural Studies', in G. Morris (ed.) *Moving Words: Rewriting Dance*, London: Routledge.

Morris, Geraldine (2000) 'The Role of History in Performance Interpretation', in *Dance History: The Teaching and Learning of Dance History*, Conference Proceedings of the European Association of Dance Historians, Twickenham: EADH.

Perpener, J. O. (2001) *African-American Concert Dance: The Harlem Renaissance and Beyond*, Urbana and Chicago, Ill.: University of Illinois Press.

Ralph, R. (1995) 'On the Light Fantastic Toe: Dance Scholarship and Academic Fashion', in *Dance Chronicle*, 18, 2: 249–60.

White, H. (1978) *Tropics of Discourse*, Baltimore, Md.: Johns Hopkins University Press.

Chapter 2

Alexandra Carter

DESTABILISING THE DISCIPLINE

Critical Debates about History and their Impact on the Study of Dance[1]

DANCE HISTORY IS NOW WELL established as a vital component of dance studies. Whether engaged with as a 'named' course or integrated within broader fields of study, it is a part of the curriculum at many levels of dance education and training. Paradoxically, the traditional discipline of history has come under attack from critical and cultural theories which question the very nature and status of knowledge, and how that knowledge is retrieved, organised, recorded and received. These debates about the construction and reception of knowledge arose from postmodern, poststructuralist and feminist theories. Although the challenges to the accepted modes of engaging with history which are presented by these critical perspectives have, in themselves, been challenged (see Appleby et al. 1994), my purpose here is to identify their relevance to the teaching and learning of dance history. That is, how theoretical debates about history might impact on the pedagogy of dance history. The examples are drawn from western theatre dance but the general principles are relevant to an engagement with the histories of all dance forms.

Debates about the nature of knowledge have arisen from a variety of critical and cultural perspectives. Poststructuralist thought has influenced our conception of the very nature of 'history' itself, such as the assumption that the historical endeavour coheres around the retrieval of 'facts' which are, in themselves, 'true'. The postmodern attitude to the role of the 'author' has given rise to a questioning of the role of the historian, who is now seen not as neutral recorder of events but as active creator of them. Discourse theories have exposed how knowledge is constituted not by limited logocentric modes of engagement with the world but by a vast variety of influences; this calls into question the reliance on written sources as privileged evidence for recreating the past. Cultural studies impacted on traditional thinking about the hierarchy of knowledge in which certain events are deemed more significant than others. Similarly, attacks on his-story came from feminist writers who exposed the gendered nature of historical construction. In all, the gaps and silences in historical records have been exposed not as 'empty' or unworthy of research but as a product of culturally constructed, hierarchical perspectives on the 'what', 'who', 'when' and 'how' of the past.

In terms of the teaching and learning of dance history, these challenges can be explored in relation to:

- the totalising nature of history and the status of 'facts';
- the role of the historian;
- the nature of and attitudes toward sources; and
- the privileging of certain kinds of 'knowledge'.

The totalising nature of history and the status of 'facts'

The writing of history is the writing of stories about the past. These are narratives, which imply a traditional narrative structure of beginning, middle and end. This structure is a way of 'using story to give shape to experiences as a way of understanding them' (Husbands 1996: 46). But it also, argues Hutcheon, 'imparts meaning as well as order' (1989: 62). The packaging of dance history into neat periods or 'shapes' with a beginning, middle and end not only enables the organisation of a curriculum ('next week we'll do the Romantic period') but it gives meaning to those periods, making them discrete and self-contained in the specificity of their characteristics. The dangers inherent in this packaging are that those activities, those periods of time, which don't fall neatly under prescribed labels don't fall anywhere at all. They are less researched, under-recorded, not studied. Why is *Coppélia*, a very popular ballet in our repertoire, far less well known and less written about than *Giselle* or *The Sleeping Beauty*? Might it be that, created in 1870, it is on the cusp of the waning Romantic era and the impending Neoclassical age of the Russian Imperial ballet – but it doesn't fall neatly into either? We all know that modern dance started in Britain in the mid-1960s with the policy change of Ballet Rambert and the establishment of London Contemporary Dance Theatre and School – but did it? As Nicholas demonstrates in Chapter 11, the history of modern dance in Britain is far richer than this commonly accepted 'starting point' suggests.[2] Of course we need to organise our teaching and learning and our textbooks, for there are clusters of characteristics which can be ascribed to particular times and phenomena; certain conditions of production and reception which result in particular kinds of dance works. But we also need to be conscious that nothing neatly starts or finishes. There are dance works which sit firmly within a period but don't conform to the characteristics which have been identified. For example, our notion of the Romantic period is based on the supernatural ballets of spirits and sylphs and we tend to forget all the 'national' ballets presented during the same period which were different in their aesthetic concerns. One of the historian's problems, therefore, is 'to decide how and where to insert an analytic knife into the seamlessness of time, and to recognise the motivations for whatever incision is made' (Southgate 1996: 113). We need to define parameters, 'the Romantic period', the 'Neoclassical', the 'Modern', the 'Postmodern', but we need to be aware of the flawed finality indicated by these capital letters and the fact that these packages are tied by historians, not necessarily produced by neat, all-inclusive, clusterings of events themselves.

Implicit in the above debate is the notion of continuity, that is, a sensitivity to traces left behind and embedded in what is to come. But the postmodern challenge to totalisation also rejects the imperative of continuity. As Hutcheon, drawing on Foucault, suggests,

> instead of seeking common denominators and homogeneous networks of causality and analogy, historians have been freed . . . to note the dispersing interplay of different, heterogeneous discourses that acknowledge the undecidable in both the past and our knowledge of the past.
>
> (Hutcheon 1989: 66)

In our own learning, teaching and research, we can acknowledge that events, or repertoire, might not 'fit in' to a linear notion of history. We tend to see the past as a line stretching back from the present. As Chapman says in relation to ballet history,

> the dance historian sets off on a voyage through the past with the rudder of his (*sic*) modern prejudices steering his course. He seeks significance in terms of what he knows of the theatrical dance of today. His explanation of historical development is couched in terms of the progressive accumulation of traits similar to the major features of twentieth century ballet.
>
> (Chapman 1979/80: 256)

It is a fascinating project, for example, to look at a reconstruction of the *ballets de cours* of the seventeenth century and identify features which can be 'traced through' to our ballet vocabulary and repertoire today. This helps to enhance appreciation of why we are studying history at all. But history is not just a line from past to present; it is a web, a 'dispersing interplay' of discourses. (See Tomko, this volume Chapter 8, for an extension of this debate.) As such, our histories can accommodate activities which do not seem to contribute in any obvious ways to the 'development' of the art form but, in their time, were a vital part of it. My own work on the ballet in London in the Victorian era is a case in point. Although I would argue strongly that this period disrupts the notion that British ballet was 'born' in the 1930s, the ballets were also, in their own right, a central part of the entertainment scene of London and many provincial cities. As such, they are worthy of study not for their place in the continuum, but for their place in their time.

We can argue, therefore, that the study of history comprises not the study of neat boxes of knowledge, which embody uncontested facts, but is analogous to the study of clouds. Clouds have the capacity to change shape, to present different images, depending on who is looking at them, and when and why.

The role of the historian

> (H)history is a shifting discourse constructed by historians and . . . from the existence of the past no one reading is entailed: change the gaze, shift the perspective and new readings appear.
>
> (Jenkins 1991: 14)

This is what can make the study of dance so vital; it is not just that new sources are found which lead us to reformulate our accounts, but new ways of looking, 'shifting perspectives' which can offer new readings of old sources. As Jenkins argues, sources in themselves don't say anything:

> The claim that bias can be expunged by attending to 'what the sources say' is undercut by the fact that sources are mute. It is historians who articulate whatever the 'sources say'.
>
> (Jenkins 1991: 38)

The biases in historical record are strengths, so long as we are aware of what they are. It is the biases, the different perspectives on the past, that stop it solidifying. Ramsay Burt's *The Male Dancer* (1995) could not have been written twenty years ago, or certainly would have been written differently, for the explanatory models which he uses to grant meaning to the past (Hutcheon 1989) did not exist. As a result, we see the male dancer afresh.

The difference between the traditional model of history which strives for an unachievable neutrality and objectivity and more recent models is that the latter acknowledge their bias:

> What is foregrounded in postmodern theory and practice is the self-conscious inscription within history of the existing, but usually concealed, attitude of historians towards their material.
>
> (Hutcheon 1989: 74)

This notion does not, of course, make the endeavour a free for all, but it develops a consciousness that the study of history is a creative activity. Created, that is, by both the historian and by the recipient. It involves the imaginative piecing together of various accounts in order to produce meanings; it may necessitate speculation where there are gaps and asking questions as to why there are gaps. In our studies, one of the key questions we can ask is: who wrote this? Why is Nijinsky so privileged in primary source accounts of the Ballets Russes, and Karsavina barely mentioned? Why was Nijinska, until recently, written out of these accounts? We might ask who wrote them, what were their sexual proclivities, what attracted them to the performers and how has that personal attraction become embodied in seemingly neutral accounts of the Ballets Russes? Sally Banes's book (1998) is not really about 'Dancing Women'; it is about about dancing women in America – because the author is American and that is her realm of expertise. Not much, if anything, may be known about the writers whose works we study but a quick look at their autobiography on the flyleaf will indicate nationality, gender, profession. This information does not invalidate their writing; it just alerts us to where the authors are 'coming from'. Historians make meaning; we need to be aware of who is making the meaning and from what perspective that meaning is made.

Attitudes towards sources

Although a case has been made that dance poses a special challenge to the historian because of its ephemerality (see, for example, Berg in Fraleigh and Hanstein 1999), such a claim is only partially tenable, for all of the past is ephemeral; it exists only in records of the events, not in the events themselves. As suggested, 'hard' evidence such as artefacts or documents do not have meaning in themselves, for meaning is ascribed through various interpretative frameworks or points of view. While we might be personally better informed if we could have seen Nijinsky dance, it is the exploration of what that dancing might have 'meant' and how it meant different things to different people which is the interrogative and imaginative task of the historian.

Writers and readers of history, therefore, make meaning from sources, for

> the development of historical understanding is always the result of an active dialogue between ourselves, in the present, and the evidence in whatever form the past has left behind.
>
> (Husbands 1996: 13)

In an ideal world, those who learn about dance history should be able to juxtapose those sources, compare them, consider their biases, their explicit or otherwise theoretical frameworks. What, for example, are the different stances taken by David Vaughan in his *Frederick Ashton and his Ballets* ([1977] 1999) and Julie Kavanagh in *Secret Muses* (1996)? What do these books tell us, in their different ways, not only about Ashton, but also about the changing nature of biography? But we do not work in an ideal world and it is not always possible to compare sources critically. What can be done, as already suggested, is to consider the nature of the source as well as its content, even at a simple level. Who wrote it, when and where? If distinguishing a theoretical stance is not always easy, discerning a personal bias is easier. How useful is the source? Are there chapter headings, a contents page, an index, a bibliography? For whom is it written – the intended recipient? It is becoming more common now to tackle educational assignments which address the nature of the sources, or the research methods, rather than the rewriting of history culled unimaginatively from books. It isn't easy, however, to be persuaded by the validity of these tasks. For a history module I teach in a university, an essay assignment demands a critical analysis of selected historical sources. A monitoring questionnaire on the module produced the comment that 'it was a pity that the assignment did not relate to history'.

In most history curricula, time is short and there will be a tension between how much of it we spend on engaging with historical methods and how much on historical content; there's not much point in establishing Ivor Guest's credentials if you don't know what Ivor Guest has written about. But on the other hand, a critical approach to sources is a lifelong, transferable skill which has the potential to inform how we read the daily newspaper, watch the television news, hear the political broadcast. A healthy scepticism about 'facts', about 'truth', about how these are constructed and by whom, will stand scholars in good stead as discriminating citizens.

A key source in the study of dance, however, is not the traditional written one, but the visual: the dance itself. Here, the adoption of a critical attitude towards the works we see is still vital – no, that's not Coralli/Perrot's version of *Giselle* we're viewing but Grigorovitch's new choreography of 1990, based on Petipa's of 1884 and Coralli and Perrot's of 1841. Marwick in 1989 (p. 323) devotes a page to the use of visual sources as if they are a novel idea. Ten years later, Simon Schama, in a Radio 3 talk in November 1999 (Schama 1999), is still calling for a wide variety of source material as well as 'text-bound' research. It is in the use of visual sources where dance study has the edge over many other disciplinary endeavours.

The privileging of 'knowledge'

A further debate in macro-history which inevitably impacts on dance concerns the notion that historiography is not value-free. It privileges certain kinds of people and activity and it is these that constitute the canon. As Laakkonen says, 'Canons guide our thinking of what is considered to be good and worth knowing . . . our way of writing and interpreting history' (2000: 60).[3] She claims, however, that canonisation and its implicit rules have resulted in a limited understanding of our past. Traditional history has been accused of celebrating 'the achievements of . . . dead white European males rather than showing the contribution of women, minorities, gays or other oppressed and excluded groups' (Appleby, et al. 1994: 5). Now, as Hutcheon claims for a postmodernist perspective, we can consider 'the histories . . . of the losers as well as the winners, of the regional . . . as well as the centrist, of the unsung many as well as the much sung few' (Hutcheon 1989: 66). This is now happening in our dance literature: Burt and Kavanagh have written about homosexuality and the dance artist; Lynn Garafola rescued Nijinska (1987/88). She also, in her extensive account of the Ballets Russes (1989), put audiences back into the picture, thus explicitly acknowledging the full interplay of people and events, the range of discourses which produce historical phenomena. But that interplay is still limited. Although Jowitt (1988), for example, looks at the working lives of performers, the whole notion that dance performance is a job is still underexplored. The glamour of the ballerina is fascinating, but so too is the question 'how much did she get paid?' We know about the big names, and we will probably never know the actual small names, but we can be alert to the notion that the dance event is produced not only by individual creative artists but by unacknowledged armies of dancers, walk-ons, administrators, scene builders and movers, front-of-house, publicity and marketing people and so on. We cannot, as said, name all these but we can acknowledge that context is not just background, but context is what produces the artistic event, and shapes our perception of it. The state of an employment market at a particular time; the financial imperatives – if Terpsichore was in sneakers in America in the 1960s (Banes 1986), it was not just an aesthetic choice but an economic one – all this impacts on how dance is produced and received. This information can be found in our dance books, as history cross-fertilises with other disciplinary perspectives such as sociology, cultural studies and ethnography, but it is not easy to disentangle. Nevertheless, by being alert to the notion that history is produced by this interplay of a huge variety of discourses, we can bring it closer, acknowledging it as part of everyday life that was – and is.

In conclusion, one of the attacks upon postmodern and other critical perspectives is that they result in a deep cynicism of the whole historical project. They appear to unravel the nature of historical knowledge until we can't see what is left; they seem to undermine the professionalism of historians, trivialise the value of their archival research, and doubt the integrity of all sources. But there is a difference between cynicism and scepticism. As Appleby et al. (1994: 6) point out, 'skepticism is an approach to learning as well as a philosophical stance' but 'complete skepticism . . . is debilitating, because it casts doubt on the ability to draw judgments and make conclusions'. Part of the skill of a historian is the ability to 'draw judgments and make conclusions', for history is not an exercise where all is relative and anything goes. But we can, perhaps, promote the development of a questioning attitude. As postmodern dance is an attitude to dance making, not a predetermined set of procedures and outcomes, so with history. An awareness of the debates would encourage the loss of a 'theoretical innocence' (Jenkins 1997: 2) about history and nurture an incredulity towards its metanarratives (Lyotard, in Jenkins 1997). We may not, or cannot, change the syllabus content but we can introduce a critical engagement with sources. It is important to be realistic, of course; as I've said, it's a struggle sometimes to read one source, let alone engage with several. But even that one book or article can be read with an inquiring mind about not just its content, but its status as a source. The role of the historian can be invested with qualities of both reason and imagination; students of all ages can see that they, too, are historians. They can learn that dance history is produced by many other histories and, in turn, has the potential to contribute to those other histories.

Students have so much to learn and teachers have so much to offer, in so little time; we have to be realistic about what can and cannot be done. It is not possible to argue or make judgements if there is no awareness of the nature or sides of the argument; the engagement with historical content is paramount. But it is possible to argue, for historical theory is necessarily imbued in its content; it is just a question of whether or not we choose to disentangle it. As Geyl (in Southgate 1996: 109) claimed, 'History is argument without end.' By nurturing an inquiring attitude towards how history is made, by whom and for what purpose, we can see our own creative role within it. History is an essentially human endeavour in which we attempt to make sense, with the emphasis on 'make', of what Simon Schama describes as 'the past, in all its splendid messiness' (1991).

Notes

1 This chapter is based on 'Partners in Time: A Critical Examination of the Changing Nature of "History" as a Discipline', paper given to the European Society of Dance Historians Conference, Twickenham (Carter 2000).

2 See also Nicholas (1999) on modern dance activity around the period of the Festival of Britain in the 1950s.

3 In her paper (2000), Laakkonen disentangles the various means by which the canon in constituted.

Bibliography

Appleby, J., Hunt, L. and Jacob, M. (1994) *Telling the Truth about History*, New York, NY: W. W. Norton.

Banes, S. (1986) *Terpsichore in Sneakers: Postmodern Dance*, Middletown, Conn.: Wesleyan University Press.

—— (1998) *Dancing Women: Female Bodies on Stage*, London: Routledge.

Burt, R. (1995) *The Male Dancer: Bodies, Spectacle, Sexualities*, London: Routledge.

Carter, A. (2000) 'Partners in Time: A Critical Examination of the Changing Nature of "History" as a Discipline', in *Dance History: The Teaching and Learning of Dance History*, Conference Proceedings of the European Association of Dance Historians, Twickenham: EADH.

Chapman, J. (1979/80) 'The Aesthetic Interpretation of Dance History', *Dance Chronicle*, 3, 3: 254–74.

Fraleigh, S. and Hanstein, P. (eds) (1999) *Researching Dance: Evolving modes of Enquiry*, London: Dance Books.

Garafola, L. (1987/8) 'Bronislava Nijinska: A Legacy Uncovered', *Women and Performance*, 3, 6: 78–88.

—— (1989) *Diaghilev's Ballets Russes*, Oxford: Oxford University Press.

Husbands, C. (1996) *What Is History Teaching? Language, Ideas and Meaning in Learning about the Past*, Buckingham: Open University Press.

Hutcheon, L. (1989) *The Politics of Postmodernism*, London: Routledge.

Jenkins, K. (1991) *Rethinking History*, London: Routledge.

—— (ed.) (1997) *The Postmodern History Reader*, London: Routledge.

Jowitt, D. (1988) *Time and the Dancing Image*, Berkeley, Calif.: University of California Press.

Kavanagh, J. (1996) *Secret Muses: The Life of Frederick Ashton*, London: Faber.

Laakkonen, J. (2000) 'The Problem of Canon in Writing and Teaching Dance History', in *Dance History: The Teaching and Learning of Dance History*, Conference Proceedings of the European Association of Dance Historians, Twickenham: EADH.

Marwick, A. (1989) *The Nature of History*, 2nd edn, London: Macmillan.

Nicholas, L. (1999) 'The Lion and the Unicorn: Festival of Britain Themes and Choreography in the Postwar Decade', unpublished PhD, University of Surrey, Roehampton.

Schama, S. (1991) 'A Room with No View', *Guardian*, 26 September.

Schama, S. (1999) 'Sounds of the century' lecture, BBC Radio 3, 13 November.

Southgate, B. (1996) *History: What and Why? Ancient, Modern and Postmodern Perspectives*, London: Routledge.

Vaughan, D. ([1977] 1999) *Frederick Ashton and his Ballets*, London: Dance Books.

Chapter 3

Lena Hammergren

MANY SOURCES, MANY VOICES

WHY HISTORY? KEITH JENKINS reflects upon this question in his thought-provoking book written at the end of the last century (Jenkins 1999). He concludes that we no longer need history as we have known it; we do 'not need to go to history' in order to find 'all the imaginaries we need to think the future' (ibid.: 199–200). In this statement, he refers to what historians have usually considered the primary goal of any historical study of a reflective nature: we investigate the past in order to learn about the future. Inspired by his intention (although not fully by his conclusions, since I still believe that certain conceptualizations of the past help us to think about the future) I will focus this text on the question: why source material? Or, to formulate it more precisely, how do we conceive of sources and what can we make of them? To raise these questions is to highlight a part of the process of constructing historical narratives that we sometimes regard as less 'problematic' in nature compared to the more troublesome undertaking of applying theories. In this chapter I will query the process of assembling, choosing and interpreting documents from which dance histories can be told.

Source criticism

Every scholar who has spent hours in archives will be aware of the daunting task of conflating often disparate sources into a single, unified history. One of the traditional tools historians use to address this problem is source criticism, a process which often starts by dividing source material into primary and secondary sources. The former category generally includes material that is 'close' in time to the object of study and may be considered 'raw material' (e.g. diaries and dance performances); the latter involves sources produced 'farther away' in time, and they emphasize interpretation (e.g. history books and performance reviews). Historians also propose a hierarchical relation between these two categories, deeming primary sources to have the potential of being more 'true' to the object than secondary sources. In this view, a personal letter and a dance written and performed respectively by Isadora Duncan are more likely to reveal her intentions or aesthetic ideals than would an analysis of her work by a dance historian, written several years later.

Yet we find an intriguing contradiction inherent in this view, and it has to do with how time is supposed to affect the historian's ability to evaluate the importance of events or the agency of an individual artist. The German historian Oskar Bie has provided us with a good example of how time might change our evaluation of a dancer. In 1906 he published his first version of *Der Tanz* (The Dance), and in 1919 he wrote a second, revised edition. In the two editions we find interesting changes concerning Bie's judgement of Isadora Duncan's importance. In 1906 he rejects her influence on modern dance (Bie [1906] 1919: 305). In the later edition he gives voice to an altered opinion, and argues that she did indeed lead dance into a new phase of development, even though she never fully realized her intentions (Bie [1906] 1919: 362). We might explain this evaluative turn as a result of the passage of time in between the two editions. In 1919 Bie would have had more sources supporting the judgement of Duncan's influence on contemporary dance than in 1906, a year perhaps too close in time to her breakthrough as an artist. However, because we lack enough information on exactly why Bie changed his mind (was he influenced by other critics' opinions, had the audiences' reception changed, or had he simply watched more performances by Duncan?), we might, instead of deeming him wrong in 1906, look at the two editions as equally 'true'.

This view could direct our interest to focus on the question of when and why an individual artist becomes part of the dance canon rather than on the historian's ability to make the right evaluations or whether the sources are primary or secondary. It is quite interesting to note that some of today's historians use German dance histories from the 1920s as 'evidence' when they are referring to Duncan's influence in Germany during the early years of the twentieth century (e.g. Partsch-Bergsohn 1994: 3–4). This is not wrong, but Bie provides one example of how differently we could interpret the reception of Duncan in Germany if we were to choose a source from an earlier date, more contemporary in time to the object of study.

From an international perspective it is also important to stress the need for analyses of local sources. We often use a shared canon of source material, which can be reinterpreted many times in different contexts, but national or regional sources hitherto not investigated or not addressed by international dance histories can offer us possibilities for new interpretations or complementary analyses. Amy Koritz has emphasized these circumstances in her cogent research on dance and literature in early twentieth-century British culture. From a British perspective, she addresses the historical stature accorded to Maud Allan in comparison to some other contemporary dance artists. Koritz argues that 'a dance history written from the point of view of the English public would not give the same status to St Denis, or to Duncan . . . as either is commonly accorded in the United States' (Koritz 1995: 31–2). Thus, it is easy to understand that the way we choose and use source material might result in many different historical narratives.

Sources as social constructions

Instead of trying to distinguish between sources' classification as primary or secondary, we can look at them as parts of discourses. The word discourse has multiple meanings, and I use it here to signify the codes and conceptual systems by which we manifest and make understandable different aspects of our lives, to ourselves and to others. Thus, we can distinguish between discursive topics (the subjects that we are 'talking' about), discursive media (the documents in which the discourse is manifested), and the set of codes and conventions forming the discourse. If the development of dance is the chosen topic, we may find it in discursive media or sources such as history books, encyclopedias, or oral statements. In order to analyse the discourse, we then need to look at each discursive medium's particular manner of expressing the discourse.

One excellent application of this view has been made by David E. Nye in the field of the history of science (Nye 1983). He assumes that 'all evidence has been given a form', which is connected to the socio-cultural systems that produced the sources (p. 12). Our contemporary view on historiography has made us aware of the role of the historian's interpretation of sources. The questions we put to the documents affect the answers we receive. But Nye clarifies one additionally important aspect to the commonly expressed notion that sources are 'mute'. An object is imbued with patterns of meaning already in the act of becoming a document, for example when it is included in an archive or inserted into the layout of a newspaper. As a result, primary sources cannot be perceived as 'raw material' in comparison to the assumed interpreted nature of secondary sources.

Let me give as an example two different collections of dance reviews, and how the act of collecting gives rise to different interpretations of the reviews. Both collections are part of the Dance Museum's archive in Stockholm. The first is a collection made by the two Swedish sisters Marja and Rachel Björnström-Ottelin, who made careers as modern dancers in Europe during the 1920s and 1930s. In their scrapbooks, all the reviews are neatly arranged in chronological order, and most of the clippings come with a note from the agency providing the clipping service. This was a service available by subscription, and it reveals the sisters' awareness of the importance of documenting their careers. All the reviews in the collection have dates and names of newspapers, the kind of information you would usually expect in a proper documentation of press clippings. The second example is a scrapbook once belonging to Edgar Frank, who was a dancer in the German choreographer Kurt Jooss's early company. The company visited Sweden for the first time in 1934, and in 1935 Edgar Frank returned as a Jewish refugee. Frank's clippings usually lack information either on the newspaper's name, its date or the name or byline of the critic who wrote the review. These informative details are often simply cut off as if they were judged unnecessary. In every review, however, one finds Frank's name underlined in red, regardless of how much or little is written about him and whether the criticism of his dancing is negative or positive.

Applying Nye's view on sources, let us focus our attention on the documents' different material forms, and on the acts of collecting and transforming the clippings into source material. The two collections represent contrasting strategies with regard to how they formulate dancing careers as expressions of individual differences, and as part of a specific time and socio-cultural context. Edgar Frank was a dancer on the move. At the time of the Swedish performance, Jooss and his company had just left Germany because of the emerging Nazi politics. Based on this contextual information, Frank seems to need clippings as a mirror of his life. His name underlined in red exists as a vital link between a nomadic existence and a desire to belong, or to be at home within himself, regardless of the continuous change of geographical locations. Frank's clippings provided him with an image of permanence and stability, and because his future held uncertainty to such a high degree, that was perhaps all that was needed. Recording informative details on newspaper names and critics' signatures were deemed less important than identifying his own name, and marking it in bold red. The sisters' agenda was very different. Browsing through their collection of scrapbooks one gets an impression of the sisters acting as professional archivists of their own life stories. The meticulous documentation is a strong expression of the will to shape a career, an example of the sort of self-fashioning activity which is evident in other parts of the collection as well. One finds different versions of letters to agents, notes on spelling and translation. In an outline to a letter addressed to the German theatre director Max Reinhardt, someone has added the comment: 'Use a lighter and more original tone, and bear in mind that the man has to read several hundred [letters] per week.' So, in my interpretation, Frank's clippings speak of an existential need for permanence and equilibrium, whereas the sisters' manner of collecting documents is employed to improve their professional dance personas.

Because documents are saturated with such codes of meaning, Nye argues, there is no hierarchical distinction between primary and secondary sources. To dance scholars following in Nye's footsteps, this would mean that we do not privilege some documents over others. We do not make hierarchic choices between descriptions of a dance made by the choreographer, reconstructions of the same dance, photos of the original dancers, or personal reminiscences about the performance of the dance documented many years after its premiere. Rather, these different sources may render simultaneous versions of the dance under consideration. Given this situation, the historian will look for the particular relationships which can be found between the sources. In Nye's words, we search for 'patterns of translation, displacement, and contradiction' (Nye 1983: 18).

Accordingly, using the famous reconstruction of *Le Sacre du Printemps* by Millicent Hodson and Kenneth Archer as an example, it could be interpreted as a translation or a contradiction. Instead of searching for its degree of 'truthfulness', one would look into the notion that an assumed origin was created long after the premiere of the dance in 1913 (for this idea of an assumed origin, see Lion 2001). We may choose to conceive of the reconstruction as a translation of an origin in the sense that documents have been translated into movements, sound and stage setting. But because the origin is lost, that is, it has disappeared from repertory and the reconstruction has replaced it as another kind of 'authentic origin', we could perceive it as a contradiction in relation to the 1913 version. This is of course not the end of the story concerning *Le Sacre du Printemps*. With the use of different documentary realms, the dance(s) will take on other kinds of relationships. Using the many excellent workshops and writings on the method of reconstruction, produced by Hodson and Archer, as a distinct cluster of documents, dance as an object of study takes on another guise, namely that of a scientific method including source criticism (Archer and Hodson 1994). Here, we can speak of a relationship of displacement. *Le Sacre du Printemps* exists simultaneously as an example of Nijinsky's individual artistic talent, and as an instance of scientific research. In the first case the ballet is constructed as a high point in a developmental conceptualization of twentieth-century dance history; in the second, the ballet adds to the status of dance research as a respectable enterprise among other established academic disciplines. The 'same' ballet gives rise to several different but interrelated historical voices.

From a theoretical perspective, it is important to acknowledge that Nye includes the mapping of structural relationships between different realms of documents, in a framework of semiotic history, based on the linguist A. J. Greimas's semiotic square, a system of binary opposition. Written in the 1980s, Nye's book was to a large extent influenced by the writings of Hayden White (e.g. White 1973) and in particular his critical view on causation as historians' fundamental mode of explanation. Nye, in his turn, questioned traditional biography, hence he labelled his book an anti-biography. But he was also explicit in stating that a semiotic history was used only as a 'temporary weapon, helping to clear the ground for a new kind of history' (Nye 1983: 29). His emphasis on semiotics/structuralism, does not, I argue, disqualify Nye from being an inspiration today. His analytic treatment of source material is still valid as a methodological tool in an era of postmodern historiography.

Individual life stories

Some of the examples I have presented so far are generated within the area of biographical research, and this particular kind of study lends itself very well to reflections on the use of source material and the different historical narratives we can construct with the help of documents. One of the basic assumptions in this discussion is a slightly simplified notion, for argument's sake, of traditional biographies as texts applying 'unmasking, unveiling, and uncovering' as central, conceptual metaphors (Nye 1983: 24). In addition, they strive for biographical and historical realism by placing documents in chronological order, thus achieving the presentation of an individual as a unitary presence, and often disregarding contradictory tendencies and interpretations.

Intertextuality

If we look at memoirs and biographies as specific genres of historical narratives, we can apply intertextuality as one method with which we can escape the traditional typecasting of biographies as texts aiming at uncovering an individual's personality behind the public persona. The intertextual approach focuses on the object of analysis – for example a text, a dance, a film – in relation to other texts, dances etc., as well as in terms of the relationship between the interpreter and the object of study. One initial phase of intertextual methodology is the identification of intertexts, which are conceived as 'a corpus of texts, textual fragments, or textlike segments of the sociolect that shares a lexicon and . . . a syntax with the text we are reading' (Riffaterre 1984: 142). A sociolect is a kind of social 'dialect', used by a group sharing not only a lexicon and syntax, but also a culture's codes of conduct, values and myths. It is in this sense that we can argue that autobiographies and biographies are genres which make use of a shared set of narrative codes. These codes can in turn be worked upon in different ways, either by individual texts or by groups of texts. From this it follows that we can speak about generic codes as well as other kinds of intertexts interacting with the text we are studying, for example different critical theories, cultural practices of various sorts, and contextual material.

Several scholarly studies of autobiographies offer intriguing examples of how the narratives are adjusted to generic and time-specific conventions. In an analysis of nineteenth-century women's autobiographies, Thomas Postlewait has revealed how well they are adapted to narrative codes found in contemporary popular and picaresque novels (Postlewait 1991: 253–4). Likewise, David E. Nye points out how businessmen's careers in the nineteenth century were moulded after heroes in novels, the narratives typically describing how the person 'rose from obscurity and poverty to a promising position in middle class life, not through years of hard work, but through a single meritorious action' (Nye 1983: 107). With the help of a dramatic peripety, the businessmen's life completely changed after 'stopping a run-a-way [*sic*] horse, protecting a chest of money for a stranger, or saving a drowning child' (ibid.).

In dancers' memoirs from the early twentieth century, we find striking similarities. Both Loie Fuller and Isadora Duncan begin their narratives by evoking childhood memories. Fuller describes a ball she attended as a baby, only six weeks old, and how she was carried from one person to another, enthralling everyone with her charm (Fuller 1908: 9–10). Duncan starts her story at an even earlier point, by remarking on how her mother's pregnancy affected her choice of career. Duncan vividly describes how she had already started dancing while in her mother's womb, as an effect of the only nourishment her mother could take – iced oysters and champagne, the glamorous food of the goddess Aphrodite (Duncan 1927: 9). Both Fuller and Duncan refer to images from a time they could not themselves have remembered, and they do so in a particularly artful manner.

To begin a life story with childhood reminiscences has long been a narrative convention. Most dance artists use it in the same manner as Fuller and Duncan in order to point out how their future careers were decided very early in life, and they depict dance as a kind of 'natural' or universal force impossible to avoid. An interesting exception to this generic convention is the American ballerina Gelsey Kirkland's autobiography. She also starts by telling the reader about her birth, but since her story is a tragedy marked by drug addiction and mental collapses, she uses a self-conscious and ironic tone and emphasizes her awkward appearance as a baby, indicating that she was fat and had a pear-shaped head, making a dancing career seem unlikely (Kirkland 1986). From a generic perspective, it is important to acknowledge that the confessional narrative mode, which could be used by a female dancer writing in the 1980s, was not part of the accepted literary codes for a woman writing an autobiography at the time around 1900.

Another generic tendency in both Fuller's and Duncan's memoirs is that, in contrast to autobiographies by nineteenth-century actresses, they give more room for their characters' agency. In nineteenth-century memoirs, one often finds stories about other people's agency and importance in changing the development of the author's career. Postlewait notes the recurring use of 'the crucial meeting – the encounter that provides the opportunity or catalyst for success' (Postlewait 1991: 260). Moreover, in women's memoirs these pivotal meetings occur with powerful men, who thereby take over the role of propelling the narrative forward. In Fuller's and Duncan's memoirs there are traces of this convention, but overall there is a much more outspoken agency directly linked to themselves.

Paying attention to autobiographies' literary or generic qualities does not mean that they can be used only for locating fragmentary pieces of factual information. Perceived as discourses giving voice to specific socio-cultural codes and values, autobiographies are no less valid than other kinds of sources. On the contrary, they give us ample opportunity to compare and relate them to one another and to discover all those existing modes of producing an individual identity that can be found in the process of transforming documents into historical narratives.

Structure and agency

Intertextuality has been used here in order to highlight history's multiple voices. Its focus on generic relationships might, depending on the purpose of the research, need to be complemented by another perspective, that is an analytic approach that can emphasize the notion of individual agency but still give equal opportunity to multiple historical narratives. This perspective involves looking at the object of study from the viewpoint of structure and agency. Within the eclectic grouping of theories known as cultural studies, the tensions between structure and agency as explanatory and interpretative modes have been clearly outlined. This became particularly apparent when researchers turned to studies of popular culture and subcultures. In order to analyse these cultural fields, it was necessary to concentrate on how groups of people interact with socio-cultural regulations. Studies like these often focused on themes of 'pleasure, empowerment, resistance and popular discrimination' (Storey 1993: 185). This became a contested area within cultural studies, and the problem can be summarized as follows. There are always social structures and rules governing an individual's actions within a society: economic, political, educational and gender systems, to name a few. But if this were true for all human actions, there would be hardly any possibility for individual agency. On the other hand, if we believe that agency is possible, how can we understand the workings of social structures and their regulative power? One way to address this problem has been to mediate between the two perspectives and be constantly aware of how they constitute each other. This mediation can be conceptualized in theoretical terms as a joining together of structuralism and hermeneutics. In short, the former focuses on society's structural grids and explains how they are constructed and function, and the latter focuses on the interpreter's or historical subject's process of understanding and communicating life and interpersonal relationships. Several instances of dance scholarship based on mediations between structure and agency could be mentioned in this context. One recent example is Nadine A. George's compelling article about the African American Whitman Sisters performing on the vaudeville stage in the beginning of 1900 (George 2002). She shows how the sisters cleverly undermined the contemporary fixed sexual, gender and racial identities, that is how different performance strategies were used in order to resist and upset audience expectations.

Structure, as it has been referred to so far, concerns larger social systems and practices. But I will also use it with a more stratified purport, to single out particular layers of meaning with regard to readings of different types of source material. I will exemplify it with a discussion of interviews employed as sources for interpretations of structure and agency. As Nye has remarked, memoirs and biographies can be said to reveal to their readers the private persona behind a public, professional individual. The same might be said about interviews, in which a reporter probes a person with questions aimed at getting behind the professional mask, of revealing how things 'really are'.

In the beginning of the twentieth century, interviews were still quite a novelty in European newspapers, having appeared as a true media genre only during the late nineteenth century. In Sweden, as in many other countries, whenever there was a guest performance, including a dancer with an assumed 'star quality', reporters stood in line in order to conduct their interviews. It is useful to investigate how individual dancers use the interview, that is how they express agency with regard to the interviews' structural feats of intimacy and news event. The famous French ballerina Cléo de Mérode (visiting Sweden in 1903 and 1904) readily answers many kinds of personal questions, which Isadora Duncan (visiting Sweden in 1906) refuses to do. She prefers to talk about her school in Germany, the importance of physical education, and about art. In this sense she reveals a clever marketing strategy, adapted to her professional persona. But de Mérode, who seemingly adjusts to the reporters' expectations, expresses agency of a different kind. She allows the reporters to sit in during her meetings with the theatre director as well, and shows a very strong-willed and efficient business mind. She is a career woman who is clearly aware of how she can make use of the reporters' interest in her private person. Both de Mérode and Duncan act on the 'rules' of the interview, albeit in different ways, and thereby transform a structure of assumed intimacy and unmasking into one that reveals the workings of clever, professional entrepreneurs.

The Canadian-born dancer Maud Allan exemplifies agency in a different manner. In an interview conducted by a Swedish journalist in 1908, Allan paints a nice and highly respectable picture of herself and her family, which artfully manipulates the truth. Had she revealed the true story, it would have been a journalistic scoop, since Allan's brother had been executed for murdering two girls in 1898. Allan's agency consists of creating a higher social, rather than artistic, status for female dance artists. Although her story is quite remarkable in its details, one can find many examples during the period under consideration in which interviews were used as a means to heighten social position.

Development over time

Having focused my discussion on the research of individual artists whose lives do not stretch too far over time, one might very well wonder what will happen once these multi-narrated biographies become included in other kinds of historical research spanning longer periods of time. Research on individual life stories is usually labelled a form of micro-history, thus it is reasonable to reflect upon the relation to its opposite category, macro-history.

Generally, construction of a narrative covering shorter or longer periods of time follows one of two different trajectories: a diachronic or synchronic perspective. The former focuses on long-term analyses of certain historical features (for example, tracing the development of classical ballet from the Renaissance to modern times); the latter pays attention to relationships between specific features, often occurring during a shorter time-span (for example, the interrelation between different forms of theatrical dancing during the early twentieth century). These analytic perspectives also affect the way in which we use source material, and David E. Nye's views on sources could be neatly placed within the category of synchronic history. What diachronic and synchronic perspectives have in common, however, is that they both rely on some kind of tropological or discursive figure, that is figures of thought which underpin the entire conceptualization of the historical narrative. We are all familiar with the tropological figure of rise-and-fall used to describe the Romantic ballet in the nineteenth century, but there are other possibilities of narration. Deborah Jowitt has replaced that metaphor with the dichotomy of flesh and spirit, which thereby changes the reading of the period (Jowitt 1988). The development of western modern dance has often been conceptualized as a family tree, beginning with the pioneers and continuing with the first and second generation of modern dancers. Each group breaks away from its predecessors in order to shape its own dance aesthetics. In comparison, we can look at the development of theatre dance in Africa, which has been analysed as a continuous fusion of old and new movements (Adewole 2000: 126), or at history writing in India, which has been labelled a 'stratified stockpiling' (de Certeau 1988: 4). If we choose to emplot biographies of, for example, Fuller and Duncan as psychobiographies, using 'the true self' as the explanatory and narrative figure, we get a completely different narrative than we would if we were to use the opposition between dance as autonomous art and dance as popular culture, a recurring narrative motif in western dance history. If we use sources usually associated with 'unmasking' we find impressive manifestations of professionalism (for example, in responding successfully to a reporter). If we juxtapose the psychobiography with the cultural dichotomy of dance as art and dance as popular culture, we find everyday tactics of compromises, failures and triumphs in response to larger social structures. Every micro-history or biography can be read and contextualized in this manner. Thus it can be used to point out certain tendencies in macro-history.

The important task in rethinking dance history from this perspective is not to judge 'who is right', but to learn to discern the emplotment strategies used by historians, and how it affects the dance history being told. And, accordingly, to begin to understand and perceive sources as profoundly ambiguous, because they are part of a polysemic structure of meaning making. This involves an act of reading which emphasizes how a particular source always has more than one meaning, depending on the larger system into which it is activated.

Finally, I would like to return to Keith Jenkins and use one of his references concerning a more overarching view of history, which deals with the notion of historical time, and thus historical narratives, and present it as a kind of summary of this chapter. Jenkins cites Elizabeth Deeds Ermarth, who has provided perhaps the most compelling trope so far for dance scholars to be inspired by: rhythmic time. "I swing therefore I am. In this conjugating rhythm, *each move forward is also digressive*, also a sideways move. A postmodern narrative . . . keeps alive . . . an awareness of multiple pathways and constantly crossing themes", (Ermarth cited in Jenkins 1999: 174). I swing – hence I will understand that the life of a historical subject is not a curriculum vitae but a series of paratactical moves with many beginnings, middles and ends.

Bibliography

Adewole, F. (2000) 'African Theatre Dance: Aesthetics, Discourses and the Stage', in *Dance History: The Teaching and Learning of Dance History*, Conference Proceedings, of the European Association of Dance Historians, Twickenham: EADH.

Archer, K. and Hodson, M. (1994) 'Ballets Lost and Found: Restoring the Twentieth-century Repertoire', in J. Adshead-Lansdale and J. Layson (eds) *Dance History: An Introduction*, London: Routledge.

Bie, O. ([1906] 1919) *Der Tanz*, 2nd edn, Berlin: Verlag Julius Bard.

De Certeau, M. (1988) *The Writing of History*, trans. T. Conley, New York, NY: Columbia University Press.

Duncan, I. (1927) *My Life*, New York, NY: Boni and Liveright.

Fuller, L. (1908) *Quinze Ans de ma Vie*, Paris: Librairie Félix Juven.

George, N. A. (2002) 'Dance and Identity Politics in American Negro Vaudeville: The Whitman Sisters, 1900–1935', in T. F. DeFrantz (ed.)

Dancing Many Drums: Excavations in African American Dance, Madison, Wis.: University of Wisconsin Press.

Jenkins, K. (1999) *Why History? Ethics and Postmodernity*, London: Routledge.

Jowitt, D. (1988) *Time and the Dancing Image*, New York, NY: William Morrow & Company.

Kirkland, G. with Lawrence, G. (1986) *Dancing on My Grave*, Garden City, NY: Doubleday & Company.

Koritz, A. (1995) *Gendering Bodies/Performing Art: Dance and Literature in Early Twentieth-century British Culture*, Ann Arbor, Mich.: Michigan University Press.

Lion, K. (2001) *Les Sacres: En Socio-kulturell Analys av tio Versioner av ett Våroffer*, PhD thesis with English summary, Stockholm: Theatron-serien.

Nye, D. E. (1983) *The Invented Self: An Anti-biography from Documents of Thomas A. Edison*, Odense: Odense University Press.

Partsch-Bergsohn, I. (1994) *Modern Dance in Germany and the United States: Crosscurrents and Influences*, Choreography and Dance Studies Series, Volume 5, Chur, Switzerland: Harwood Academic Publishers.

Postlewait, T. (1991) 'Autobiography and Theatre history', in T. Postlewait and B. McConachie (eds) *Interpreting the Theatrical Past: Essays in the Historiography of Performance*, 2nd edn, Iowa City: University of Iowa Press.

Riffaterre, M. (1984) 'Intertextual Representations: On Mimesis and Interpretative Discourse', *Critical Inquiry*, September, 11, 1: 141–62.

Storey, J. (1993) *An Introductory Guide to Cultural Theory and Popular Culture*, London: Harvester Wheatsheaf.

White, H. (1973) *Metahistory: The Historical Imagination in the Nineteenth Century*, Baltimore, Md.: Johns Hopkins University Press.

Chapter 4

Helen Thomas

RECONSTRUCTION AND DANCE AS EMBODIED TEXTUAL PRACTICE

Introduction

SINCE THE MID-1980s, we have witnessed an increasing concern to reconstruct and preserve dances from the early American modern dance era in particular, and early twentieth-century modern ballet (Copeland 1994). Canadian dance 'professionals' have also sought to recover the barely documented Canadian modern dance tradition (Adams 1992). There has also been an interest in reconstructing the work of German modern dance innovators such as Rudolf Laban (Rubidge 1985), Mary Wigman (Manning 1993) and Kurt Jooss (Lidbury 2000). Increasingly, too, internationally renowned choreographers of today like Merce Cunningham and Paul Taylor set their earlier 'company made' dances on other contemporary dance companies across the globe, as well as on their own. Taylor and Cunningham have also set their work on classically based companies (Kane 2000). Dance preservation, in effect, has become a minor industry. This 'professional dance' interest has been accompanied by the development of healthy debates within dance scholarship regarding the politics of reconstruction and preservation. For example, in 1984, *The Drama Review* produced a dedicated issue on reconstruction (in theatre, music and dance), which opened up the debate to a wider audience than the dance notation/reconstruction/history audience where it traditionally resided (*The Drama Review* 1984). The 1992 Society of Dance History Scholars Conference at Rutgers University, New Brunswick, entitled *Dance Reconstructed: Modern Dance Art, Past, Present, Future* (proceedings published in 1993), opened up a number of divergent practical and theoretical issues. These were developed further in the first major European conference on the topic, which was held at Roehampton Institute in London in 1997. The impetus for *Preservation Politics: Dance Revived, Reconstructed,*

Remade, which addressed ballet and modern dance forms, stemmed from 'strong signals' emanating from both the profession and dance scholars (Jordan 2000). In this chapter, I explore some of the theoretical issues that dance scholars have raised in regard to reconstruction and preservation (see Thomas 2003 for a broader discussion of the issues).

The absence of a 'usable' past[1]

The first question we might want to ask is: why reconstruct past dances in the first place? The answer to this from the perspective of dance scholarship generally refers back to dance's ephemeral nature and the need to search for a usable past upon which to build a substantive tangible tradition. Dance, as a performance art, unlike fine art or literature, does not leave behind it material objects, which remain 'relatively' stable in the sense that they can be touched, felt or looked at in their extant context. Rather, dance, according to Marcia Siegel (1968: 1) 'is an event that disappears in the very act of materializing'. Despite advances in technologies for recording dance, the majority of dance events unfold in what phenomenologists term the 'vivid present' – the here and now. A few dances do 'live on' over time or at least for some time by being kept in repertory. These have mostly been passed down in a performative manner from dancer to dancer. Drama is also a performance art but it is possible, for the most part, to refer to a script upon which the 'original' performance was based (I will return to the question of 'the original' later). Western music, too, has a long-established 'universal' system of notation and composers and performers are musically literate. Many attempts have been made to develop movement notation systems over the past five centuries, some of which were published and were popular in their time, although they soon died out (Hutchinson 1977). The twentieth century witnessed the rise of various systems of notation, some of which gained a considerable impact in dance and related areas of movement (see Hutchinson Guest 1984 for a historical survey of dance notation and Davies 1975 for a survey of major systems of recording movement and dance developed in the twentieth century). As yet, there is no one universally accepted system of dance notation, although Choreology (devised by Joan and Rudolf Benesh [1956] for recording ballet) and Labanotation (US) or Kinetography Laban (Europe) (based on the system invented by Rudolf Laban [1928]), have made increasing gains in terms of development and usage since they were invented. Choreographers and dancers of today, unlike their counterparts in music, are generally not literate in movement notation (Van Zile 1985–86), although a few, such as Cunningham, prefer to develop a method for their own use. Moreover, choreographers are generally more interested in creating new works as opposed to reworking old ones.

The overwhelming fact is that the traces of thousands of past choreographies can be found in scattered fragments which marked the existence of the privileged few dancers/choreographers over the many: critical commentaries; treatises of the famous dancing masters; dance histories; photographs; snatches on film here and there; the bodily memories of dancers who performed in them (if they are still alive) and/or transmitted their bodily knowledge to other dancing bodies; the mind's eye of the audience members who witnessed them and so on.

It is hardly surprising, then, that the history of dance is generally viewed as a history of 'lost' dances. One of the positivist reasons offered for reconstructing past dances is that filling in the 'blanks' of the dance 'story' offers a more inclusive and therefore more truthful picture of dance history. On one level, this viewpoint seems more democratic in regard to, for example, excavating and revealing African American concert dance artists' contributions to the development of the mainstream concert dance tradition in America, a subject which has been shrouded in a veil of silence in dance history and criticism until recently. John Perpener's (2001) detailed history of the careers of eight African American concert dance artists, who were mostly written out of dance history, attempts to do just this (see also de Frantz 2002). In the process, he highlights the unspoken but embedded assumption in European–American aesthetics that 'whiteness was a prerequisite for the universality in *art*' (Perpener 2001: 203) [my emphasis]. 'Whiteness was the background against which all other points of view were projected in a dichotomy of superiority and inferiority' (ibid.).

But on another level, the concern to fill in the blanks of the dance story shows signs of exclusivity too. It is overwhelmingly theatrical, 'high art' past dances that are deemed suitable, worthy candidates for reconstruction. Thus, what gets reconstructed or preserved remains highly selective. This selective preservation is underpinned by a vertical (hierarchical) concept of culture, which stems from the 'culture and civilisation tradition' in which culture is defined as 'the best that has been thought and said'. In this case, high art *per se* is the yardstick by which all other cultural forms and practices are measured. Thus, it sustains the high art/popular cultural divide, which postmodernist cultural criticism has so thoroughly challenged in recent years. By contrast, there is a sustained history of recording social or 'folk' dance traditions in central and eastern Europe, which is underscored by a broader, horizontal model of culture, which has its roots in the folklorist tradition (see Giurchescu 1999 and Felföldi 1999) and the notion of culture as a way of life of a people or 'folk'. In this chapter, the problematics of dance reconstruction will be aired with reference to the vertical dimension, with examples drawn from early modern dance and modern ballet. However, it should be noted that many of the key concerns regarding authenticity, reproducibility and interpretivity, which animate debates on the reconstruction of early modern dances and modern ballet, are also visible in the ethnochoreological tradition of central and eastern Europe.

Advocates of dance reconstruction/preservation often rationalise the venture on the grounds that it offers the possibility of a kind of permanency to this ephemeral form, which in turn will facilitate a continuing cycle of cultural reproduction and perhaps enhance dance's traditional lowly status as an art form. In so doing, they sometimes unwittingly shift from the particular to the general by appealing to a well-worn trope concerning the universality of dance. The following quotation is a case in point:

> Knowledge of our dance heritage – kinaesthetically, visually and culturally – gives meaning and context to the dance works of today. Dance has been an essential and significant part of man's past, and too often it has been undervalued because of its ephemeral nature and lack of appropriate technological and notation systems to document dance's rich contributions to culture. As an art form and cultural expression, dance deserves rightful recognition.
>
> (Pernod and Ginsberg 1997: 4)

The idea of permanence in regard to those other arts which advocates of reconstruction often invoke has, of course, already been questioned in music (see Taruskin 1995), literature (see Thompson 2000) and fine art also, as the intentionally temporary artworks and installations created by contemporary artists show only too well. I will return to the concern to create a usable past on which to establish a firm dance heritage later on in the chapter. Having explored the reasoning behind the desire to reconstruct dances in the first place, I now wish to consider why this minor dance preservation industry has arisen in recent years.

Sally Kriegsman (1993) suggests a number of related social, biological and artistic reasons for the drive towards reconstruction and preservation in the context of dance in the US. To begin with, HIV/AIDS has had a significant impact on the theatre arts community in general. A number of performers and choreographers have had their life cut short before they had the opportunity to fulfil their promise and have their work recorded. Second, as modern dance choreographers, dancers and teachers become old or die, the possibility of passing down dances is lost. But this is also the case with ballet. When Nancy Reynolds (2000: 52) embarked on her video programme to 'retrieve fragments of Balanchine choreography no longer performed', she went initially to older dancers such as Dame Alicia Markova who had worked with him, almost by chance rather than design. However, she soon found an increasing sense of urgency to work with older dancers when one of the three famous 'baby ballerinas' who performed with the Ballet Russe de Monte Carlo in the 1930s,

Tamara Toumanova, died before she could assist Reynolds with the 'original' *Mozartiana*. Third, America historically is a polyglot culture and new immigrants to the US often seek to preserve their 'native' dance traditions in their new social setting and thereby pass on their cultural traditions. Fourth, the field of dance has become aware of the richness and diversity of 'home grown' dance forms. Kriegsman notes the desire to explore and celebrate the influences of African traditions on African American and 'mainstream' modern dance practices, which had previously gone unrecognised. In times of rapid change and fragmentation, she suggests, a search for 'roots' can offer a sense of continuity. Fifth, rapid developments in 'electronic reproduction' and computer technology have made it increasingly possible for choreographers and performers to have a record of their own work at little cost. As Kriegsman notes, 'a choreographer born today has a camera in her hands ready to record her first crawl' (p. 16). In so doing, choreographers and performers can 'own' their own heritage. Finally, public scrutiny and external validation have become increasingly important to artistic survival in contemporary culture. Electronic recording of created dance works may be offered as records of choreographic achievement through which the artistic value of a choreographer may be externally judged in the present and the future. I would also suggest that the increasing process of rationalisation into almost every crevice of everyday life is a contributing factor in the drive to reconstruct, preserve and catalogue dance history and bring it in line with the economics of exchange. This is particularly evident in regard to the increasing concern with 'intellectual' (or creative in this case) property rights.

Addressing the 'why now' question, as Kriegsman is only too aware, leads to a number of other related questions, some of which are implied above. For example, what and who gets performed and recorded? What are the political and ethical consequences of reconstructing past dances? In this chapter I address these and other questions which emerge out of the discussion. But perhaps we are running on ahead of ourselves here. There appears to be an implicit assumption as to what reconstruction is. I therefore commence the next section by trying to define reconstruction. As will become clear, this is not as simple as it first appears.

'What is in a name?' Revival, reconstruction, re-creation, co-authorship, reinvention . . .

Dance researchers often use the terms reconstruction, revival and re-creation interchangeably, although some have sought to make a clear distinction between them. For Selma Jean Cohen (1993), for example, a revival is carried out by the choreographer him/herself. A reconstruction is made by someone else who researches the 'work'. A re-creation is concerned to capture the 'spirit of the work'. Ann Hutchinson Guest (2000: 65), on the other hand, uses the term revival to refer to a work that has been brought to life by someone using a notated score, rather like 'a musician bringing a music composition to life from a notated music score'. Unusually, Hutchinson Guest is highly 'literate' in a number of movement notations. Vaslav Nijinsky, the legendary dancer and choreographer of Diaghilev's Ballets Russes, recorded his first ballet for Diaghilev, *L'Après Midi d'un Faune* (1912), in his own system of notation. The ballet, however, was handed down over the years from dancer to dancer, without reference to Nijinsky's complex notation score. Hutchinson Guest and Claudia Jeschke deciphered the original score and subsequently translated it into Labanotation in the late 1980s, which in turn led to 'revivals' of the ballet in Naples, Montreal and New York (Hutchinson Guest 1991).

A reconstruction, according to Hutchinson Guest (2000), involves 'constructing a work anew' from a wide range of 'sources' and information, with the intention of getting as close to the original as possible. Millicent Hodson and Kenneth Archer's staging of Nijinsky's *Le Sacre du Printemps* (1913) for the Joffrey Ballet in 1987 and *Jeux* (1913) in 1996 would fall into this category. Archer and Hodson's (2000: 1) primary concern is to 'preserve only masterworks' of the twentieth century that are historically relevant and have 'contemporary relevance'. They aim to 'ensure that the reconstruction is a reasonable facsimile of the original'. They insist that in order to take on the task of bringing 'lost jewels' back to life, they have to ensure that the end product (the reconstructed work) will be founded on at least 50 per cent 'hardcore evidence for dance and design' (p. 2). Robert Joffrey, who commissioned *Le Sacre*, estimated that the 1987 reconstruction represented 85 per cent of the original Ballets Russes production in Paris, which caused a riot when it was premiered in 1913.

A re-creation for Hutchinson Guest (2000) is based on an idea or a story of a ballet (or dance), which has been lost in the mists of time. The re-creation may involve using the original music or idea. This idea of re-creation roughly corresponds to Cohen's notion. In the late 1980s Eleanor King, who performed in the early Humphrey-Weidman company, staged two versions of an early but little-known Doris Humphrey solo, *The Banshee* (1927), largely based 'on her own memories and imagination' (Dils 1993: 225). Ann Dils considers that King's first re-creation of the solo, which was performed by Dawn De Angelo, 'seemed very close to Humphrey's dances from the period' with its abstract choreographic scaffolding and 'the steely revelation of body parts . . . that builds a sense of dread in the audience, rather than being an imitation of a banshee' (p. 226). De Angelo performed the solo in leotard and tights. King's other version, the Kabuki banshee, performed by Mino Nicholas, was very different. Here the banshee was stylistically presented like a Kabuki actor. Nicholas's 'face was painted white and his eyes were outlined in red' and he donned a 'long white wig, cut to form a mane like a Kabuki lion' (ibid.). This costume was in stark contrast to that worn by De Angelo, which in itself was different from the 'moldy green costume described in Humphrey's letters' (ibid.). In 1927, Humphrey was attempting to distance her dancing from the orientalism of Denishawn. Thus the costuming and makeup used in the Kabuki version seems somewhat at odds with Humphrey's ideas when she created the solo. There were also differences in the stylistic qualities of the movement. In the Kabuki version, Dils argues, King built the dance around the specificities of Nicholas's movement tendencies and his muscularity. The dance, according to Dils, 'was changed to meet the performer, instead of expanding the dancer's movement range and stretching the audience's perceptions to see a tenuous female sprite actualized by a bulky male performer' (ibid.). While King's first version might be considered a re-creation in the spirit outlined above, it may also be seen as a 'co-authored' work, as it was based on King's embodied memories of Humphrey's early style and her imagination. The Kabuki version, on the other hand, could be viewed as a 're-invention' (see Franko 1995) of Humphrey's 1927 solo for today's audiences. Perhaps through her extensive experience as a choreographer in her own right, King defamiliarised or distanced herself from the Humphrey solo as she had known it and on which she also based her first re-creation for De Angelo, to make something anew for Nicholas. Dils suggests that the Kabuki version is less valuable than the first re-creation because it shaped the dance to the demands of the performer rather than expanding the vision of the performer to the emergent Humphrey style of the late 1920s. Paying attention to the performative elements of reconstruction, Dils argues, presents present-day dancers with new challenges and 'expands the possibilities of dance moving beyond what is comfortable and expected to ways of performing that are essentially new and surprising for current audiences' (1993: 227). At the same time, however, it could also be argued that King's two very different versions of *The Banshee* reveal that 'authoring' and therefore the question of ownership of intellectual or creative property rights, is a more complex story than we might at first imagine.

There is no doubt in Hutchinson Guest's mind that the revival is the nearest to the 'original' dance work, because it is 'authored' by the choreographer's own hand through the notated score. From her perspective, the productions of *L'Après Midi d'un Faune*, based on her translation of Nijinsky's score, fit the criteria for a revival of the original production performed in Paris in 1912. In other words, they constitute 'the real thing', whereas reconstructions are less authentic. Indeed, she suggests that reconstructions might be better thought of as 'reconstitutions'. She further suggests that, for the sake of accuracy, reconstructions such as Hodson and Archer's 1996 version of Nijinsky's *Jeux* (1916) should read 'Choreography by Millicent Hodson based on existing evidence of Nijinsky's original ballet', not 'choreography by Vaslav Nijinsky' (Hutchinson Guest 2000: 66). She also proposes that ballets that have been passed on through memory, as with the numerous handed-down productions over the years of *Faune*, should indicate this in the programme notes.

As shown above, there are different terms used to speak about the activity of taking dances out of the shadows of time and putting them on to the stage. Although I have only scratched the surface of the debates, it should be evident that behind almost every discussion of reconstruction, revival, and so on, are assumptions (implicit and explicit) regarding authenticity, reproducibility and interpretivity.

Authenticity, reproducibility, interpretivity and *The Dying Swan*

In this section I am using the term 'reconstruction' in the broadest sense of the word to refer to bringing back past dances (lost and found and preserved) to the stage, or in some cases on the page. As indicated at the beginning of the chapter, the debates on reconstruction have usually been conducted in relation to early modern dance or early twentieth century 'modern' ballet. I have chosen to focus on a particular case study of a now classic short ballet solo, *The Dying Swan*, choreographed by Mikhail Fokine in 1905, to shed light on questions of authenticity, reproducibility and interpretivity.

In the latter part of the 1990s, Fokine's granddaughter, Isabelle Fokine, was hired to teach her 'version' of *The Dying Swan* to the Kirov Ballet, who have had their own proud tradition of performing Fokine's ballets, including *The Dying Swan*, over many decades. In 1997, Isabelle Fokine was the central protagonist in a weekend arts television programme, *The 'Dying Swan' Legacy* (Fox 1997), which explored her sense of how this dance and others choreographed by her grandfather, such as *Spectre de la Rose* (1913), should be performed. Her convictions and rationale were set against the views of critics, historians, former ballerinas and members of the Kirov Ballet. The programme provides a fascinating example of competing perspectives on authenticity and their ramifications, despite the fact that *The Dying Swan* is not considered to be a particularly 'revolutionary' ballet. Indeed, as the critic Clement Crisp notes in the television programme, it has become something of a cliché. Unless otherwise stated, all references to this discussion of *The Dying Swan* are drawn from the programme. The words and views of the various critics, historians and dancers on the ballet cited in this discussion are also taken from the programme.

At the beginning of the programme, Isabelle Fokine asserts that her version of *The Dying Swan* and her approach to teaching it stems from her 'upbringing as a dancer' and her 'own family's beliefs' and 'family heritage'. Isabelle Fokine situates her claim to the authenticity of her *Dying Swan* in terms of her own performance practice and, more importantly, in the fact that she has privileged access to Fokine's ideas, notes etc., which he passed down to his son, who in turn passed them down to her. In other words, she has direct access to 'the oracle' for performing and teaching purposes. *The Dying Swan*, as Isabelle Fokine notes, does not make 'enormous technical demands' on a dancer but it does make 'enormous artistic ones because every movement and every gesture should signify a different experience', which is 'emerging from someone who is attempting to escape death' (ibid.). *The Dying Swan*, however, is probably associated more with the acclaimed early twentieth-century ballerina, Anna Pavlova, for whom the dance was created, than with the choreographer. Pavlova popularised the dance through her numerous tours, which were received by enthusiastic audiences across the globe for over twenty years. A film of her dancing *The Dying Swan* was made in 1924. Judith Mackrell, the dance critic, points out that because the ballet was made on Pavlova's body, the 'bird-like quality' of her movement for which she was noted became part of the choreography. Irina Baronova, also one of the three 'baby ballerinas' who performed with Ballet Russe de Monte Carlo from 1932 to 1940, notes that she considered the ballet to be closely connected to Pavlova – so much so that she never wanted to dance it herself, although she performed all the other roles that other great ballerinas before her had danced. *The Dying Swan*, according to Baronova, belonged to Pavlova; it was 'her very special thing' (Pavlova asked to be buried in the costume). Hence, both Baronova and Mackrell propose that Pavlova played a large part in the creation of the dance and its subsequent development through her continuous performance of it.

As Crisp notes, it would be impossible to obtain an accurate sense of what the dance looked like when it was first performed in 1905. The Hollywood film of Pavlova performing the ballet was taken many years later. If, as seems likely, Pavlova altered the dance over time to accommodate changes in her style and her ageing dancing body, then a large question is left hovering over the idea of an original authentic version and the likelihood of reproducing this or any other dance exactly 'as it was'. Many other leading ballerinas have also performed the ballet over the years, including Fokine's wife, Vera Fokina. Can we say with any confidence if their interpretations were more authentic or inauthentic than Pavlova's?

According to Isabelle Fokine, the way in which her grandfather had choreographed and recorded *The Dying Swan* is significantly different from the manner in which it is performed today. Her aim is to restore it to its original state. The ballet, she observes, often appears as if it is a variation of *Swan Lake* (Pepita-Ivanov version 1895); 'it looks like Odette at death's door'. However, she argues, the ballet 'in essence' is 'not about the beauty of a ballerina' being able 'to transform herself into a figure of a swan'. The ballet, she maintains, 'is *not* about a swan, it is about *death* and the swan is simply a metaphor for that' [my emphasis]. She continues:

> So what the *original* choreography offers the ballerina in general doing her own series of gestures, is a very textured piece . . . There are moments when the gestures express extreme fragility, her vulnerability, her surrender, her longing, her desperation, her yearning for love. [my emphasis]

Isabelle Fokine reasons that if her grandfather had genuinely considered this dance to be an improvisation, then 'he would not have recorded it in the great detail that he did'. Fokine, however, did not record the dance in 1905. It was recorded later and was published in 1925. Fokine, as indicated above, worked with other dancers and, as Crisp suggests, his restaging of the dance for Markova in 1941–42 could be deemed to be his '*last* thoughts' [my emphasis] on the subject. According to Markova, her version differed significantly from previous versions in that it was danced 'completely *en pointe de bourrée*'. Crisp implies that the notion of a definitive version of *The Dying Swan* is simply a Fokine invention.

The Kirov presented two versions of *The Dying Swan* at the Coliseum in London on two successive evenings in 1997. We are informed that these were their own and Isabelle Fokine's respectively. According to the dance critic Debra Crane, they were remarkably different. The first performance, according to Crane, was more like Odette in *Swan Lake*, while the second performance was more dramatic. Isabelle Fokine claims that she sought to offer the Kirov an 'authentic alternative' to their interpretation of the ballet. The Kirov, on the other hand, as Crane points out, retains *The Dying Swan* and other Fokine ballets, such as the *Polovtsian Dances* (1909), in the repertoire. As such, she notes, 'they have decades of performing these dances and they would need to be convinced as to the accuracy of Isabelle Fokine's version'. From the confrontations between the Kirov dancers and Isabelle Fokine evidenced in the programme, particularly in regard to the *Polovtsian Dances*, it is clear that the dancers had not been convinced. On several occasions in the programme the dancers openly protest that Isabelle Fokine's version of the dance is contrary to the way they have 'always danced it'. The Kirov dancers consider that their approach to Fokine is faithful to their tradition, which has been passed down from dancer to dancer. Isabelle Fokine, however, argues that the Kirov dancers' performance could be enriched 'with a degree of authenticity', which she could 'bring to their production'. Relying on memory to pass on dances, she suggests, is fallible, while she can return to the choreographer's sources and notations. These notations etc., to a large extent, become in the end the definitive 'dance text'. Isabelle Fokine's assertion that 'there is a definitive version of *The Dying Swan* because of the detailed records he [Fokine] left' is given a legal edge in the credits of the programme, which inform us that 'Fokine Ballets are protected by international copyright law and cannot be performed without a licence from the Fokine Estate Archive'.

Conclusion

This story of the legacy of *The Dying Swan* raises questions about the origin of a work of art and the search for a definitive, authentic version. It also shows that the attempt to reconstruct a dance on the basis of the choreographer's intentions is just as problematic, despite the fact that in this instance the choreographer maintained that his description of the ballet is the definitive version as he taught it to Madame Pavlova (Fokine 1925). Vera Fokina, not Pavlova, executed the 36 poses from the ballet, which accompanied Fokine's 'detailed description' of the dance, which was published twenty years after the first performance. The extent to which the choreographer is the sole 'author' of the work is also questioned here. Choreographers do not generally construct dances in the abstract, even although some may now work with computers and virtual bodies. Dancers are not simply vehicles for expressing the choreographer's intentions. There is of necessity a degree of collaboration between choreographer and dancer, if not always co-authorship in the creative process. The ownership of the work, however, mostly remains firmly in the hands of the choreographer. In an increasingly commodified and bureaucratised system of exchange, intellectual property rights are progressively mapping on to the agenda of contemporary performance practices. The case study shows that a dance work is not 'fixed' in either performance or in writing and that through the process of handing down dances from one dancer to another or by working from a dance script, description or score, different, often competing, interpretations emerge. This, then, challenges the drive towards reproducing a dance in the image of the 'original', which, as I have suggested, is bound more by myth than fact. Attempts to capture and to 'freeze frame' dances in their time may assist dancers and researchers to understand to some extent what a dance might have felt like to perform and witness and, in turn, may add to the knowledge base of the tradition. But that knowledge base, like the tradition, is always partial (biased and selective) and in light of the above discussion I suggest that it is important to be reflexive about this in the process of reviving, reconstructing, re-creating or reinventing the dance 'stories' of the past. The construct of tradition with which I would want to work is one that lives and breathes through embodied textual practice (on or off the stage), not one that is locked up in 'performance museums' (Franko 1993).

Note

1 The American cultural commentator, Van Wick Brooks, coined the term 'usable past' in his writings on American culture in the early twentieth century. Aaron Copland used the term to describe his concern in the 1920s

to search out former American composers who explored 'the American scene' in order to find a basis for developing a style of music that would be recognised as American in character.

Bibliography

Adams, L. (1992) 'The Value of Dance', *Dance Connection*, 10, 3: 24–6.

Archer, K. and Hodson. M. (2000) 'Confronting Oblivion: Keynote Address and Lecture Demonstration on Reconstructing Ballets', in S. Jordan (ed.), *Preservation Politics, Dance Revived, Reconstructed, Remade*, London: Dance Books.

Benesh, J. and Benesh, R. (1956) *Introduction to the Benesh Dance Notation*, London: A & C Black.

Berg, S. (1993) 'The Real Thing: Authenticity and Dance at the Approach of the Millennium', *Dance Reconstructed: Modern Dance Art, Past, Present, Future*, Proceedings of Society of Dance History Scholars Sixteenth Annual Conference, Rutgers University, New Brunswick: SDHS.

Cohen, S. J. (1993) 'Dance Reconstructed', *Dance Research Journal*, 25, 2(Fall): 54–5.

Copeland, R. (1994) 'Reflections on Revival and Reconstruction', *Dance Theatre Journal*, 11, 3: 18–20.

Davies, M. (1975) *Towards Understanding the Intrinsic in Body Movement*, New York, NY: Arno Press.

De Frantz, T. (ed.) (2002) *Dancing Many Drums: Excavations in African American Dance*, Madison, Wis.: University of Wisconsin Press.

Dils, A. (1993) 'Performance Practice and Humphrey Reconstruction', in SDHS, *Dance Reconstructed: Modern Dance Art, Past, Present, Future*, Proceedings of Society of Dance History Scholars Sixteenth Annual Conference, Rutgers University, New Brunswick: SDHS.

Felföldi, L. (1999) 'Folk Dance Research in Hungary: Relations among Theory, Fieldwork and the Archive', in T. J. Buckland (ed.) *Dance in the Field: Theory, Methods and Issues in Dance Ethnography*, Basingstoke: Macmillan.

Fokine, M. (1925) *The Dying Swan, Music by C. Saint-Saëns: Detailed Description of the Dance by Michel Fokine; Thirty-six Photographs from Poses by Vera Fokina*, New York, NY: J. Fischer & Brother.

Fox, Gerald (1997) *The 'Dying Swan' Legacy*, produced and directed by Gerald Fox, London Weekend Television: South Bank Show.

Franko, M. (1993) *Dance as Text: Ideologies of the Baroque Body*, Cambridge: Cambridge University Press.

—— (1995) *Dancing Modernism/Performing Politics*, Bloomington, Ind.: Indiana University Press.

Giurchescu, A. (1999) 'Past and Present Field Research', in T. J. Buckland (ed.) *Dance in the Field: Theory, Methods and Issues in Dance Ethnography*, Basingstoke: Macmillan.

Hutchinson, A. (1977) *Labanotation, or Kinetography Laban: The System of Analyzing and Recording Movement*, illustrated by D. Anderson, New York, NY: Theatre Arts Books.

Hutchinson Guest, A. (1984) *Dance Notation: The Process of Recording Movement on Paper*, London: Dance Books.

—— (1991) 'Nijinsky's *Faune*', *Choreography and Dance*, 1: 3–34.

—— (2000) 'Is Authenticity to be Had?', in S. Jordan (ed.) *Preservation Politics: Dance Revived, Reconstructed, Remade*, London: Dance Books.

Jordan, S. (ed.) (2000) *Preservation Politics: Dance Revived, Reconstructed, Remade*, London: Dance Books.

Kane, A. (2000) 'Issues of Authenticity and Identity in the Restaging of Paul Taylor's *Airs*', in S. Jordan (ed.) *Preservation Politics: Dance Revived, Reconstructed, Remade*, London: Dance Books.

Kriegsman, S. A. (1993) 'Dance Reconstructed: Modern Dance Art, Present and Future', *Ballett International*, 6: 15–17.

Laban, R. von (1928) *Schrifttanz: Kinetographie Methodik*, Vienna: Universal Edition.

Lidbury, C. (2000) 'The Preservation of the Ballets of Kurt Jooss', in S. Jordan (ed.) *Preservation Politics: Dance Revived, Reconstructed, Remade*, London: Dance Books.

Manning, S. A. (1993) *Ecstasy and the Demon: Feminism and Nationalism in the Dances of Mary Wigman*, Berkeley, Calif.: University of California Press.

Pernod, J. and Ginsberg, A. (1997) 'Dialogue: New Work and Reconstructed Work in the Context of Dance Repertory', *Dance Research Journal*, 29, 1: 1–5.

Perpener, J. O. (2001) *African-American Concert Dance: The Harlem Renaissance and Beyond*, Urbana and Chicago, Ill.: University of Illinois Press.

Reynolds, N. (2000) 'Inside Artistry: The George Balanchine Foundation', in S. Jordan (ed.) *Preservation Politics: Dance Revived, Reconstructed, Remade*, London: Dance Books.

Rubidge, S. (1985) 'Old Modern Dances Revived', *Dance Theatre Journal*, 3, 4: 38–9.

Siegel, M. B. (1968) *At the Vanishing Point: A Critic Looks at Dance*, New York, NY: Saturday Review Press.

SDHS (Society of Dance History Scholars) (1993) *Dance Reconstructed: Modern Dance Art, Past, Present, Future*, Proceedings of Society of Dance History Scholars Sixteenth Annual Conference, Rutgers University, New Brunswick: SDHS.

Taruskin, R. (1995) *Text as Act: Essays on Performance*, Oxford: Oxford University Press.

The Drama Review (1984) 'Reconstruction Issue', 28, 3 (t103): 2–98.

Thomas, H. (2003) *The Body, Dance and Cultural Theory*, Palgrave: Basingstoke.

Thompson, A. (2000) 'Shakespeare: Preservation and/or Reinvention', in S. Jordan (ed.) *Preservation Politics: Dance Revived, Reconstructed, Remade*, London: Dance Books.

Van Zile, J. (1985–6) 'What Is the Dance? Implications for Dance Notation', *Dance Research Journal*, 17, 2 and 18, 1: 41–7.

Chapter 5

Chris Roebuck

'QUEERING' THE KING

A Remedial Approach to Reading Masculinity in Dance

Introduction

IT IS WIDELY ACCEPTED IN dance scholarship that male dancers in western classical theatre dance have long been a source of tension, a predicament that has been sustained by the twin forces of prejudice and ignorance.[1] Three hundred years ago, however, the situation was very different. As Terry (1978: 7) explains:

> At six years old, this Frenchman was pretty much his own boss. His father was dead, so he didn't have to ask his approval (although his father had enjoyed the dance), and his mother was more concerned with politics and guiding him in such matters. So he did as he pleased and he danced throughout most of his life. He could because he was King. He was Louis XIV.

What happened to male classical dancers in the transition from amateur *ballet de cour* to professional ballet today? Have they, as many social commentators and historians would suggest, been the most spectacularly visible but innocent victims of widespread changing socio-political and aesthetic attitudes about gender representation?[2] Could the way that men are represented (and represent themselves) in dance literature also be at least partially to blame? Or is it possible that ballet practice itself should shoulder some of the responsibility, wherein what would later contribute to the sense of unease that now surrounds male ballet dancers might be traced back to the noble style of dancing developed in Royal French courts during the seventeenth century? If so, might not this *ballet de cour* also provide a possible antidote to the current malaise?

'Dancing? A flicked wrist and a sneer said it all'[3]

Since the 1980s, when feminist dance scholarship problematised the patriarchal codes through which aspects of gender and sexual identity are produced, the issue over what model of masculine identity male dancers in classical ballet are meant to represent has become more intense and politicised. The traditional view is that, through both the choreography and narrative, men in ballet articulate 'acceptable' masculine values such as gallantry, virility and rationality. To defend this 'ideal' model, any possible source of unease is adroitly blamed on off-stage behaviour (see Birdwhistell 1969). This strategy of segregating performance from detrimental outside forces, however, has done little to dispel the belief that, because they engage in an activity historically associated with the spectacular display of women's bodies, these men represent a corruption of these ideological values.

According to dualistic gender codes, to be on display is associated with loss of power which is regarded as a feminising position. This, in the world of ballet, is a code for homosexuality (see Burt 1995). Is this the underlying cause of much of the prejudice and ignorance that surrounds men in dance? If so, it might explain why it is a subject that more traditional studies in dance history seem reluctant to address directly.[4] The link between men in ballet and homosexuality was, however, only forged during the twentieth century. As Burt (1995: 12) points out, 'There is as yet no firm evidence of gay involvement in ballet before the time of Diaghilev and Nijinsky.' Yet, he adds, problems concerning men in dance can be traced back to nineteenth-century Romantic ballet. Rather than homosexuality, the major cause for concern at this time was changing attitudes towards class wherein the male dancer was caught in the crossfire of a middle-class loathing of anything that referred to what they perceived as an aristocratic degeneracy on the one hand and a similar disgust with suggestions of the 'vigour and fecundity of the working classes' (p. 26) on the other.[5] Although much of this class prejudice has now dissipated, the idea that the male dancer is a source of unease has remained. By the beginning of the twentieth century, that unease was identified with homosexuality.

Surprisingly, perhaps, the idea that ballet promotes 'orthodox' models of masculinity can often be found in some of the early feminist dance research. Those values so cherished by traditionalists are, however, read as indicative of how classical theatre dance has always reflected and promoted an institutionalised gender and sexual inequality. By looking at factors such as narrative devices, movement symbolism and the imbalance between male choreographers and female dancers, ballet is categorised as a direct representation of the ways in which mainstream culture continually conspires to empower heterosexual men and subjugate those deemed 'Other' (women and homosexual men). This definition then forms the basis of an antidotal strategy in which the classical arena is placed on the bottom rung of a 'politically correct' ladder while postmodern practices are set at the top. That many of these *avant-garde* works are devised and performed by women and openly gay practitioners is used as evidence to substantiate a politically motivated belief that, in comparison, ballet is a patriarchal institution that has only ever been concerned with the promotion of a limited number of 'acceptable' male models.[6]

These two somewhat ahistorical and 'sweeping' (traditionalist and early feminist) interpretations of how classical dance produces identity have, however, been questioned by post-feminist researchers such as Lynn Garafola (1997), Sally Banes (1998), Susan Manning (1998) and Alexandra Carter (1999). In order to break free of what Carter (1999: 92) describes as the 'straitjacket' effect produced by politically essentialist strategies that stress the victimisation of women and stigmatise men, two key issues are now being addressed. First, a shift away from what Carter sees as a 'myopic' (p. 95) view of the ballet in which only a fraction of the repertoire is examined which is then 'taken as generic'. This, she argues, 'negates the richness of the ballet heritage and the diversity of its [male and female] incumbents'. Second, by adopting a 'historical and materialist' approach to reading individual works, postfeminist scholars are discovering 'a much more complex range of representations than has previously been suggested' (Banes 1998: 3).

Another key element to this methodology is an emphasis upon performance dynamics in that, although the narrative may be misogynist or patriarchal and describe the female character as weak or passive, 'the physical prowess of the dancer performing the role may saturate it with agency' (Banes 1998: 9). Likewise, while the male role may be depicted in the libretto as powerful and dominant, lending support to essentialist models of masculinity, telling instances in the choreography 'can undermine or render ironic the narrative flow' (p. 10).

For dance history scholars, however, although this 'historical and materialist' approach to reading individual works from previously neglected areas of the repertoire is useful, the use of performance agency as a means of deconstructing ideological formations of identity remains problematic. For example, it is difficult to see how such a paradigm can be applied to works of which only written documentation and a few artistic sketches remain, such as those of the *ballet de cour*.[7]

The *ballets de cours*

It is nearly dawn on the morning of 23 February 1653. So far, members of the French Royal court have been treated to an almost twelve-hour *melange* of dancing, singing, poetry and elaborate stage effects depicting various scenes of village life, demonic activity and Greek myth. At the climax of *Le Ballet Royal de la Nuit*, and to herald the rising of the sun, the magnificently dressed King Louis XIV (1643–1715) appears as *Le Roi Soleil* to lead the entire cast in a grand ballet.

Circled by masked courtiers according to the then controversial cosmology of Copernicus, the young king was portraying Apollo, one of the many Greek gods who had passed into the allegorical conventions of fifteenth-century Christian Europe. As the god of music, medicine, prophecy and archery (whose arrows, like piercing rays from the sun, had the power not only to bestow life but to destroy), the king symbolised physical light and mental illumination. By enshrining himself as the corporeal emblem of knowledge, truth and moral purity, Louis was sending out a clear signal not only to the local masses but also to the *haute monde*. As Bryson (1997: 61) explains,

> If Louis XIV has himself represented in painting . . . as one who dances, it is because his dance, in its widest sense, orchestrates the entire milieu, from its mode of dress down to its actual revenues. Instead of gold as the infrastructure subtending court culture, the infrastructure becomes the king's manipulation of spectacle and prestige, and his orchestration of the courtier's bodies into a kind of permanent dance of power.

Louis's overt politicisation of court ballet, according to Mark Franko (1993: 133), would not have been lost on his erudite audience for whom 'choreography was an academic pursuit'. Aware of this *connoisseurship*, Louis was able to use his dancing to symbolise his desire to change the political structure of France from oligarchy to absolutism. The king, no longer a first among equals atop a feudal system, was now proclaiming himself as the personification of a new sense of Baroque individualism. This deliberate fusion of art and life, according to Franko (1993: 38), also marks the beginning of what would later be considered key to the problematic status of classical male dancers, wherein 'performance is no longer, from this perspective, the representation of things to be interpreted but the active interpreting of historical reality'. What has become disadvantageous to men in dance today was, however, highly lucrative for Louis. As Bryson (1997: 60) suggests, for the king, dance imagery was a direct means to a political actuality:

> The king's image is where the king generates his personal authority, and in relation to that image all the lesser levels of the court hierarchy are measured: the king as solar centre of personal spectacle, round which all the lesser satellites of power revolve.

If France was the geographic and cultural centre of Europe, Versailles (no longer Paris) was the political centre of France, and the *ballet de cour* was the symbolic centre of court life, then Louis was the sun around which it all revolved.[8] The King, according to Bryson, was no longer 'the reflection of a power located elsewhere, but power's actual locus' (p. 60).

To secure his new prominence and to keep himself ahead of the rest of the court, Louis kept his dancing masters busy inventing new steps and positions for him to execute. These were then formalised, recorded and quickly learned by those who wished to curry favour from a king who was dictating the prerequisite standard in bearing and elegance of deportment. Furthermore, as Garafola (1997: 4) explains, during this time there was no differentiation between the sexes when it came to technique: both male and female courtiers were expected to execute all the new *pas* if they were to remain fashionable. But just how difficult or demanding was this choreography? Although no reliable evidence exists that describes Louis's own abilities as a dancer, aspects of his costume and some of the rules that govern conduct at court provide possible clues.

The king's spectacular sun costume was an extremely elaborate confection complete with plumed head-dress and highly decorated short skirt, worn over stockings, that emphasised the young King's slender and elegant frame. In such an outfit it is hard to imagine the King executing the large leaps and multiple turns that today are a prerequisite for, and define the masculine status of, male classical dancers. For Louis, the emphasis was not on athletic power, which would have been considered vulgar, but on his central position in the choreography. As Garlick (1997: 24) points out, in accordance with the strictures of court etiquette,

> in the ballroom, the nobleman (and above all the king) was expected to refrain from excessive displays of virtuosity, demonstrating only those skills which would pass for natural grace. A similar decorum may have applied when the king appeared on stage in the figure of a god or king.

Furthermore, and according to Franko (1993: 67):

> According to conventions established by the Renaissance *basse danse*, airborne movement was grotesque in that it recalled the actions of vainglorious or mad men through its achievement of height as an image of swollen pride; movement closer to the earth and resembling walking in a measured manner connoted authentic nobility and good judgement.

By today's standards, the model he portrayed through his costume and 'measured' movement seems to defy categorisation according to what are now considered to be the traditional balletic codes of gender representation. In contrast to what both recent male practitioners and theorists describe as a 'universal' masculine model, the King's identity was constructed on the expression of autonomous power through the use of a genderless movement vocabulary set in a genteel kinesphere that is now more associated with the feminine. Of course, this identity would not have been considered inappropriate at the time as this was a period in history when male courtiers were expected to take as many pains over their outward appearance and deportment as the women. As Eva-Elizabeth Fischer (1998: 38) remarks, during the Renaissance, difference between the sexes for the nobility was based solely upon a slavish attention to fashion and etiquette and 'sexuality was locked out'.

For Louis, the means to power was not achieved through outward manifestations of any 'innate' gender or sexual code but through an artificially heightened and spectacular visibility. His body, with its sexual signification masked by his costume, is transformed into a hollow and genderless political vessel. At the very moment of aligning himself as an object of adoration, his own individual identity is surrendered: the king as a symbol of power becomes disassociated from Louis the man. In the equation between power and identity not only is sexuality locked out but the body, as something of flesh, is erased. As Rudolph zur Lippe (quoted in Franko 1993: 194) explains, as dance became the tool of absolutism in the late sixteenth and early seventeenth centuries, it lost the human potential for self-realisation. By manipulating the physical display of the court dance to legitimate his double status as real and ideal body, Louis underwent a process of self-alienation.

As an 'alien' vision of sexless and bodiless identity, the King corrupts the 'natural' bond between the male body and the masculine code. Rather than integral, power is revealed as the result of stylised gestures and acts inscribed on the body. In his role as the sun, and tied to neither a purely masculine nor feminine vocabulary of expression that is then articulated through the deconstruction of the metaphysical divide that separates 'masculine' power from 'feminine' display, Louis can be read as a prototype of what theorists would later define as a queer identity.[9]

Louis: the prototype queer?

In his solo role of 'Le Roi Soleil', Louis exploited both the intellectual and the aesthetic (the political and the spectacular) dimensions of court ballet to promote his ambition for autonomy. Unencumbered by issues surrounding 'politically correct' gender and sexual representation on the one hand and, on the other, untouched by any accusation of deviancy that currently compartmentalises male ballet dancers, he had nothing to prove beyond his capabilities as absolute monarch. But how can his Baroque individualism be understood as corresponding to a prototypical queer praxis? To answer this requires, first, an engagement with the disjunctive schism between dance history and theory and second, an examination of one of the key tenets of queer theory: a non-axiomatic concept of 'difference'.

On this schism between history and theory, Franko (1993) suggests that, in recent dance scholarship, developments in theory are too often biased towards advances in late twentieth-century practice. This, he contends, has led to a situation wherein theoretical developments are either misattributed or even dehistoricised. Rather, Franko claims, dance theory is not a 'purely postmodern gesture' but is 'intrinsic to the earliest significant practices of Western theatre dance' which, in turn, can be traced back to the intellectual and aesthetic function of Baroque court ballet. 'Theory and practice', he contends, 'share *one* history' (1993: 132) [original italics]. As such, by 'cultivating a theory of dance, we engage in a fundamentally baroque pursuit: a form of questioning and a questioning of form developed at the historical site of western theatre dancing . . . our spectatorship *is* baroque' [original italics].

According to Franko, the link between baroque and postmodern thinking is an emphasis upon the materiality of the body as 'text'. While, in court dance, Louis's body was the inscribed and dynamic locus of a new theory of identity politics, postmodern theory emphasises the body as an agent of meaning whose unique historicity effects a material resistance upon more modernist concepts of the unified and disembodied subject. In both instances the body is not only coded with meaning but becomes the locus of both aesthetic and political change. Furthermore, as Franko suggests (p. 135), codes of behaviour and deportment originating in the *ballet de cour* that are still in evidence in classical theatre dance's vocabulary today create a 'dialogue between forms and periods on the basis of style, vocabulary and theory rather than history alone'. This dialogue also extends to the model of identity articulated by Louis in his dancing and the non-axiomatic concept of difference described by queer theorists.

On this concept Eve K. Sedgwick (1990: 22) comments that, although there are a tiny number of 'indispensable' axes such as gender, race, class, nationality and sexual orientation, these tend to 'override all or some other forms of difference and similarity'. Focusing on what she sees as a postwar 'condensation of sexual categories' (p. 3) into only two discrete specifications (namely heterosexuality and homosexuality), she goes on to speculate whether it is still possible to identify differences within sexuality that could retain 'the unaccounted-for potential to disrupt many forms of the available thinking about sexuality' (p. 25). This 'condensation' is particularly prevalent in dance history, wherein scholars have tended to read ballet as a coded representation of two other discrete specifications, those of male and female culture.[10] Fundamental to this anthropological framework is a concept of difference based on social experience. Elsewhere, Michèle Barrett (1987: 32) takes issue with this model by arguing that it tends to assume a level of cultural essentialism in which 'the identities that people construct from their experience are never seen as problematic'. She contends that the authority of a separatist approach, wherein 'men have one reality, women have another' (p. 31) should, however, be challenged. To this end, Barrett advocates a more deconstructive approach to the concept of difference in which differences within, as well as between, the genders are considered.[11]

Key to both Sedgwick's and Barrett's radical and sceptical form of identity politics is a great deal of specificity when dealing with representations that includes attending to what people take pleasure in, how this is tied to historically specific circumstances and the representational dynamics and dilemmas in which they find themselves.[12] For dance analysis, this translates as a closer inspection of not only how the male role corresponds to, or goes against the grain of, contemporaneous attitudes on gender but also how individual dancers can exploit certain roles at key moments in history in order to say something about themselves as men.[13] Moreover, Sedgwick and Barrett's anti-essentialist criteria are sympathetic to Banes's 'historical and materialist' approach to reading dance in two ways. First, they not only expose the contradictions and instabilities that regulatory definitions of gender try to suppress but, second, they also provide a new conceptual framework that avoids a tendency towards negative (misogynistic, homophobic) rhetoric that has rendered problematic previous scholastic investigations into representations of identity.

As a corrective, difference, not as difference *from*, but as *pure* difference, is used to mark an escape from concepts of identity that, according to cultural theorists Horne and Lewis (1996: 1), are modelled on 'heterosexist norms'; norms that, for too long, have remained unchallenged both in scholarship and cultural practice. In their place, emphasis is given to the exploration of forms of identity that are marginal, temporal, contingent and hybridic. The unresolved heterogeneity of this hypothetical concept of a *pure* difference is the link between queer theory and the model of identity articulated by Louis in his dancing.

As *Le Roi Soleil*, Louis's 'difference' is without an axiomatic opposite. As such, he is incapable of being assimilated into any extant codes of identity that are used to support the mechanisms by which dance history claims to know gender and sexuality. Moreover, the figure and movement style of Louis, read as a disruption of the dualisms through which traditional dance forms are said to define difference (subjectivity/objectivity, active/passive, masculine/feminine etc.) provides a materiality and historical context to more abstract models conceptualised in queer thinking.

Fischer was earlier quoted as suggesting that, during the Renaissance, sexuality for the nobility was 'locked out'.[14] Rather, by applying Sedgwick and Barrett's theoretic to the *ballet de cour*, it is the visual and behavioural codes through which sexual *difference* is determined that are not in evidence. Sexuality is still present because whenever there is a human body it is coded, even if biological determinants are masked by non-gender-specific codes of conduct and fashion. As Carter (1999: 97) explains, 'the body may in one sense be surface, written on, "inscribed" by ideologies of gender, but it also has depth – and consciousness'. That Louis, in his dancing, cannot be categorised according to dualistic codes does not necessarily mean that his is a non-identity.

Elsewhere, some critics have argued that queer theory tends to imply that the identities that individuals and similar-interest groups assume for themselves operate on an even playing field (see Eldeman 1995 and Jagose 1996). Rather, they contend that although the two major axioms of gender and sexual object-choice are not all-encompassing and inclusive, they are still magnetic and exert a force at either end of the spectrum within which queer identity politics operates. As such, while acknowledging the fluidity, transience and hybridity that Louis, in his 'queerness', articulates, his self-fashioned identity is not a free-floating entity that exists in a vacuum, but is both subject to and the result of a highly specific socio-historical, economic and political context. Moreover, according to Seidman (1993: 133), while queer theorists have tended to strive towards avoiding the self-limiting, fracturing dynamics of identification by consistently refusing to name the subject (a form of negative dialectics) they 'presuppose these very identifications and social anchorings'. Instead of aiming for this extreme deconstruction of identity which, Seidman suggests, is impossible anyway, he advocates a more socio-historically aware application of queer identity politics that interprets identities as strategic systems that have both a pragmatic revisionist purpose and an antidotal value. This is the 'visionary' agenda of this investigation wherein Louis, while anchored in a specific socio-historical and political context, can also be interpreted as the visionary articulation of a prototypical queer identity whose anti-essentialist materiality provides a remedy to the current deadlock between those who are either for or against ballet's identity politics.

Conclusion

The tensions that surround masculine representation in classical dance forms are set to remain for as long as scholars and practitioners alike persist in employing old-fashioned and essentialist strategies to evidence their claims. Moreover, and as Burt (1995: 30) points out, a somewhat 'blinkered' and sanitised approach to biographical material evident in some historical research can act as a paralysing force that can 'channel and block our understanding and appreciation of representations of masculinity'. Ultimately, for those who either champion or criticise male classical dancers (and ballet itself) as exponents of a conservative masculinity, theirs can only be a pyrrhic victory. For both sides of the argument, the same dualist hierarchy is a prerequisite. As such, any notion of 'otherness' is categorised as deviancy and, by default, the 'ideal' model (along with all its supportive mechanisms) prevails.

Only very recently has any escape from this *impasse* become available in the language of queer theory and its strategic assault on what Warner (1993: xxvi) describes as 'the desexualised spaces of the academy'. The full potential of a queer approach to reading representations of identity, however, is yet to be fully realised in a dance scholarship that, in relation to more established areas of art criticism and history, is a comparatively new field of discourse.[15] As such, dance history scholars cannot rely on the same level of stability and conceptual autonomy available to those working in other fields and this sometimes results in an over-cautious approach to the application of non-dance discourses. Voices of concern stemming from those engaged in dance study who remain sceptical as to the benefits of adopting what they consider to be the extreme level of deconstruction associated with oppositional theoretical strategies are yet to be assuaged.

To counter this apprehension, and taking account of the problems associated with the wholesale application of a yet untested theoretical model in order to rewrite dance history, the approach adopted here has been conditioned by certain key factors. First, and in acknowledgement of what some critics see as a tendency towards ahistoricism, the application of queer theory is attuned to the reading of a specific identity, that of Louis XIV in his role as *Le Roi Soleil*. Second, the historical materiality of the king, as a dynamic figure who is the embodied source of power, is recognised as exerting a resistance to hypothetical models of identity.

To this end, a vital lesson can be learned from history. Instead of having to rely on dualist and hierarchic constructions of gender and sexual identity, the figure of Louis, as the Sun King, read through the lens of a historically sensitised queer theory, offers a positive insight into the direction that future analyses of masculine representation might take.

Notes

1 See introductions to Birdwhistell (1969), Terry (1978), Bland and Percival (1984) and Burt (1995).

2 For a discussion on how widespread changes in twentieth-century western cultural practice have contributed to a sense of crisis surrounding masculinity see Segal (1997), Middleton (1992) and Simpson (1994).

3 See Terry (1978: 2).

4 In dance historiography, this unwillingness to discuss homosexuality is particularly pronounced. For example, in Terry (1978) there is only the briefest mention of the relationship between Nijinsky and Diaghilev in

which the term homosexual is neatly avoided. Elsewhere, in Bland and Percival (1984), this subject is handled far more clumsily. Seeking to solve the 'mystery surrounding his [Nijinsky's] personality', they state: 'To many people, he seemed to have literally dropped out of the skies as a pure and unsullied spirit of the dance, only to be corrupted by Diaghilev who has been accused of contributing to his insanity through his sophisticated embraces' (p. 102). Their suggestion that the 'pure and unsullied' Nijinsky was not homosexual before meeting Diaghilev is both tortuous and misleading. It also displays a homophobic attitude that risks erasing gay men's contributions to dance.

5 He also got in the way of the erotic spectacle enjoyed by the predominantly male audience and, after the Romantic period, virtually disappeared from the ballet stage to be replaced by the female *en travestie* dancer.

6 See Garafola (1997) and also Thomas's (1998) review of Burt's *The Male Dancer* (1995).

7 As Franko (1993: 1) remarks, because contemporary reconstructions of *ballets de cours* 'accent past facts of performance, they tend to leave us with an aesthetic carapace'. As such, 'what has been missing in most reconstructions is precisely the uniqueness of the original as a quality of the performance' (p. 12). The reason for this, he argues, is because 'the early seventeenth [century] lacks explicit sources elucidating its dance vocabulary and style'.

8 As Bryson (1997: 61) remarks, at Versailles, 'dance is no longer an adornment, a decoration, an epiphenomenon of power; bodily orchestration, discipline, and spectacle are the heart of the state apparatus'.

9 A detailed account of the term 'queer' (and its history) is beyond the scope of this chapter. Because it is used to cover an ever-widening terrain within the shifting sands of identity-politics, both as a concept and as an act, however, a brief characterisation will be given here. As an 'umbrella' term, queer delineates categories of identity in which chromosomal sex, gender and desire are, according to heterosexist codes, mismatched (hermaphroditism and transvestism for example). As such, to be labelled 'queer' signals a resistance to dominant systems of gender that tend to view heterosexuality as a stable origin and promote the illusion of a shared universality. As an action, 'queering' effects an extreme deconstruction of notions of authentic identity formations, exposing them, rather, as arbitrary, contingent and ideologically produced. As Jagose (1996: 7) remarks, 'queer is always an identity under construction, a site of permanent becoming' and, as such, can be represented as 'ceaselessly interrogating both the preconditions of identity and its effects'. While many critics recognise queer theory as an important development within identity politics, however, it is not without problems. For example, some commentators argue that, because far too

often it is used uncritically as a 'catch-all', it is losing its initial potency as a site of contestation. Others, meanwhile, argue that it tends towards ahistoricism and, as such, places little or no value on formations of identity that minorities have had to carve out for themselves. As a corrective, the concept of queer being articulated here is attuned to a specific historical context and is used to give a name and agency to aspects of representation that dance history has previously ignored.

10 For example, the anthropologist Ted Polhemus (1993: 11) argues that dance is the metaphysics of culture in which '*for any given individual* the experience of gender identity is an absolute boundary which is existentially insurmountable' [original italics].

11 For a more detailed discussion of the concept of 'difference' see Barrett (1987).

12 See also Horne and Lewis (1996) and Steven Seidman (1993).

13 An example of this is Burt's (1995) reading of Nijinsky wherein, he argues, it was not only the combination of his exotic Russian 'otherness' and his allegiance to the *fin de siècle* aesthetic movement in the arts but also his homosexuality that led to his dancing such 'unorthodox' roles as the Golden Slave in *Schéhérazade* (1910), the Spirit of the Rose in *Le Spectre de la Rose* (1911) and the Faun in *L'après Midi d'un Faune* (1912).

14 As Franko (1993: 1) suggests, Fischer's notion of a noble body purged of sexuality may be misleading because, as with twentieth-century reconstructions of *ballet de cour*, it 'brings a chastened body to mind, a masked and quasi-desexualized body enacting rituals of opaque self-transparency'.

15 This situation is beginning to change, however, and for an example of how queer theory is now being introduced to dance analysis and history see Burt (2001).

Bibliography

Banes, S. (1998) *Dancing Women: Female Bodies on Stage*, London: Routledge.

Barrett, M. (1987) 'The Concept of "Difference"', *Feminist Review*, 26, July: 29–41.

Birdwhistell, R. L. (1969) Introduction to 'The Male Image', *Dance Perspectives*, 40, Winter: 9–11.

Bland, A. and Percival, J. (1984) *Men Dancing: Performers and Performances*, London: Weidenfeld and Nicolson.

Bryson, N. (1997) 'Cultural Studies and Dance History', in J. C. Desmond (ed.) *Meaning in Motion: New Cultural Studies of Dance*, Durham, NC: Duke University Press.

Burt, R. (1995) *The Male Dancer: Bodies, Spectacles, Sexualities*, London: Routledge.

—— (2001) 'Dissolving in Pleasure: The Threat of the Queer Male Dancing Body', in J. C. Desmond (ed.) *Dancing Desires: Choreographing Sexualities on and off the Stage*, Madison, Wis.: University of Wisconsin Press.

Carter, A. (1999) 'Dying Swans or Sitting Ducks: A Critical Reflection on Feminist Gazes at Ballet', *Performance Research*, 4, 3: 91–8.

Eldeman, L. (1995) 'Queer Theory: Unstating Desire', *GLQ: A Journal of Lesbian and Gay Studies*, 2, 4: 343–6.

Fischer, E. E. (1998) 'Clothes Make the (Wo)man – How Role Images Continue to Dance', *Ballet International: Tanz Aktuell*, 8, 9: 38–41.

Franko, M. (1993) *Dance as Text: Ideologies of the Baroque Body*, Cambridge: Cambridge University Press.

Garafola, L. (ed.) (1997) *Rethinking the Sylph: New Perspectives on the Romantic Ballet*, Middletown, Conn.: Wesleyan University Press.

Garlick, F. (1997) 'Dances to Evoke the King: The Majestic Genre chez Louis XIV', *Dance Research*, 15, 2: 10–15.

Horne, P. and Lewis, R. (eds) (1996) *Outlooks: Lesbian and Gay Sexualities and Visual Culture*, London: Routledge.

Jagose, A. (1996) *Queer Theory*, Melbourne: University of Melbourne Press.

Manning, S. (1998) 'Coding the Message', *Dance Theatre Journal*, 14, 1: 33–7.

Middleton, P. (1992) *The Inward Gaze: Masculinity and Subjectivity in Modern Culture*, London: Routledge.

Polhemus, T. (1993) 'Dance, Gender and Culture', in H. Thomas (ed.) *Dance, Gender and Culture*, London: Macmillan.

Sedgwick, E. K. (1990) *The Epistemology of the Closet*, London: Penguin.

Segal, L. (1997) *Slow Motion: Changing Masculinities, Changing Men*, London: Virago.

Seidman, S. (1993) 'Identity and Politics in a "Postmodern" Gay Culture: Some Historical and Conceptual Notes', in M. Warner (ed.) *Fear of a Queer Planet: Queer Politics and Social Theory*, Minneapolis, Minn.: University of Minnesota Press.

Simpson, M. (1994) *Male Impersonators. Men Performing Masculinity*, London: Cassell.

Terry, W. (1978) *Great Male Dancers of the Ballet*, New York, NY: Anchor Books.

Thomas, H. (1998) 'Bodies, Politics and Performance', *Dance Research*, 16, 2: 29–43.

Warner, M. (ed.) (1993) *Fear of a Queer Planet: Queer Politics and Social Theory*, Minneapolis, Minn.: University of Minnesota Press.

Chapter 6

Judith Chazin-Bennahum

A LONGING FOR PERFECTION
Neoclassic Fashion and Ballet

> The late eighteenth-century's fascination with classical dress parallels its intriguing new discourse with the body and the classical body. Dressed in soft, slender drapery, women returned to an idealized, ritualized experience of democracy, of equality, of the recognition that clothing has transformative values. The revealed body becomes the means through which the evolving meanings of political and social life in Greece and Rome are reinvented as circumstances change.
>
> (Porter 1999: 13)

A BRIEF RESURGENCE OF INTEREST in classical antiquity began before the French Revolution in the 1780s and ended after Napoleon's reign in 1815. This wasn't necessarily a new preoccupation with antiquity that was established during the Renaissance and later found recognition especially in the theatre of Racine and Corneille during the era of Louis XIV. For comic relief at that time, Molière enjoyed parodying mythic characters in his comédie-ballets. Mythological themes had been *de rigueur* in opera, theatre and ballet for centuries.

Radically different in the neoclassicism of the late eighteenth and early nineteenth centuries is its embodiment in clothing, in feminine fashions and in masculine and feminine costumes on stage. The men of the time did not have the courage to sport togas or tunics. A variety of sources are responsible for the importance of neoclassicism to clothing and costume – discoveries in archeology; the shift to historical accuracy in costumes for mythological plots; Enlightenment attitudes toward clothing strongly influenced by English modes; a blending of Boulevard costume practices with the Opéra's and pleasure in the revelation of the female body. Essentially, neoclassicism was the movement that freed the body in a sartorial switch from heavy, glittering embroidery and amplified skirts to the white, columnar lines of the tunic.

Neoclassicism engendered a remarkable shift in the aesthetics of clothing as "the female body lost its extremely defined waist in the 1780s and gained a soft, long skirt line with indented material, typical of the chiton, to permit free movement of the legs" (Hollander 1993: 117). The female body took on a new personality; it was reborn. The look of the breasts became round and full or "two well-defined hemispheres", rather than the eighteenth-century, pushed-up and bumpy look.

Flowing, transparent tunics revealed and idealized the female body, and especially recognized that this creature not only had legs to stand on, but also had an exciting sexual attraction in the new attire. However, the dresses were more suited to the climate of Greece. Sometimes the muslin was dampened so that it clung to the body in imitation of the folds of the Greek dresses (Laver [1969] 1995: 152). The new fashion greatly enhanced a young girl's figure, which also accounted for its great popularity. "This was the first time in the history of fashion that there had been any such revival of a bygone mode. It was also the first time that a fashion had been introduced which was especially attuned to the young" (Ewing 1971: 44). During this time, children's fashions, which were simple and easy to wear, began to influence adult clothing (Boucher 1983: 303).

The new style replaced a highly formulaic and artificial dress form that had suited an arrogant aristocracy. Their living spaces were not designed for relaxed, easy access to salons and daily meetings. On the contrary, room proportions seem eminently small to our tastes today. The eighteenth-century royal body deliberately forced itself into those spaces with the court costume and all its accoutrements – paniers, lace, feathers, jewels, large wigs, and high-heeled shoes with buckles. The steel corset provided the framework for this architecture that pushed the breasts up and emphasized a wasp waistline. Women's forms produced a sensuality adapted to the *règles de jeux* that permitted them to seek power where they could. Small, mincing steps gave the impression of the inflated royal bottom moving like a floating ship maneuvering itself through the wicked waters of the court. These exaggerated raiments were obviously not worn by all classes of society, but they represented the power and the glory all looked to and respected. The aristocracy lived in a coveted, hermetic environment that paid little attention to the wider world. But travellers, artists and intellectuals from all fields began to affect the culture of the time.

Archeological revelations and writings by Johann Joachim Winckelmann (1717–68) threw light on Greek influences in Roman art and architecture. The 1738 discovery of art and artifacts in Italy's Pompeii and Herculaneum brought a new and lively awareness of the ancient world. In 1750, books of engravings and other pictures helped to publicize and popularize the draped gods of Pompeii and Herculaneum. Excavations of ancient amphora and Greek artifacts were unearthed and sent to the British Museum by Sir William Hamilton. He published his *Illustrations of Greek Vases* in 1770 and twenty years later married Emma Hamilton when he was ambassador to Naples.

Implicit in the neoclassic costume revival was the fact that Greek vases and sculpture, as well as Roman imitations, were not just archeology, or ethnographic proof of other cultures' artifacts, but forms of art with clear aesthetic and ideological intentions. Art informed the stage, as it should, and the audience liked it because the vision it held spoke the truth to them. The sculptures of the Elgin Marbles recalled a past where the principles of democracy were born and ideals of philosophy and behaviour were pronounced. One particular book, *Travels of Anarcharsis* by the Abbé Barthélémy, encouraged many people to return to the past. It was a fourth-century evocation of Philip of Macedonia's reign. The beauty of the Greek past helped to restore brotherhood and "invited people to identify with it" (Starobinski 1988: 166). Costumes for the stage and clothing on the street became "expressive" of the new French citizen, one who believed in freedom and the more personal self.

Even the queen needed to express herself. In the 1780s, under the influence of Marie Antoinette, Vigée-Lebrun's portraits, and English style or *à l'anglaise*, the chemise dress came into fashion. Yielding to English influences in local gossip and chatter, in 1783 Marie Antoinette rebelliously asked Vigée-Lebrun to paint a portrait of her in a "chemise" with her hair unpowdered and unwigged. The result of this portrait was the style *chemise à la reine*. Revolutionary in its simplicity, in its early form it was merely a tube of white muslin with a drawstring at the neck and a sash at the waist. One of the explanations for the origins of this dress was that the style was first borrowed from Creole women by the ladies of Bordeaux and was the forerunner of the muslin gowns worn during the next thirty years (Delpierre 1997: 109). The light color gave the shape and quality of draping a lovely aura. "Coming from the French West Indies (where indigo grew, giving the dresses a bright bluish-white hue), it was popularized by Marie Antoinette and from her court spread all over Europe" (Ribeiro 1983: 15). Vigée-Lebrun painted Marie-Antoinette twenty-five times.

Political relations between England and France became an important factor in this fashion. When wars led to the British Blockade, ports of entry that provided particular products such as silks or feathers were closed and fashions of the moment changed. The use of cotton was particularly suited to the tunic line of Greek statuary. "Newly fashionable fabrics such as printed cotton and fine muslin were widely worn; when silk was worn it was often silk gauze, to provide the fluttering, floating look popular in the 1780s, or painted silk from the East" (Ribeiro 1983: 15).

Early on, England began to import cotton yarns via the East India Company when it was founded in 1600. It brought in costly fabrics such as calico from Calcutta and fine muslins from Mosul, Iraq. The East India's monopoly of trade with India ended in 1813 when the West Indies began to supply large quantities of raw cotton. Further supplies were found in America, Mexico and Peru. "By 1800 the cotton industry had overtaken the woolen one in Britain. As early as 1791, 38,000 black people were transported to the cotton plantations of America, which was more than half the total European slave trade for that year" (Ewing 1984: 63). Sadly, the slave trade increased as a result of fashion.

Discussion of this central moment in fashion history focuses on the newly discovered female body. One reason for the popularity of the soft material and lines without corsets was that breast feeding was slowly gaining in popularity due to the works of Locke and Rousseau, with encouragement from leading women thinkers. Enlightenment writers disputed the contemporary need for uncomfortable opulence and ostentation as it reflected undemocratic notions. The Philosophes promoted a realignment of values in French social and political institutions and babies were included in this narrative. A mother could more comfortably nurse a baby with that kind of clothing. "Breastfeeding became fashionable! To call attention to this change in attitude about women's bodies, women also walked around with breasts showing" (Browne 1987: 52).

The fashion in the street dictated that a new shoe shape be worn with the tunic style of dress. Neoclassic fashions called for sandal-like small heels or heelless slippers tied about the ankles with satin ribbons. The ribbons secured the shoe on the foot and created the impression of a Greek sandal. This petite slipper began to grace the ballet studio as well. The discomfort of wearing a shoe smaller than one's natural size could be endured as the young girl was trained from an early age to bear pain (see Swann [1982] 1984).

> The developing fashionable ideal had evolved a very narrow, light, flexible heelless slipper, constructed with a sole slightly too small for the wearer. The fabric of the upper, wrapping closely around the foot, compressed the bones together and encouraged them into a slender, elongated elegance demanded by the mode.
>
> (Squire 1974: 153)

Private gatherings were the site of dance improvisations in neoclassic garb. Mme Récamier, dear friend of Mme de Staël, often danced for others in her tunic and shawl. In the last two decades of the eighteenth century, the notorious Emma Hamilton (wife of Sir William and lover of Lord Nelson) created a performance art, improvisational *tableau vivant* entitled "Attitudes". Inspired by her husband's revelatory book on Greek statues, she performed different pictorial moments while draped in soft materials, a living embodiment in these poses.

> In a marvelous way, according to her contemporaries, she could thus give new life to ancient figurations . . . one has to emphasize their

> broad resonance in the fashion and taste of society that neoclassical aestheticians believed, somewhat ingenuously, could be modified simply by appealing to the classical ideals of simplicity and purity.
> (Falcone 1996: 244)

At the Opéra any fashion became institutionalized so that the breath of fresh air that came with neoclassic attire rapidly installed itself as irreplaceable. "Rather quickly the antique style imposed new conventions that were as unrealistic as those that came before: the required flesh colored tights, the filmy tunic, the supple ballet slipper necessary to execute the pirouettes, which predicted the next design of the point shoe" (Christout 1965: 96).

In the myth ballets, the short, light, transparent tunic for dance became common with the radical tendency to reveal the woman's body on stage. This is confirmed by a review in the *Mercure de France*, 26 November, 1791, of the opera *Diane et Endymion*, in which Mlle Saulnier "wore a costume of almost transparent simplicity . . . She appeared almost naked, yet her bearing banishes any licentious thought. She brings to mind those beautiful Spartan women on the banks of the Eurotas, who, to borrow a phrase from Rousseau, were clothed only in public respect" (Guest 1996: 331–2). In an earlier article on 20 November, 1791, in the *Chronique de Paris*, Victoire Saulnier is praised for her performance in the same opera: "We must give her credit for being almost the only dancer at the Opéra to have adopted an authentic costume" (ibid.).

At the Archives Nationales, in cluttered boxes with folders of the Opéra's accounts and spending, a document lists the *tunique blanche* as the favored costume for dancers, probably the *corps*, from 1800 onward. Accessories were tights, flower or laurel crowns, tambours for Terpsichore, and so forth. This confirmed the shift to a more uniform, simplified profile for the *corps de ballet* and was a recognition that ballet technique could more easily be explored if the dancers were wearing less cumbersome attire.

The value of this filmy *tissu* was that the shortening of the dress and the use of transparent material in its construction led to the introduction of *maillot*, or tights, a combination of long stockings with skin-tight knickers. The invention of this garment is generally attributed to Maillot, a costumier at the Opéra at the beginning of the nineteenth century.

The *Maître de Ballet* of the Opéra, Pierre Gardel, discovered during the Reign of Terror that he could keep his head and satisfy the early revolutionaries as well as audiences if he reverted to the popular mythological themes. Under the prophetic influence of Noverre and Angiolini, Gardel produced the romanticized myths as ballet-pantomimes with dancers who could act and who gave their movements and gestures an expression of feelings that we associate with romantic literature. *Télémaque dans L'isle de Calypso* and *Psyché* in 1790, and in 1793 *Le Jugement de Paris* succeeded beyond all expectations. Later, during the

Empire, it was natural for Gardel and other choreographers at the Opéra to appeal to Napoléon's conservative taste for antiquity. Each of Gardel's myth-based ballets became so popular that they still remain on the lists of the most well-attended performances at the Opéra. Certainly, their touching stories and the more emotive manner of presentation gave them tremendous impact. The transformations enhanced their visual splendor. Since Gardel's teacher was the distinguished choreographer Jean-Georges Noverre, he emphasized carefully structured scenarios and dancing with gestural power.

Télémaque dans L'isle de Calypso (February 23, 1790) tells the story of Ulysses's son who returns to Calypso's island where he discovers true love. Télémaque's tunic and mantle displayed the gentle lines of a draped dress to the knee with decorated hem and neckline. Calypso's revealing skirt fell above the knee. A rope-like belt defined a high waistline over a sleeveless bodice that hung over the skirt as seen in pictures of Greek women. Sandals were the preferred shoe.

The ballet *Psyché* (December 14, 1790) depicts the tale of the young goddess upstart who attempts to compete with Venus while falling madly in love with Cupid, Venus's son. Psyché endures classic suffering for her sins while the stage is filled with dazzling scenic spectacles. What contributed to the fortune of this ballet was her costume. The *robe à la Psyché* became one of the most touted fashions of the time. *Le Journal de la Mode et du Goût* of December 25, 1790, mentioned that this costume was tastefully designed to suggest one breast exposed. The dressmaker, Mme Teillard, offered the *robe à la Psyché* for sale at her shop (Guest 1996: 325). However, it is doubtful that women actually wore one breast exposed on stage; sources of the time do not confirm this practice. For a brief period after Napoléon, dancers wore as little as possible, although there is no mention that their breasts actually were nude. A few society women did indeed expose one breast in social situations. It was a sensational as well as suggestive gesture.

In *Le Jugement de Paris* (March 6, 1793), gods and shepherds dance together while Paris takes his time falling in love with Oenone. First, Paris must judge "the most beautiful", a contest between Venus, Minerva, and Juno, and of course decides that Venus merits the title of most beautiful woman in the world. Ultimately, he chooses the lovely young Oenone for himself. In *Le Jugement de Paris*, historical accuracy gave way to convenience as the dancers no longer wore the traditional Greek cothurnes, but lightly sported the modified Phrygian sandal in which they could move much more easily (Christout 1965: 205).

Jacques-Louis David institutionalized the cult of the antique during the Jacobin period when the guillotine, also known as "La Veuve" or "The Widow", was effectively wiping out the aristocracy and clergy. David designed the Revolutionary Festivals that attracted the Parisians and French people to the streets to celebrate their goddesses of Reason and Liberty. The floats were decorated with symbols and artifacts that brought ancient Greece back to life. The dancing girls who graced these moving panoplies wore white tunics with beautiful drapery.

At the Opéra, it is believed that the artist/costumier, Jean-Simon Berthélémy initiated the antique style at the ballet when Pierre Gardel was dancing master. Berthélémy was brought in as costumier in 1787 at the Paris Opéra by Ménagéot, who was originally appointed to the position but took a more prestigious job and gave his to Berthélémy. Berthélémy succeeded Boquet as "*dessinateur en titre des costumes de l'Opéra*" or Director of Costume Designs at the Opéra, and remained until 1807 when Ménagéot recovered his original position. Boquet's tenure lasted through the middle years of the eighteenth century. He was a decorative artist greatly skilled in creating delicate Rococo confections that were firmly based on the stiff and standardized costume shape and seemed to be out of touch with trends in the artistic community. His sketches of exotic people, Indians, classical gods and furies appear sprightly, delicate and as formal as Bérain's a century earlier.

But following Boquet, a serious change was afoot. Unlike many of the Opéra's scene and costume designers, both Berthélémy and Ménagéot were academic painters who had studied in Rome and learned the standard rules of painting techniques that brought neoclassicism and draperies onto the opera stage. Berthélémy's talents as a ceiling painter and designer of historical pictures demonstrated that he understood perfectly the value of a dramatic setting. His designs depicted the perfect moment to display his costumes, showing the characters during an expressively vivid scene. Another important contribution was his insistence that there were rules to protect the design of the costumes and scenery, a kind of early copyright. He also wished that the costumes be properly maintained and catalogued by the Chief Tailor. No doubt, one of the reasons for the great success of Gardel's myth-based ballets during revolutionary times was the work of Berthélémy (see Sandoz 1979).

The Opéra tried to keep up with London and Milan in imitation of their neoclassic designs. One of the most important neoclassical choreographers, Salvatore Viganò, came from Italy and worked in London, Vienna and his native Milan. His name, as well as his wife's, appear in the programs for Dauberval's ballets in London during the 1790–92 seasons. Viganò collaborated with the exceptional designer Alessandro Sanquirico (1777–1849). At La Scala in Milan their work became the focal point of the ideals of neoclassicism. The stage picture was grand, ordered and calm, while Viganò's choreography portrayed heroic and elaborate historical spectacles. Massive theatrical effects accompanied the rhythmic pantomime telling the ancient Roman stories of *I Titani* and *La Vestale* (Clarke and Crisp 1978: 68).

Illustrations of Viganò drawn by J. G. Schadow display his costume of white, close-fitting, aristocratic breeches and a light, short-sleeved coat with flared skirts. The coat is pale blue or deep pink, lined with white and bound with a white sash tied in a bow at the back so as to leave flowing ends. There is a relaxed, light and flowing quality to the style. In another drawing, we see Viganò and his wife, Marie Medina. She wears Greek sandals and has a transparent dress gathered beneath the breasts and looks quite naked compared to Viganò who is partnering her (Beaumont 1946: 29). Viganò's carefully choreographed rhythmic interpretation of Italian myth and history centers him as one of the counterfeiters of the neoclassical tradition in Europe.

Another capable designer of Italian origin, Vincenzio Sestini, the King's Theatre costumier, was initially a singer married to the well-known soprano Giovanna Sestini. He first became a tailor, then a costumier, renowned for his neoclassic opera and ballet designs. He created dresses for the ballets *Venus and Adonis* (1793), *Iphigenia in Aulide* (1793), Mme Hilligsberg's benefit (1794), *L'Amour et Psiche* (1796), *Sappho and Phaon* (1797), and *Alessandro e Timotes* (1800). He also designed a costume parody for the caricature engraving by Thomas Rowlandson in 1791, "The Prospect Before Us", which depicted members of the King's theatre company begging in the streets. Among those in the picture are Mme Hilligsberg and "Poor Old Servini", a nickname or a mistake for Sestini, since no one by the name of Servini is known to have been with the King's company at that time.

Important changes in shoe wear also affected the way in which both the social and the professional dancer moved. The dancing shoe of minuets, waltzes and quadrilles rapidly became the ballet slipper and standard apparel for preparatory classes. Some dance historians, for example Marion Hannah Winter (1974) and Ivor Guest, alluded to the fact that rope dancers wore soft shoes for balancing and that the ballet dancers of the late eighteenth century imitated this practice. The gradual change from high heel to lower heel to sandal to slipper and finally to pointe shoe seemed completely within the concept of how women's feet looked to society, regardless of their natural shape. (See rope dancers in illustrations in Winter [1962], and Christout [1965].)

Despite discomforts, satin or silk slippers provided flexibility for the foot and enhanced the possibilities for jumping, balancing and turning. For example, when making a *demi-coupé* and stepping onto a *demi-pointe*, the foot takes a shape where, with an enforced arch or instep, the toes are extended as well, making the foot arch and point so that the line of the leg becomes much longer and vertical. These are directives about which Gennaro Magri wrote in his treatise *Theoretical and Practical Treatise on Dancing* (1779). Gradually the foot became more than a balancing device to help shift the weight, it became a mechanical tool or organ that could be strengthened and exercised and expanded in its own right. And this is exactly what began to happen in the latter part of the eighteenth century but could not really evolve until the foot was freed from the heel, however high it was.

The fame and beauty of female ballet soloists spread throughout the large cities of western Europe and brought increasing attention to the development of their virtuosic and dramatic capabilities, one outdoing the other. The neoclassic costume contributed to their renown. Mlle Parisot shocked London audiences in 1796 with her high legs flying in the ballet *Le Triomphe de l'Amour. The Monthly Mirror* (October 1796) cited Parisot's flexibility that "created a stir by raising her legs far higher than was customary for dancers". In 1798, the Bishop of Durham made an example of her immoral moves and denounced her in an intemperate speech before the House of Lords. Subsequently, the opera administration changed the colors of dancers' maillots from flesh-colored to white (Swift 1974: 98).

At the time of the Revolution, the changing neoclassic costume, as well as a more enlightened view of dance as an expressive art, contributed to the growth of popularity of the ballet pantomime or *ballet d'action*. It may have been the soft, flat slipper, or the light textiles or the maskless face or the wigless head but, more than any other change in the quality of its dancing, ballet abandoned the steppy sequences of Baroque forms and took to the air, to the notion of height, length and grandeur of movement, and began to flow more freely in the body and in space (Chazin-Bennahum 1988: 168).

Bibliography

Beaumont, C. (1946) *Ballet Design, Past and Present*, London: Her Majesty's Stationery Office.

Boucher, F. (1983) *Histoire du Costume en Occident*, Paris: Flammarion.

Browne, A. (1987) *The Eighteenth Century Feminist Mind*, Brighton: Harvester.

Chazin-Bennahum, J. (1988) *Dance in the Shadow of the Guillotine*, Carbondale, Ill.: Southern Illinois University Press.

Christout, M-F. (1965) *Le Merveilleux et le Théâtre du Silence*, Paris: Editions Moulon, La Haye.

Clarke, M. and Crisp, C. (1978) *Design for Ballet*, London: Studio Vista.

Delpierre, M. (1997) *Dress in France in the Eighteenth Century*, trans. Caroline Beamish, New Haven, Conn. and London: Yale University Press.

Ewing, E. (1971) *Fashion in Underwear*, London: Batsford.

—— (1984) *Everyday Dress: 1650–1900*, London: Batsford.

Falcone, F. (1996) "The Arabesque," *Dance Chronicle*, 19, 3: 231–53.

Guest, I. (1996) *The Ballet of the Enlightenment*, London: Dance Books.

Hollander, A. (1993) *Seeing Through Clothes*, Berkeley, Calif.: University of California Press.

Laver, J. ([1969] 1995) *Costume and Fashion*, London: Thames & Hudson.

Magri, G. (1779) *Theoretical and Practical Treatise on Dancing, Naples*, trans. M. Skeaping (1988), London: Dance Books.

Porter, J. I. (ed.) (1999) *Constructions of the Classical Body*, Ann Arbor, Mich.: University of Michigan Press.

Ribeiro, A. (1983) *Visual History of Costume in the Eighteenth Century*, London: Batsford.

Sandoz, M. (1979) *Jean Simon Berthélémy*, Paris: Editart.

Squire, G. (1974) *Dress, Art and Society*, London: Studio Vista.

Starobinski, J. (1988) *1789: Emblems of Reason*, trans. Barbara Bray, Cambridge, Mass.: MIT Press.

Swann, J. ([1982] 1984) *Shoes*, London: Batsford.

Swift, M. G. (1974) *A Loftier Flight: The Life and Accomplishments of Charles-Louis Didelot, Balletmaster*, Middletown, Conn.: Wesleyan University Press.

Winter, M. H. (1962) *Le Théâtre du Merveilleux*, Paris: Olivier Perrin.

—— (1974) *Pre-Romantic Ballet*, New York: Dance Horizons.

Chapter 7

Cara Tranders

CARA TRANDERS'S REVERIES
The Autobiography of Cara Tranders, Ballet Girl at the Empire Palace of Varieties, 1892–99
(Interspersed with the Voices of Poets, Novelists, Lyricists, Critics and Historians)

A history teacher addresses his class:

'And did I not bid you to remember that for each protagonist who once stepped on the stage of so-called historical events, there were thousands, millions, who never entered the theatre – who never knew that the show was running – who got on with the donkey work of coping with reality? True, true. But it doesn't stop there. Because each one of those numberless non-participants was doubtless concerned with raising in the flatness of his own unsung existence his own personal stage, his own props and scenery – for there are very few of us who can be, for any length of time, merely realistic . . . even if we miss the grand repertoire of history, we yet imitate it in miniature and endorse, in miniature, its longing for presence, for feature, for purpose, for content.'

(Swift 1984: 40–1)

It looms up, a large greyish shape with ill-defined edges. I like to think of it as a friendly whale in murky sea waters. Out of the dusky green of the fog, the bus that will take me to the Palace crawls to a stop. Like Jonah, I climb in. Its soft lights envelop me and the conductor greets me warmly, for he doesn't fear my travelling alone. He knows I am a dancer but he has seen my sharp eyes as I repel any potential threat to my reputation. Some people think, you know, that if you show your body to the public on stage you must be willing to show it to anyone in private. My aunt was horrified when mother told her I was hoping to be a dancer.

'A ballet girl? Are you mad, Florence? Why, what a disgrace . . . an Actress? Better put her on the streets at once.'

(Mackenzie [1912] 1929: 76)

The professional dancer is looked upon as one who has sadly misapplied talents which might have won reputation in some worthier path of life.

(Grove 1895: 1)

Aunt changed her attitude, though, when she came to see me in our new show. Escorted by Uncle (for she would never have gone on her own) she was quite dazzled by the spectacle of it all, even though Uncle himself said that he couldn't tell which one was me, being so far from the stage and us all looking alike with our wigs and red and gold costumes and all holding the same long batons in our hands.

Though all alike in their tinsel livery
And indistinguishable at a sweeping glance
  They muster, maybe
  As lives wide in irrelevance
A world of her own has each one underneath
  Detached as a sword from its sheath.

(Hardy 1917 in Gibson (ed) 1976: 492)

Uncle was a bit quiet when we left the theatre and stopped going on about it was all 'bally nonsense'. I wouldn't tell Aunty, not even to spite her, but I believe he's been back to the ballet on more than one occasion since.

I'm a very strong admirer of the ballet and the play
  But I haven't told the missus up to now!
And to watch the fairies dancing I pass may(*sic*) an hour away
  But I haven't told the missus up to now!
When I see their graceful attitudes with love I'm burning hot,
And when the angels flap their wings, they mash me on the spot,
And I feel as if I'd like to go at once and kiss the lot,
  But I haven't told the missus up to now!

(Cornell 1887)

I sink into my seat, relishing the ride from Kentish Town up to Leicester Square when, trapped by my transport, I can do nothing. My body is exhausted, for we were at the theatre at eleven this morning for rehearsal of the new production. Finishing at two, I have time to get home to give mother her late lunch, for she's poorly now and since Dad ran off there's no one but me to look after her.

What I will do when I meet that young chap of my dreams who'll want to whisk me away and look after me, I do not know. Perhaps my young man will take her in, too, because he'll be wealthy enough. Not too much out of our class, of course, because that would be unnatural, but he'll have just enough money for us to be 'comfortable', as they say. Till then, it seems I'm destined to be always tired, for I don't get the bus home after the show till gone eleven at night then it's up in the morning to tidy both mother and the rooms before I leave for the theatre.

Rehearsals were strenuous and frequent, and the girls appeared each morning with the regularity of factory workers. Their life seemed one incessant hurrying backwards and forwards from home to theatre.

(Willis in Green (ed.) 1986: 180)

She must devote herself each day to practice. At night she must report herself sober and competent. Shortly after eleven you may see her at Charing Cross waiting for the Brixton bus . . . she is the sedate, painstaking artisan of the stage, with her sick clubs, and her boot clubs, and all the petty prudences of the working class.

(Hibbert 1916: 197–8)

Some girls are lucky; they don't have to come and go but can wait at the Rehearsal Club, started by that nice Lady Magenis for the likes of us to flop around during the afternoons when we've a few hours off. My wages aren't too bad, for I'm on twenty shillings a week now and if I can be promoted to the front row of the *corps* I can make thirty five, though by the time I've paid my Sick Club and other clubs that arise from time to time, my take-home's not special. Sometimes I get fined for being late which is a bit unfair because it's always such a rush and I can't help the traffic, especially in the pea-soupers. The scene painters earn three pounds, though. This doesn't seem fair either because they just slap on paint and no one cares about where the edges are because the audience can't see that close anyway.

At least I'm lucky to have a job. We had a scare at the Empire only last year. That Mrs Ormiston Chant nearly got us closed down for good, complaining as she did to the Council. She said the ballets were immoral and I said she was an interfering old busybody who should mind where she pokes her nose but some said she wasn't accusing us, just the management of promoting licentious shows. I don't know what licentious means, myself, but it doesn't sound like a compliment.

The works (The Girl I Left Behind Me, 1893 and La Frolique, 1894) 'seemed to be for the express purpose of displaying the bodies of women to the utmost extent. There is not the least attempt to disguise that which common sense and common decency requires should be hidden.'

(Chant in Donahue 1987: 58)

My friend Emily wrote to the Council appealing to them not to close the Empire, which was ever so brave of her. She's only in the middle row of dancers, like me, but she's become a bit of a star now.

Dear Sirs,
My engagement at the Empire theatre is of subordinate character but as my position is my livelihood I am emboldened to appeal to you, not only in my own name but also in that of my two sisters and other ladies.

Emily Banbury (Empire dancer)
(LCC 1894)

Fortunately, they did renew the Empire's licence and our jobs were saved. People get mixed up, of course, and confuse those 'ladies' of the night who ply their trade in the promenade at the front of the theatre, and us ladies of the ballet. We don't want to be tarred with the same immoral brush as them, though I must say, I do envy their elegance. Some say the men just enjoy the company of these women, but quite a lot goes on at the front there. Not just women but men, too, exchange their company for money.

An anonymous letter to the LCC Licensing Committee revealed that the writer had been informed by a theatre attendant that more than half the audience in the shilling promenade were 'sodomites' and that 'he often gave them a good kicking'.

(LCC 1894)

Sometimes I wonder if it's worth being on this side of the curtain rather than out there in the promenade. Not seriously, of course, but I daydream a little when I suffer the conditions in which we have to work. Our dressing rooms are so cramped, and with a hundred and fifty of us in the big ballets, backstage is worse than Piccadilly Circus on Boat Race night. We have to fly down the stairs after our scenes to get changed for the next one, knocking over anyone who gets in the way – especially that critic chap who lurks around. All you can think of is getting to your room. We just ignore men like him – we've got a job to do.

Every few minutes half a dozen pretty girls would rush to their dressing rooms to change, leaving me heart-broken, while another contingent would arrive in fresh costume, as though to console me.

('S.L.B.' 1896: 524)

It's off with one costume and on with another, then running back up the stairs to make my next entry, panting hard but smiling. Hard, that is, panting and smiling. But we get used to it. We don't always get used to the rats, though they scarper and we just see their tails disappear. They don't like all the activity and, as you can imagine, twelve of us all cramped together in one little dressing room can be a very active occasion – elbows and legs everywhere. You're never sure whose hose you're putting on. We're not allowed out of the room during the break between the two nightly ballets when the other acts are on. It's less frantic then; we might knit or catch up with our sewing, but it's the smell we don't like. We can't help the sweat and the greasy make-up, but there's no air and it's hot and sometimes you just hold your breath, so you're panting even more. But you have to keep smiling, because the management said so and we do what they say or we'll never make the front row. If I go to the back row before I go forward, I'll just die. The back row is for those who are beginners or those who are past it. Some of the girls' mothers are in the back row. Quite companionable, being on the same stage as your mum, but you can see your future in hers if you're not careful. Mme Lanner, our ballet mistress, danced professionally until she was nearly fifty, so it can be a long career for those who are lucky, those who work hard and keep out of trouble.

Most of us are really careful to keep out of trouble. And we do work hard, even though it can be boring at times, especially towards the end of a six-month run which is quite normal for each ballet. Although we all think we can do more, most us know secretly that we're not trained to be able to display our skills. I learned at Mme Lanner's National Training School of Dancing in Tottenham Court Road, from where she gets most of the Empire girls. Not the principals of course – they come from abroad where the training's much better. That's why they star. Isn't fair, really. We are pretty well a world apart, as they don't have much to do with us and we wouldn't dare speak to them. But we watch them secretly, when we're framing their performance, and we talk about them after. Some of the girls can be quite nasty. Jealousy, really, for that's all we are on the stage – a coloured frame around a pure white dancing image. The ballerinas can go up and stay on their toes. I've tried, time and time again, but my legs won't let me do it. But they've got the muscles for it. Men don't see the muscles, though. I don't really know what they see. The ballerinas are a bit out of their class, being skilled and foreign and all that, but I suppose the men can dream.

Elly (we call her Elly behind her back, just to bring her down a bit; her name's really Elena Cornalba) wears a lovely gauzy dress in our current ballet, *Faust*. She doesn't do much else, mind. Got no 'character' to play but she does the proper steps. There's rumours that she's leaving and they're looking to Moscow for another star. That will be interesting. Management can't seem to find a permanent ballerina from Italy. Mme Cavallazzi as Faust is as strong as ever;

we know all her mime actions of course but could never do them as well as she can. I can imagine myself in that black Mephistopheles costume of Zanfretta's with those grand arm gestures which tell the story. So dramatic.

My reverie comes to a jolting halt. I like having reveries as they sound foreign and glamorous – but it's time to get off the bus. Mme Lanner will be furious if we're late; she's like a big black beetle in her bombazine. She is good at her arrangements of us *corps de ballet.* Should be by now, for she's been with the Empire since 1887 they say. Her and Mr Wilhelm work on most of the ballets together. For this *Faust* he's written the story (based on someone else's we think), so he worked more closely with her on each scene as well as designing the costumes as usual. We all know he's actually called William Pitcher and his dad is a shipbuilder, but he changed his name to sound more foreign because it helps in this business. You can't blame him. Sometimes when I'm standing there in yet another tableau I dream up names I'd choose for myself. I fancy Cara Taglioni so I could keep the same initials, but there's already been a Taglioni and I wouldn't want people to get mixed up.

Costumes – I must get into mine. I fly off the bus and walk ever so quickly to the side street entrance of the Empire where I meet up with my friend Maria. Maria used to be with the Salvation Army but there wasn't much life there and she kept banging her tambourine in the wrong place. So she came to us.

Sister 'Ria, Sister 'Ria of the Army soon began to tire
So she's sold her tambourine
Now she's nightly to be seen
Dancing in the ballet at the Empire.

(Mills and Lennard 1895)

For tonight's ballet I'm a soldier in the first scene. We play quite a lot of soldiers. There aren't any men dancers except for the occasional foreigner but they're not much liked even when they're good, like that Mr Cecchetti who was with us a couple of years ago. Went on to become a teacher of sorts, I think. 'They're all the same,' says my Uncle, 'one of those.' It took me a while to know who 'those' were and it isn't really fair because some of these gentlemen dancers were married. But you never know. The 'male' characters are nearly always played by women; '*en travestie*', they call it. Nice to know a bit of French. We know that the audience like to look at our legs when we're dressed as soldiers and we have to keep our waists trim. Difficult if one of us girls gets pregnant and wants to hide it for as long as possible. But the men can look at what they like. It's all part of the show to us. We march off after the first scene in *Faust*, being careful to keep in time and not rush, for we have a brisk break of one scene before the third, in which I'm a will-o'-the-wisp. It's the last scene that's the worst. We play angels, with lovely golden wigs, but we have to climb these very steep ladders backstage and perch on the top, sticking our heads through a hole in the backdrop, so our faces appear like 'angels in the sky'. We're terrified, because we're so high up and the ladders wobble and it's freezing cold up there, but we have to keep smiling. I imagine it must look good from the audience's point of view but we don't feel much like angels when we're up there, I can tell you.

A crystal stair, and in the air
  the angels hover round . . .

No more those angels deck the sky –
those angels hail from Peckham Rye,
  From Bow or Kentish Town.

('J.M.B.' 1896: 524)

No wonder we get coughs and colds or worse, all this going from those damp and muggy dressing rooms up those cold stairs to the stage, then hot again under the lights. That's why the Sick Club is so important, to help us through those times when we're poorly.

The little painted angels flit
  See, down the narrow staircase, where
The pink legs flicker over it!

Blonde, and bewigged, and winged with gold,
  The shining creatures of the air
Troop sadly, shivering with cold.

(Symons 1895: 21)

Sometimes, as I said, the work does get a little boring, though we do two ballets a night. This *Faust* is quite different to the other recent one, *On Brighton Pier*, which has nice popular melodies and we had to learn to move a bicycle around on the stage to show how modern we were. Will Bishop used to make us laugh. He's not a 'real' dancer, of course, but he entertains us with his clog dancing and in *Brighton* he had a really clever masher dance – you know, showing off as a young man about town. The management like these different kinds of ballets – sometimes a really up-to-date work, or one celebrating Britain's Empire; sometimes one from fairy tale or legend. Keeps everyone happy. The Alhambra are doing *Titania*, based on a Shakespeare play, but they're not as good as us. They say we just hold up the scenery which is a typical thing to come from an Alhambra girl. Admittedly, the movements we're given in all of the ballets are pretty much the same, and are not that difficult in themselves – but it's just the same at the Alhambra. We march a lot, and strike poses, drawing attention to the ballerina. The management always ask Mme Lanner to get a vision scene in, a 'transformation', as the audience love these. There'll be tinkly water music and the flimsy curtain at the back of the stage will be drawn back to reveal another tableau, a 'transformed' picture within the picture of the stage. Clever, really. The best bits for us are when we waltz or galop as then you can really be carried away with the music and feel that you're really dancing. We're not on our toes but we are still an important part of the show. Often there are long periods when we do nothing at all, just stand in position. Sometimes I try to find faces in the audience but of course you can't see them individually in that great sea of half darkness. My mind wanders then. I think about mother at home and feel the pity for her, all day in that room. That's why I try to get home in the afternoons but it makes my day such a squash. I always seem to feel tired. Sometimes I use those tableaux when the ballerina is doing her thing to plan the next days' meals. A neighbour gave us some beef dripping, so we can have that with bread tomorrow. Nice and nutritious.

Suddenly I saw a beautiful girl whose face was strange to me. She was exotic, with passionate lips and eyes, magnetic. Then she . . . that is you . . . fixed her eyes on mine without surprise, without hesitation, as if drawn by some instinct, your eyes fixed on mine at every turn you made as you danced with the others.

(Symons in Beckson 1977: 160)

Yes, beef dripping would be lovely. Useful thinking time, these tableaux are, so long as I don't forget to move on the sixteenth beat after the big crash of the drums. (For *Faust* they've had an organ built and it's a lovely sound – sort of heavenly but majestic.) You don't often miss your cue, though. Even if your mind has wandered you sense it from the girls when it's time to move as their breath and their muscles prepare. We've been working together so long we almost dance as one, especially when Mr Wilhelm dresses different groups of us in different colours. We must look like an artist's paint palette. Green's my favourite as it goes with my eyes. Not that anyone could see my eyes.

. . . the members of the corps de ballet . . . become convenient units in the development of the (colour) scheme.

('T.H.L.' 1893: 344)

The important thing, though, is to keep looking at the audience as if you can really see them. We know we've got to 'communicate'. Not go over the top on our character, of course (it's a bit difficult going over the top on being a daisy, anyway), but just sharing our joy of dancing and trying to look attractive.

That's important because many of the people in the audience really do love the ballet.

London audiences now began to regain an appreciation of the technical basis of the Dance and Ballet which they had lost . . . thus, they were enabled the better to understand the Russian ballet when it eventually arrived and achieved instant success.

(Perugini 1925: 1177)

Some of them just come for a night out, because the Empire means all that is 'home' to them, especially when they've been away in our colonies.

Something more than a mere music hall . . . it was . . . an Englishman's club, an Empire club, famous wherever Englishmen fought, worked, adventured. Britishers prospecting in the Klondyke, shooting in jungles, tea-planting in Ceylon, wherever they fore-gathered in cities of Africa, Asia and America would bid one another goodbye with a 'See you at the Empire one day when we're back in town.'

(Booth 1929: 142)

We know that some men also come to eye us up and some of the girls even walk out with men they've met at the stage door. I personally don't like to hang around with those johnnies – I'm in too much of a rush to catch the bus – but I don't blame those who do. Some of the dancers from the Alhambra used to go the Crown public house, just off Leicester Square, where they'd meet the young men who claimed they were poets. The girls used to try and explain how the ballets worked and how the steps were performed and they'd get really angry because the men didn't seem to take them seriously. These men belonged to some club – the Rhymers Club, I think. Violet Piggot had an affair with one of them called Arthur. He seemed very keen at first but some of these men don't seem to realise that you can't go to the public house in all your stage finery and in your real clothes, and close-up, you look rather different. What do they expect, a dancing will-o'-the-wisp in a pub? Arthur turned quite nasty, apparently, and dropped Violet pretty quickly. We hear these stories all the time. At least this Arthur writes nicely about the ballet in the *Star* and the *Sketch* and stories come down to us girls about what he, and other writers, have said about the new ballets. They're nearly always complimentary, thank goodness. One critic said how much the dancing of the rank and file (that's us) had improved; that made us glow. Sometimes there are photographs and I was nearly in one of the *corps* photos once, but I didn't get chosen in the end. The girls have to pose for these in whatever position pleases the photographer, often with their arms bent up and their hands behind their heads. This doesn't appear anywhere in the ballet, of course, but the more worldly amongst us know that this position pushes up your bust, making you more attractive. The drawings on the covers of the Empire programmes don't look much like us in real life, either. You'd think we danced half naked, which is nonsense because we always have our fleshings over legs and arms, or that we all look the same when we're actually all shapes and sizes. But I suppose the management like to present an image of us that will draw in the crowds. And if we don't get the crowds, there won't be the money to pay our wages, so we don't complain.

We do try to look attractive, those who can, that is. It's all part of showing off our skills. One critic, a Mr Bensusan who is probably so ashamed that he has to write under the letters 'S.L.B.', said in a review of an Alhambra work that so long as us ballet girls have good looks talent goes for nothing. That made us cross but it is all part of the attraction of the ballets. For some girls, this is all they care about. Most of us, though, are proud of what we do. The ballet goes way back in to history, and we're part of that history. We get nearly two thousand people in on full nights (I shake a little when I think about it). Toffs; artists; soldiers on leave; men about town and ordinary people including, more and more, the women. No one knows what they think about the ballet. I imagine they get a different kind of pleasure in watching, perhaps imagining themselves as us, perhaps just enjoying all the colour and lights and movement and a night out. No one tells us what the women think.

What do I think? I think a lot. My body is nearly always exhausted, but I wouldn't do another job. It's wonderful, really, to be able to dance, to be part of such a long artistic tradition. I know I'll never be a real ballerina, but that's all right. My job is secure, more or less, and the work is varied compared to the factory or even the office, where so many young girls work nowadays. And it's a million times better than the domestic. The ballet can take me out of my own domestic, out of the worry about home. When I'm dancing, I can dream, and sometimes my mind is empty as my body just takes over. But I also think a lot. About my aching arms, holding this heavy pole at the exact right angle; about how late the bus will be in the fog; about how Cornalba can't get that crisp finish to her pirouettes; about what I would look like if I were out there in front like her and how that applause would be for me alone as I dazzled them with my spins and turns and jumps and balances. My legs would be strong as iron; my arms as light as muslin. My smile would be confident, my gaze at the audience assured as I returned theirs. I think about a man who will come along and look after me and mother. But he'll have to know the real me from the pretty picture he sees on stage. Yes, I think a lot. But nobody knows what I think. My thoughts won't go down in history. But the ballet will, and I'm proud to be a part of it.

The history teacher addresses his class:

'Children, you are right, there are times when we have to disentangle history from fairy-tale. There are times . . . when good dry textbook history takes a plunge into the old swamps of myth and has to be retrieved with empirical fishing lines. History, being an accredited sub-science, only wants to know the facts. History, if it is to keep on constructing its road into the future, must do so on solid ground . . . At all costs let us avoid mystery-making and speculation, secrets and idle gossip . . . and above all, let us not tell *stories* . . . let us get back to solid ground.'

(Swift 1984: 86)

Bibliography

Beckson, K. (ed.) (1977) *The Memoirs of Arthur Symons: Life and Art in the 1890s*, University Park, Pa.: Pennsylvania State University Press.

Booth, J. B. (1929) *London Town*, London: T. Werner Laurie.

Cornell, C. (1887) Music score: 'I Haven't Told the Missus up to Now', London: Francis Bros. & Day.

Donahue, J. (1987) 'The Empire Theatre of Varieties Licensing Controversy of 1894: Testimony of Laura Ormiston Chant before the Theatres and Music Halls Licensing Committee', *Nineteenth Century Theatre*, 15, Summer: 50–60.

Gibson, J. (ed.) (1976) *The Complete Poems of Thomas Hardy*, London: Macmillan.

Green, B. (ed.) (1986) *The Last Empires: A Music Hall Companion*, London: Pavilion.

Grove, L. (1895) *Badminton Library of Sports and Pastimes: Dancing*, London: Longmans, Green.

Hibbert, H. G. (1916) *Fifty Years of a Londoner's Life*, London: Grant Richards.

'J.M.B.' (1896) 'An Earthly Paradise', *Sketch*, 1 January: 524.

LCC (1894) MIN/10,803, 13 October, London Metropolitan Archives, 40 Northampton Rd., LONDON ECIR 0HB.

LCC (1894) MIN/10,803, 15 October, London Metropolitan Archives, address as above.

Mackenzie, C. ([1912] 1929) *Carnival*, London: Martin Secker.

Mills, A. J. and Lennard, A. (1895) Music score: 'Sister Ria', London: Francis, Day & Hunter.

Perugini, M. E. (1925) 'Where Are We Going?', *Dancing Times*, August, 1171–7.

'S.L.B.' (1896) 'Behind the Scenes II': The Empire', *Sketch*, 1 January: 523–4.

Symons, A. (1895) *London Nights*, London: Leonard Smithers.

Swift, G. (1984) *Waterland*, London: Picador.

'T.H.L.' (1893) 'A Chat with a Costumier: Wilhelm at home', *Sketch*, 8 March: 343–4.

Chapter 8

Linda J. Tomko

CONSIDERING CAUSATION AND CONDITIONS OF POSSIBILITY

Practitioners and Patrons of New Dance in Progressive-era America

FOR HISTORIANS, ONE OF THE MOST perplexing aspects of Michel Foucault's *The Order of Things* ([1966] 1971) was perhaps its bracketing of causation. Foucault neither exploded nor reinvigorated the search for causal explanation that was so typical of Euro-American historical inquiry in the nineteenth and twentieth centuries. He simply set aside the issue and turned to a different problem. *The Order of Things* pursued the notion of "episteme" as a kind of master mode of knowing or apprehending, invoked by and characteristic of a given era, which was displaced by a different mode in a following era. Resemblance, the figure for the Renaissance, for example, gave way to classification or the taxonomic urge in the seventeenth and eighteenth centuries. Shifts between epistemes occurred by some sort of rupture; Foucault sought and proffered no reason for the change. Nor was he concerned to pinpoint agents of change. For twentieth-century studies of dances past, and dance's past, this sidelining of causation and agency presented a radical departure from what may be termed modernist models of analysis. In their search for origins and their tracings of "influence" and teacher–student "family trees", modernist dance studies have frequently sought to locate the sources of change, and principal actors, that shaped genres like ballet or modern dance.[1] For dance history in particular, adherence to Foucault's example seemed to require a break with principles of professional history just as the field was beginning to gain recognition as an academic discipline.

Displacing causation and agency, Foucault studied instead the conditions of possibility for relations and networks that framed social existence. In *The Order of Things* and other works, he scrutinized the constitution of knowledge, the circulation of power, and the designation of sameness and difference (Gordon 1980:

229–59). Foucault's reorientation of inquiry was liberating in several respects, and it intersected with other poststructuralist concerns. It abetted new interest in matters of representation – how representation worked, how its products circulated, how its operation participated in relations of domination and subordination. Interest in representation proved especially beneficial to studies that analyzed dance practices as means through which people presented and interpreted themselves, *to* themselves. Jane Desmond's "Dancing out the Difference" (1991), for example, read Ruth St Denis's dance–drama *Radha* for its orientalizing effects. Susan Manning's "Black Voices, White Bodies" (1998) parsed the metaphorical minstrelsy by which white women's modern dancing bodies on the concert stage stood in for absented African Americans. Foucault's redirection of inquiry also contributed to a larger reconsideration by poststructuralist writers, such as Judith Butler (1988), of the unitary, authentic self, and subjectivity. Such reconceptualization has proposed the self and subjectivity to be multiple, even fragmentary, and as constituted in several and varied kinds of relationships. This vein of theory has helped dance scholars to show ways in which performance and compositional strategies have troubled and challenged sanctioned modes for embodying cultural characteristics such as gender roles, the sense of belonging to a nation, and class position. Mark Franko's "Where He Danced", for instance, considered the potential of Kazuo Ohno's butoh work *Suiren* to provide an alternative registration of maleness via cross-dressing conceptualized as "through dressing," suggesting a model of gender performance that allows gender attributes to recombine "at uneven intervals and to unequal degrees" (Franko 1995: 107).

Foucault's liberating effect also extended to concern with identity, conceived as something comprised in and by its relation to something else. Identity has attracted increased scholarly attention as the understanding has dawned on researchers and general readers alike that, at the end of the millennium, flows of people, like flows of capital, technology, media, and ideas, are increasingly global in scope (Appadurai 1990). In "Welcome to the Jungle: Identity and Diversity in Postmodern Politics", Kobena Mercer (1990) seconds the sense of key cultural studies writers that the relations and elements comprising identity are capable of varied or multiple accenting. "Social identities are structured 'like a language'," Mercer explains, "in that they can be articulated into a range of contradictory positions from one discursive context to the next since each element in ideology and consciousness has no necessary belonging in any one political code or system of representation" (p. 57). Mercer cites 1980s Britain as a case in point, where the rearticulation of black identity made it a force to be reckoned with. He quotes Stuart Hall on this point, emphasizing the possibility for *re*articulation: "What was being struggled over was not the 'class belongingness' of the term [black], but the inflexion it could be given, its connotative field of reference" (p. 57). For Americans, the much-discussed racial profile of golf champion Tiger Woods offers a ready example of variable accenting. With parents of Thai,

African American, white, and American Indian heritage, Woods in the American South during the 1950s would have been immediately classified as black. There, any black heritage trumped all other heritage to legally designate a person black. In 2002, Woods's multiple heritages are equally likely to be trumpeted, especially on the West Coast and in gateway cities for late twentieth-century immigration to the United States. Here the particular decade in the twentieth century, the region of the US, and the metropolitan politics of immigration create the conditions of possibility for different inflection of Woods's identity. Recuperating neither causation nor agency *per se*, the attention scholars pay to conditions of possibility indexes a concern that – perhaps surprisingly – poststructuralist inquiry about identity shares with classical historical analysis: how change (or, here, variable accenting) occurs over time.

It is to conditions of possibility for new dance innovation that this essay turns. In the early twentieth-century United States, a cluster of women movement practitioners took the opportunity to press for and to fashion dance practices that contested and confirmed current cultural issues. The persons and practices of Loie Fuller, Isadora Duncan, and Ruth St Denis are not new to dance history and analysis. Until the advent of gender and feminist analysis, historians failed to make much of the shift in the sexual division of labor for dance that Fuller, Duncan, and St Denis catalyzed. When they took unto themselves the right and responsibility to compose their own dances as well as perform them, these women redistributed, and regendered, the creative roles typically allocated to men in nineteenth-century commercial theatre. The impact of their assertions has been felt for a century. Further attention to matters of gender illuminates the salience of middle- and upper-class white women's reform and study movements in creating conditions of possibility for this significant shift in theatrical performance and representation.

Ideology and opportunity

The changes in dance practice launched by Duncan, St Denis, and Fuller in different ways capitalized on almost a century of vibrant efforts to parse women's roles in US society. A "separate spheres" ideology of gender roles had circulated since the early nineteenth century, exerting powerful force. It assigned women to the private sphere of the home and family and men to the public world of work and politics. Although this formulation appeared to speak to and for all women and men, it patently ignored the situation of working-class women, slave women, and later free women of color who toiled in the paid labor force. Despite this disjunction between its enunciation and its effective reach, separate spheres ideology proved quite powerful at organizing expectations about middle- and upper-class white women's appropriate activity. It charged women to be pious, pure, domestic, and submissive. It also assigned them the primary responsibility for nurturing children and maintaining the home. Potentially limiting, these charges in fact offered springboards for women's entry into certain kinds of public sphere activity.

In the early years of the nineteenth century, the renewed religious fervor of the Second Great Awakening added force to women's separate spheres responsibility for spiritual matters. It helped propel women to join and participate in tract and Bible study societies in the public sphere. By forming themselves into voluntary societies, such groups adopted a strategy for social action that others in the period had already come to recognize as distinctively American. Alexis de Tocqueville remarked in *Democracy in America*:

> Americans of all ages, all conditions, and all dispositions constantly form associations. They have not only commercial and manufacturing companies, in which all take part, but associations of a thousand other kinds, religious, moral, serious, futile, general or restricted, enormous or diminutive . . . Wherever at the head of some new undertaking you see the government in France, or a man of rank in England, in the United States you will be sure to find an association.
> (de Tocqueville [1840] 1945, II: 114)

Using this strategy, women in the 1830s and 1840s formed societies to promote "moral reform", that is to expose, protest, and attempt to eliminate prostitution and the sexual double standard. They worked prodigiously in female anti-slavery societies of their own forming; in male-led abolitionist organizations they constituted a growing proportion of the membership and a crucial labor force for petition drives. Conflicts within mixed-sex anti-slavery societies over women's public speaking and potential leadership wracked the movement and helped precipitate women's formation of women's rights groups. In each of these types of activism, women capitalized on the responsibilities assigned to them by separate spheres ideology and entered the public sphere of social interaction to pursue those charges.

A similar pattern obtained with the Women's Christian Temperance Union (WCTU) which was the largest grassroots women's organization in the US. Adopting a women's suffrage plank "for home protection", the WCTU also established model eating houses, reading rooms, speakers' bureaus, even temperance societies for children. It consistently played upon separate spheres expectations to validate and mobilize women's public sphere activity.

The several women's reform movements discussed above occupied different points on the continuum of period theorizings about the sources of social problems that women mobilized to address. Earlier in the nineteenth century, poor relief and moral reform societies typically identified the poor person or the prostitute as the source of his or her own predicament – the problem was one of individual personal morality. By the end of the nineteenth century, more and more reform movements subscribed to an environmental analysis. The country's shift to mass production industry in some cities while sweated labor continued in other areas, the nation's demographic shift from rural to urban settlement and crowding, and the persistence of ward politics began to receive credit as sources for turn of the century problems like crime, tenement decay, infant mortality, and continuing poverty and prostitution (Walters 1978: 192, 213–16). The perceived structural nature of social problems further enabled women's organizations to claim a "municipal housekeeping" role for themselves, again extending the responsibility for family welfare to achievement of that goal through public sphere activity. Environmental analysis stimulated the US settlement house movement, which specifically addressed the needs and perceived problems that came with large flows of immigrant people from Central and Southern Europe. With women strongly represented, settlements constituted an early kind of social welfare network in a country whose government provided none.

Strands of the post-Civil War women's club movement responded in different ways to women's public sphere activity. Founded in 1868, Sorosis brought together professional women at a time when opportunities for higher education and professional training remained extremely limited for women. Also founded in 1868, the New England Women's Club tended to bring together middle-class women who did not work outside the home. Clubs like this one sprang up across the United States. Pursuing cultivation and self-improvement, they functioned as voluntary study clubs focusing on music, literature and poetry, painting, and drama. By the 1890s, women's culture clubs turned increasingly to municipal reform issues, without, however, relinquishing interest in culture study.

Opportunities seized: platforms and patrons

Fuller, St Denis, and Duncan seized the several opportunities afforded them by the women's reform and culture club movements in the late nineteenth century. The rationales for and social action by female voluntary society organizations provided the dance innovators with much-needed platforms for launching a performing career and, certainly for St Denis, even sustaining it. In addition, the voluntary organizations supplied a nexus in which women claimed new authority as artistic arbiters and cultural custodians at the turn of the century.

Loie Fuller

Of the three innovators, Loie Fuller capitalized on the potential available through women's social movements in perhaps the most specific and contained way. In the 1890s and early 1900s she achieved prominence for her daring combination of electrical light and sensuous fabrics that she undulated and manipulated (with help from concealed rods) to form moving images of fire, flowers, and streaming motion. She scrabbled hard to reach that point, however. Historical accounts have frequently made mention of Fuller's early temperance lecturing, but without pursuing it further, when they cited the emerging artist's early stints in breeches roles, temperance dramas, and stock theatre. It was historian Sally Sommer, however, who voiced two additional, important insights. She noted the capacity of temperance's "moral instruction" to mediate the suspect qualities of women's theatrical performance, and she discerned the value that Fuller attached to the power she was able to wield in the very process of performing (Sommer 1979). These insights enable a much more nuanced reading of Fuller's autobiographical account of her early temperance identification. In unpublished writings – possibly drafts for her *Fifteen Years of a Dancer's Life* – Fuller recounted a temperance lecture she single-handedly conducted in Monmouth, Illinois.[2] Having newly taken up residence there with her family, Fuller says she scouted the town and decided out of the blue to book an available hall and publicize a speech to be given by herself. An audience arrived at the appointed hour, she claims, and listened to her discourse on everyday matters, then traditional temperance topics and some *ad hoc* extensions of the same. For example, she reports that she queried the audience whether saucy children or debtors fleeing their obligations should be considered intemperate. By the conclusion of her two-hour talk she earned $85, which she said she gave to her father.

This early temperance lecture may have actually taken place. Or, the report of it may have been apocryphal, a retrospective construction that Fuller used to fashion a self-portrait that exuded agency and control. If the lecture took place as reported, Fuller drew cannily on the model of female temperance speakers who preceded her in order to constitute herself as a legitimate public performer. And she drew from subject matter that their reform movement had already validated in order to attract a bona fide audience. These would have been fine skills to hone for the later stints of temperance lecturing that have not been questioned as part of her career. If the Monmouth scenario is a retrospective fiction, it nonetheless illuminates ways in which temperance as a social movement offered women a template with which to conceptualize parts or dimensions of their lives. For Loie Fuller, the temperance connection offered an instrument with which to authorize herself as a performer, at a very early age, when female stage performance still struck many as illicit. Further, the way in which she used these tools to author her own coming-to-be highlights the self-fashioning that this reform movement made possible for women during a particular period in American life, a salience that we have only recently been able to discern.

Ruth St Denis

Ruth St Denis's interaction with women's voluntary organizations advanced the cultural claims of both parties. The aspiring actress and dancer incorporated backbends and fabric manipulation characteristic of "skirt dancing" in the "eastern"-inflected dances she created for her own solo performance. As Suzanne Shelton (1981) pointed out, St Denis had clearly absorbed the vogue for things oriental that swept nineteenth-century America, and she pursued further reading of her own. Following employment in David Belasco's commercial theatre productions, she was determined to present her own production of *Radha*. This she styled an East Indian dance drama. Through a connection found by her mother's friend, St Denis presented a private performance of *Radha* for Mrs Kate Dalliba and her salon guests, and she received several society invitations to perform as a result. Still with her mother, she made the rounds of theatrical managers, seeking a theatrical engagement. She won the interest of theatre manager Henry B. Harris. Harris presented her in a showcase concert to an audience of male managers. Among appearances that St Denis garnered from this were "two-a-day" stints at Proctor's Theatre. This vaudeville job was not her desideratum, but there Mrs Orlando Rouland, wife of the painter and enthusiastic orientalist, viewed her performance. Mrs Rouland took up the cause of securing a "legitimate" theatre gig for St Denis, soliciting the financial support of numerous friends. The result was their rental of the Hudson Theatre and sponsorship of a ladies' matinee performance. For this March 1906 show, St Denis performed *Radha*, *The Cobras*, and *Incense*.[3]

In response, Harris himself booked St Denis for engagements during the next months at the Hudson Theatre. At the same time, the matinee's success prompted a spate of engagements by women's culture clubs, reform groups, and society hostesses. These included an appearance sponsored by Mrs Herbert Saterlee, the daughter of financier J. Pierpont Morgan, for the meeting of the Thursday evening club, a Manhattan arts and literature study club. St Denis was one of several performers for a membership that included architect Sanford White and society leader Mrs Cadwalader Jones. In April St Denis appeared in a benefit for the People's Symphony, held at the Waldorf Astoria. Several days later in Washington, DC, she performed in a benefit sponsored by Mrs A. C. Barney. The event raised funds for a settlement house – the Barney Neighborhood Club – and the Hospital for Incurables. In May she appeared at Fenway Court, the Boston home of society leader Isabel Stuart Gardner. This evening benefited the Holy Ghost Local Hospital for Incurables in Cambridge, and it was Mrs Gardner who recommended that St Denis be invited to perform. The patrons cited for the latter performance illuminate the confluence of society figures, professional men, and reform-oriented women. Charles Eliot, president of Harvard, and Charles Eliot Norton, professor and vice president of the Hospital, were patrons together with Reverend Samuel Crothers. The program was coordinated by Norton's daughter Elizabeth. Lady patronesses included Mrs J. J. Storrow, wife of the financier and herself a supporter of the settlement house movement, arts and crafts proceedings and, later, the playground and Girl Scout movements. Additional patronesses drew from Boston's artistic and financial elite: Mrs R. H. Dana, wife of the writer; Mrs William Wharton, wife of the financier; and Mrs Rudolphe Agassiz, wife of the academic. These examples from New York, Boston, and Washington illuminate the range of performance platforms that the female network of culture clubs, reform, and charity organizations created for St Denis. The visibility they provided was matchless.

In June 1906 she sailed to Europe, and the next two years saw the consolidation of her reputation as an artist of the first water. When she returned to the US, Harris booked St Denis for concerts in his Hudson Theatre and backed production of the new work *Egypta*. Harris also underwrote St Denis's tour to Midwest and East Coast cities with the "Indian" solos and a cross-country tour of *Egypta*. He lost money on both ventures. To repay him St Denis turned to vaudeville and secured more salon dates. Harris lost his life, and St Denis her chief sponsor, when the *Titanic* sank, and St Denis again turned for support to a network of female patrons. Some patrons engaged her purely to provide novel entertainment for guests; the reform and study club connection was manifest in other gigs. In Chicago, she was persuaded to donate or forgo her fee to dance at the annual charity ball sponsored by Mrs Potter Palmer. The press coverage was outstanding and the proceeds of the event went to support an array of reform and charitable projects. In March 1914, back in New York, St Denis danced at a birthday party given for Anna Howard Shaw, leader of the National American Women's Suffrage Association, in New York City.

St Denis recast her career when she joined forces with Ted Shawn and in 1915 formed the Denishawn school and dance company. She would not have survived the turbulent years as a solo artist had she not drawn on the support networks offered by women's clubs, reform groups, and society salon engagements. These offered a third type of performance platform that handily troubled the burgeoning polarity between "high culture" legitimate theatre gigs and "low culture" vaudeville jobs that subsequently characterized modernist rankings of aesthetic production. At the most fundamental level, women's organizations and society gatherings supplied crucial platforms for performance that sustained St Denis's innovations as a choreographer and dancer.

In turn, the female patronage network supplied an arena in which female sponsors actively claimed a role as arbiters of American culture. In newspaper coverage of the ladies' matinee sponsored by Mrs Rouland and friends, one jaundiced reporter explicitly connected interest in St Denis's production with ongoing investment by women's culture clubs in orientalist literature and other fare (*New York Times* 1906). In another account, the comments of a named sponsor voiced the express commitment and undeniable excitement of sponsoring something new and offering new standards of taste.

> "She is a genius", declared Mrs [Charles C.] Worthington, "and too imaginative and original for the vaudeville, it seemed to us, though if our taking her up gives her a 'boost' – is that what you call it? – in the business way, why, we are more than pleased. And it's such fun to be in on something absolutely new – as this certainly is, for she has gotten it all up herself, out of books and things. I believe she has never been abroad."[4]

For women to lay claim to aesthetic leadership was something new in late nineteenth- and early twentieth-century America, where men typically took the lead in planning and funding the new libraries, symphonies, and museums of the era. What seems clear about cultural leadership at the turn of the century is that while men participated strongly in launching edifices for new arts enterprises, women were claiming a place in the sun via their culture club concerns, their growing representation in arts and crafts societies, and, particularly germane here, their sponsorship of new dance practices. Offering performance platforms to St Denis at crucial junctures in her sojourn as a soloist, female American patrons rewrote their gender roles and reconstituted their social agency to include cultural arbitership.

Isadora Duncan

Isadora Duncan primarily pursued her career outside the United States after 1900. The tours and return visits to America that she made in the next decades registered indelibly, but it was in the earliest stages of her career that she took advantage of the support offered by women's patronage networks.

As both Fuller and St Denis had to do, Duncan spent some time working in commercial theatre productions, in this case in plays and pantomimes, and touring with the company of Augustin Daly. Located in New York, Duncan and family members conducted a teaching enterprise while she pursued engagements as a solo dancer. The slender documentation from this period in her career illuminates the transition she made from commercial theatre performer to the composer and performer of her own movement invention. In one early performance, she appeared as a supporting artist in a concert by composer and pianist Ethelbert Nevin. She danced to "water scenes" music in Nevin's *Narcissus*, *Water Nymphs*, and *Ophelia* before an audience "well-filled with fashionable people" (*New York Times* 1898). Duncan (1928) later claimed that this appearance spurred invitations from society women to perform in their drawing rooms. The surge of interest in Duncan as a performer was confirmed by a mention of the emerging dancer in the March 1898 issue of *The Director*. Oriented to dance teachers and their students, this magazine observed that "Miss Duncan is a professional entertainer, and she has been taken up extensively by well known society women" ("Emotional Expression" in *The Director* 1898: 109).[5]

Duncan asserts in *My Life* (1928) that society matrons of Mrs William Astor's ilk secured her performance at their summer residences in Newport, Rhode Island. Documentation survives for one such occasion, when Miss Ellen Mason of Boston hosted a piano recital on the lawn of her Newport home in summer 1898. The event patrons were all female and included Mrs Potter Palmer and Mrs William Astor, recognized leaders of Chicago and New York elite society. To text recited by sister Elizabeth Duncan, and violin and piano played by John Mullaly and Duncan's mother, the dancer presented the *Rubaiyat of Omar Khayyam* "done into dance" – that is, accompanied and interpreted in movement by Duncan.[6] When Duncan again danced the *Rubaiyat* in March 1899, a *New York Times* account reported that the Carnegie Lyceum event, managed by society figure Mrs Robert Osborn, "was under the patronage of a number of well-known women" (*New York Times* 1899). The Duncan family belongings were destroyed in a fire at the Windsor Hotel several days later, and in April society women again supported her, this time by sponsoring a benefit performance for the fire victim. Again newspaper reportage cited the elite status of her sponsors, who included women "from the inner ranks of the 150 of New York, San Francisco, Tuxedo [*sic*], and Chicago".[7] Shortly thereafter, Duncan sailed for London and began a different phase of her career.

Although data from this period is thin, period accounts linked Duncan's name with those of the leaders of New York and Chicago society – the Astors, the Vanderbilts, and the Palmers. For the monied New York women involved, society competition offered a potent vehicle for contesting class leadership within a felt and actual scenario of long-term, waning influence of the Knickerbocker elite, the earliest leaders in the city's colonial days (Jaher 1972, 1973). The competition played out by hostesses through dinner stylings and salon engagements, and their related sponsorship of matinee and recital events, created conditions of possibility for innovation by the emerging dancer at a key point in her career.

The practitioners and patrons considered above troubled and pressed against prevailing definitions of the ways in which artistic dancing could signify and the realms in which women could exert public leadership. It must be acknowledged that these two types of activism won gains primarily for white, middle- and upper-class women. St Denis's refashionings of orientalist source materials certainly furthered the "othering" – the reifying and derogation of other cultures accomplished by western representations of Indian and Egyptian cultures that Edward Said so cogently identified in connection with the Middle East. As well, the women's acts of recasting failed to bridge American racial divides of the era and secure presentation or reception for women of color. With these substantial limits noted, we should credit the ways in which female practitioners and patrons seized the moment to stage themselves as creators and arbiters possessing cultural authority.

Causes and agents or systems of relations?

The interpretive tradition in academic history has been relatively slow to invoke the insights that critical theory might afford for both the posing of historical questions and the framing of conclusions. Foucault's bracketing of causation and agency in *The Order of Things* jolted historians, seeming as it did to erase first principles of inquiry about the past. To work one's way through the "conditions of possibility" in a specific historical situation, as in this chapter, provides a useful perspective on distinctions that critical theory has drawn between causation and agency, on the one hand, and conditions of possibility, on the other. Causal analysis that emphasizes individuals as agents of change does embrace, it must be said, a kind of romantic faith in the individual that has characterized much western social thinking since the Enlightenment. Foucault's focus on networks and circulation privileges a systems orientation and bespeaks, it is fair to say, a scholarly investment in structural relationships as the features in society and history that matter most – and that offer the entering wedge for resistance. Foucault's sidelining of causation and agency literally helped create intellectual space for other notions of social change and operation to gain hearings. What should be the outcome of this period for reconsideration and potential recalibration of analysis? To place all analytical weight on individual actors as primary causal agents is, perhaps, hopelessly romantic, and also naïve with regard to structured inequalities that have operated over time. To place all analytical weight on system relationships and structures in a given period is to draw nigh to determinism. Neither of these alternatives alone offers viable motion. A path to pursue, I submit, is first to release the brackets tethering causation and agency. Then we need to think through the ways in which causation, agency, and conditions of possibility may be necessary to each other, even constitutive of each other – and also ways in which they are not. People and/or groups actualize the potential available in conditions of possibility; they can and do turn potentials to different account. Equally important, particular historical surrounds help conceptualize, condition, and shade the perceptions people form and choices they make. It is not too much to consider agents, causes, and conditions of possibility as different registrations or enactments of the structures and dynamism compelling change that both are capable of accessing. In the account above, nineteenth-century separate spheres ideology could very well have limited white, middle- and upper-class American women to a private space materially realized as "the home". We need to assess the interaction of agents, causes, and conditions of possibility to parse how it is that prescriptions can be upended, representations redirected, rights and power reconceptualized. Network or discourse analyses, and causal analyses acknowledging agency, are necessary to sorting out how our societies arrived at their current conjunctures. Both are necessary to forging twenty-first century action.

Notes

This chapter is based in part on research discussed in L. Tomko (1999) *Dancing Class: Gender, Ethnicity, and Social Divides in American Dance, 1890–1920*, Bloomington: Indiana University Press.

1 Two works that deployed the family tree strategy were Guest (ed. 1976), with articles written by Moore from the 1940s through the 1960s, and McDonagh (1977).
2 Fuller (1913) does not mention this early lecture nor temperance speaking 1875–77. See Loie Fuller, holograph page, no title, n.d., Loie Fuller Papers 1892–1913, folder 34, Jerome Robbins Dance Division, New York Public Library for the Performing Arts (hereafter DDNYPL); and Loie Fuller, " Before Many Years Were Over, I Had Attended Many Lectures", unpublished autobiography typescript and holograph pages, n.d., Loie Fuller Papers 1914–28, folder 204, DDNYPL.
3 On St Denis's performing career see also Schlundt (1962), Tomko (1999) and St Denis (1989: 74–5). On the March matinee, see for example *New York Times* (1906).
4 Henry Tyrell (1906) "Yes, Society DID Gasp When 'Radha' in Incense-Laden Air 'Threw off the Bondage of the Earthly Senses'", *The World*, March 25, in Denishawn Collection – Scrapbooks – Clippings, DDNYPL.
5 Additional data on Duncan's female sponsors is given in "Narcissus and Other Scenes", *The Director*, October–November 1898: 272.
6 Program, "Rubaiyat of Omar Khayyam", Done Into Dance by Isadora Duncan, Newport, 8 September, 1898, in "Duncan, Isadora/Programs 1898–1929, DDNYPL", *The Director*, September 1898: 254.
7 "A Soulful Function", unidentified newspaper clipping, hand-dated April 19, 1899, in Duncan, Isadora, Reserve Dance Clippings file, DDNYPL.

Bibliography

Appadurai, A. (1990) "Disjunctures and Difference in the Global Cultural Economy", *Public Culture*, 2, 2: 1–24.

Butler, Judith (1988) "Performative Acts and Gender Constitution: An Essay in Phenomenology and Feminist Theory", *Theatre Journal*, December, 40, 4: 519–31.

Desmond, J. (1991) "Dancing out the Difference: Cultural Imperialism and Ruth St Denis' 'Radha' of 1906", *Signs*, Autumn, 17, 1: 28–49.

De Tocqueville, A. ([1840] 1945) *Democracy in America*, originally published as 2 volumes in 1835 and 1840, this edition reprinted in 1945 and edited by P. Bradley, New York, NY: Vintage Books.

The Director (1898) undated reprint of this magazine's December 1897 to November 1898 run, New York, NY: Dance Horizons.

Duncan, I. (1928) *My Life*, London: Victor Gollancz.

Foucault, M. ([1966] 1971) *The Order of Things: An Archaeology of the Human Sciences*, reprinted 1973, New York, NY: Vintage Books.

Franko, M. (1995) "Where He Danced", in M. Franko, *Dancing Modernism/ Performing Politics*, Bloomington, Ind.: Indiana University Press.

Fuller, L. (1913) *Fifteen Years of a Dancer's Life, With Some Account of Her Distinguished Friends*, Boston, Mass.: Small, Maynard & Co.

Gordon, C. (1980) "Afterword", in C. Gordon (ed.) *Power/Knowledge: Selected Interviews and Other Writings 1972–1977 by Michel Foucault*, trans. C. Gordon, L. Marshall, J. Mepham and K. Soper, New York, NY: Pantheon Books.

Guest, I. (ed.) (1976) *Echoes of American Ballet: A Collection of Seventeen Articles Written and Selected by Lillian Moore*, New York, NY: Dance Horizons.

Jaher, F. C. (1972) "Nineteenth-century Elites in New York and Boston", *Journal of Social History*, 6: 32–77.

—— (1973) "Style and Status: High Society in Late Nineteenth-century New York", in F. Jaher (ed.)*The Rich, the Well Born, and the Powerful*, Urbana, Ill.: University of Illinois Press.

McDonagh, D. (1977) *The Complete Guide to Modern Dance*, New York, NY: Popular Library.

Manning, S. (1998) "Black Voices, White Bodies: The Performance of Race and Gender in *How Long Brethren*", *American Quarterly*, 50, 1: 24–46.

Mercer, K. (1990) "Welcome to the Jungle: Identity and Diversity in Postmodern Politics", in J. Rutherford (ed.) *Identity: Community, Culture, Difference*, London: Lawrence & Wishart.

New York Times (1898) "Society Notes", 25 March: 7.

New York Times (1899) "What is Doing in Society", 15 March: 7.

New York Times (1906) "Bringing Temple Dances from the Orient to Broadway", 25 March, 2nd magazine section: 2.

Rutherford, J. (ed.) (1990) *Identity: Community, Culture, Difference*, London: Lawrence & Wishart.

St Denis, R. (1989) *An Unfinished Life*, New York, NY: Harper & Bros.

Schlundt, C. L. (1962) *The Professional Appearances of Ruth St Denis and Ted Shawn: A Chronology and an Index of Dances 1906–1932*, New York, NY: New York Public Library.

Shelton, S. (1981) *Divine Dance: A Biography of Ruth St Denis*, Garden City, New York, NY: Doubleday & Co.

Sommer, S. R. (1979) "Loie Fuller: From the Theater of Popular Entertainment to the Parisian Avant-garde", unpublished PhD dissertation, New York University.

Tomko, L. J. (1999) *Dancing Class: Gender, Ethnicity, and Social Divides in American Dance, 1890–1920*, Bloomington, Ind.: Indiana University Press.

Walters, R. G. (1978) *American Reformers 1815–1860*, New York, NY: Hill and Wang.

Chapter 9

Ramsay Burt

KATHERINE DUNHAM'S FLOATING ISLAND OF NEGRITUDE

The Katherine Dunham Dance Company in London and Paris in the late 1940s and early 1950s

PERHAPS THE MOST SURPRISING demonstration of Katherine Dunham's place in the dance history canon lies in a humble, not particularly recent, and popular rather than scholarly US publication: Tom Tierney's 1983 Dover book of paper dolls of the 'stars of modern dance'. According to the cover text, Loie Fuller, Isadora Duncan, Ruth St Denis, Ted Shawn, Martha Graham, Erick Hawkins, and Katherine Dunham 'stand out today as the pioneers of modern dance, visionaries who brought freer, more natural movement to the art form of the dance' (Tierney 1983). With cut-out costumes one can dress the doll representing Miss Dunham for her dances *Barrelhouse*, *Rara Tonga*, and *Woman with a Cigar*, all created in 1937, and for her role as Sweet Georgia Brown in the Broadway musical *Cabin in the Sky* (1940). It is this which perhaps proves that Katherine Dunham's place in the dance history canon is assured, rather than the frequency with which her name has been mentioned in recent works of dance scholarship or the many honours and awards that she has been increasingly receiving since the 1970s. Most scholarship has concentrated on her dances from the late 1930s and 1940s and their critical reception. Much less attention has been paid to the rest of her career. She left the United States for her first European tour in 1948, and this chapter examines the period 1948 to 1952, focusing in particular on her reception in London and Paris. I argue that this period was a watershed in Miss Dunham's career. Away from the all-pervading racist climate in the United States, she and her company probably gave their best performances at this time. European critics gave her work unqualified approval of a kind that critics in the United States seem never to have been able to grant her. It was the English ballet critic Richard Buckle who wrote the first book about her work. Published in a bilingual English–French edition in 1949, it is illustrated with a fine series of photographs by Roger Wood and is still probably the single most important source of information about her choreography. In both London and Paris Miss Dunham was feted and moved in glamorously high social circles. In most of the capital cities she visited during this tour she gave lectures at universities and anthropological societies on her ethnographic research. Across Europe, and in Paris in particular, she met with important intellectuals. Some of these contacts had a direct impact on her subsequent career and have influenced the international development of 'negro dance' (as it was then called). In 1951 she made what was probably her strongest and angriest work, the controversial ballet *Southlands* which took as its subject a lynching. It is the significance of this extremely important period in Miss Dunham's life that is the subject of this chapter.

Before examining this in more detail, it is necessary first to provide some background information about Miss Dunham's career up until this date, particularly for those less familiar with her work. She was born in Chicago in 1908. Her mother was a consumptive, French Canadian teacher who died when Dunham was still an infant. Her African American father brought her up in the small town of Joliet, 55 km south of Chicago. She was a very bright student and won a place to study sociology at the University of Chicago. At the same time she studied ballet and started her own group of black dancers. Encouraged to go on to do postgraduate research, she was awarded a Rosenwald Foundation travel grant in 1936 to study retentions of African dance and music among people of African descent in the Caribbean. Most of her field work was in Haiti. Returning to Chicago, she decided to write up her primary dissertation but not take all the other exams required at that time for a Doctoral degree. This was much to her supervisor Melville Herskovits's disappointment. Instead, she contacted members of her old dance group and started a company. Several of the pieces she later performed in London and Paris – including the ballet *L'Ag'Ya* – were made in 1937 or 1938. Her dances on Caribbean subjects drew on material she had collected during her field trip. In 1939 she moved her company to New York and in 1940 they appeared in *Cabin in the Sky*. After working in Hollywood and appearing in the film *Stormy Weather* (1943), Miss Dunham and her dancers were signed up by the impresario Sol Hurok who, for the next three years, promoted their tours throughout the United States and Canada. In 1946 Miss Dunham's book *Journey to Accompong* was published in New York. In 1947 her company had a long, highly successful engagement in Mexico City where they made and premiered five new works, and her book *Dances of Haiti* was published in a bilingual Spanish and English edition by a Mexican publisher (Dunham [1946] 1983).

Miss Dunham was not a prolific choreographer. When one examines the list of her choreography compiled by Ruth Beckford (1979), she seems to have made little work after 1947. In her 1962 season in New York she was still dancing pieces she made in Chicago in 1937. By 1943 she had evolved a programme format that she would go on using until she finally disbanded her company in the 1960s. This consisted of dance pieces (and a few songs) arranged in three parts with two intervals. The first part comprised a suite of short dances adapted from the social and religious dances she had studied in the Caribbean and subsequently saw in South America. The middle section generally contained a longer, more serious work, often the three scene ballet *L'Ag'Ya* (1938), or *Rites de Passage* (1941) or, later in the 1950s, *Veracruzana* (1948). The last section consisted of shorter, more showy pieces based on African American social dances. Seen as a whole, such programmes presented the history and development of African-derived dancing in the Americas.

Miss Dunham is an intellectual, and she made pieces for specific reasons. As Vévé Clark (1983) has pointed out, many of her dances demonstrated conclusions from her ethnographic research. *Southlands* was made to convey an explicitly anti-racist message. As an intellectual, she felt guilty about giving up her university career. During the long run and subsequent tour of *Cabin in the Sky* she hired Maya Deren as her literary secretary to help her continue writing and publishing scholarly work. A comparison with Deren is revealing. It was while they were all living in Hollywood that Deren became interested in experimental film making.[1] When Deren in 1945 won the first Guggenheim award ever given to a film maker, she went to Haiti with the anthropologist Gregory Bateson. They followed in Miss Dunham's footsteps and looked at dances of possession during voodoo rituals. Bateson and Margaret Mead had done pioneering work during the late 1930s in Indonesia on trance, applying Freudian methodologies to its analysis. Interestingly, Miss Dunham didn't know of Bateson's work, despite the fact that she too had used psychological perspectives in her discussions of ritual dance. This suggests that, once she left the university environment, Miss Dunham found it hard to keep in touch with developing intellectual ideas. In the United States at that time it was almost impossible to be both a dancer and an intellectual, if you were a black woman. Europeans, however, had no such difficulties in appreciating Miss Dunham as a performer and recognizing her intellectual abilities.

For about thirty years, Miss Dunham ran her dance company without any public subsidy, ensuring a continuity in the development of African American modern dance. In 1967 she finally disbanded it and settled in East St Louis to start a Performing Arts Training Center for the University of Illinois. If she spent most of the period between 1948 and 1967 abroad, this was undoubtedly because of the racist and repressive atmosphere in the United States. It was this which caused so many African American artists during the mid-twentieth century to follow Josephine Baker's lead in settling in Europe. The racism that Miss Dunham and her company had to put up with in the United States took two main forms. Richard Buckle recounts an incident which exemplifies the first: 'There was a great occasion in Louisville, Kentucky, in 1945, when, addressing an audience where the black elements were segregated in the gallery, she swore never to return till her race could be accepted as fellow human beings' (1949: ix). While audiences in the north were not segregated, the second type of racist harassment exemplified there could take more complex and insidious forms. When Dunham and her company performed her *Tropical Review* in Boston in January 1944, most of the local newspapers mounted a campaign against her. As a result a section from *Rites de Passage* was censored for being 'outrageously objectionable'. As I have written elsewhere (Burt 2001), this was the most serious piece in the revue and the only one to have long, explanatory programme notes. Its title is that of the anthropologist Arnold van Gennep's classic 1909 study *Rites de Passage*. By suppressing this, rather than one of the more popular, lighter pieces on the programme, the Boston censor was clearly refusing to acknowledge the possibility that Miss Dunham was a serious artist. Many critics in the United States were puzzled at how Miss Dunham could be both an intellectual and dance in a frankly sexual way. 'Katherine Dunham: Cool Scientist or Sultry Performer?', the title of a feature article in the May 1947 issue of *Dance Magazine* (Pierre 1947), succinctly sums this up.

The American dance critic Margaret Lloyd, writing in her 1949 *Borzoi Book of Modern Dance*, observed that the Katherine Dunham Dance Company's *Caribbean Rhapsody*, as their programme was called, had just been ecstatically received in England. '*The Times* of London, and the *Observer*, gave it brief but positive praise. The *Dancing Times* was almost reverential before the scholarly background, the theatrical presentation. No mention was made of sex; and apparently no one suspected the presence of modern dance' (Lloyd [1949] 1979: 253). The brevity of the London notices was due to the rationing of newsprint – the *Observer* was only eight pages long. In Lloyd's opinion, the serious works in Dunham's repertoire were gradually being lost among the more popular ones. These, Lloyd argued, contained less and less dancing, hence her elliptic reference to modern dance. None of the London ballet critics mentioned modern dance because this was the first time they had seen any barefoot modern dance from the United States. Indeed the Katherine Dunham Dance Company was the first important American dance company to perform in Europe.[2]

The 1939–45 war, and in particular the bombing of London, had seriously disrupted professional dance in Britain, while in New York there was far more continuity of training and artistic development. The strength of Miss Dunham's dancers and the quality of their performance stood out for British critics. The Sitter Out in the *Dancing Times* stated:

> There is no doubt that Katherine Dunham and her artists, every one of whom deserves mention, believe in the value of their own culture, arts and traditions as a medium of artistic expression and they refuse to pander to the audience . . . Katherine Dunham has much to teach us all. Let us be wise and study her work in order that we too shall make the old traditions appear new and exhilarating.
>
> (*Dancing Times* 1948: 526)

A few critics commented on the sensuality of the show, some describing Miss Dunham's singing voice as seductive. One partially undated review from the British *Reynolds News* (1948), in the Katherine Dunham Dance Company's press cuttings book for 1948, has the headline 'Sex and magic not to be missed', and comments on her male dancers' virility 'which so much of our stage dancing lacks these days'. However, the eroticism of Dunham's dancing and choreography was not used by either the English or French press to criticize or slight her in the way a number of US critics had done.

Richard Buckle's review in the *Observer* is so short it can be quoted in full:

> In *Caribbean Rhapsody*, at the Prince of Wales Theatre, Katherine Dunham and her colourful dancers and musicians present an entertainment which disconcertingly mixes anthropology, West Indian rituals, popular dances, cabaret numbers, and reminiscences of ragtime, Blues and Charleston. Her male dancers particularly have a high standard of skill, and the troupe performs with the utmost fire and abandon.
>
> (Buckle 1948a)

Reading this, one would never guess that its disconcerted author would shortly decide to write and personally publish the first book about Dunham. Also curious is the fact that the first page of his book is not about Miss Dunham but narrates a condensed history of slavery. Unlike the United States, there were of course no slave plantations in Europe. England, nevertheless, had its own history of racism, and slave trading contributed substantially to its prosperity and the growth of its major ports during the eighteenth century. A general ignorance of this grim history meant that Buckle needed to inform his British and French readers in order for them to appreciate the significance of Miss Dunham's dances.

Some of the company's drummers were from Cuba and Haiti, but although the other performers were mostly from the United States Miss Dunham's company was mistakenly described as all 'West Indian' by writers who saw black culture in colonial terms. Jamaica and other British colonies in the West Indies were still then part of the British Empire. French newspapers described Dunham's company as Antillean. Léopold Senghor and Aimé Césaire, whom

Miss Dunham would meet in Paris, were elected members of the French national assembly, representing colonial territories. In a British context it is a remarkable coincidence that the SS *Empire Windrush*, carrying around 450 Jamaican immigrants, arrived in London about three weeks after *Caribbean Rhapsody* opened at the Prince of Wales Theatre. At the time there were very few black or Asian immigrants in Britain, and the ship's arrival is now seen as the symbolic start of the big postwar immigration boom that led Britain to become a multi-racial society. As Mike and Trevor Phillips point out, the ship's arrival didn't arouse much interest at the time although the immigrants soon found themselves subject to virulent discrimination (Phillips and Phillips 1998: 72–80).

For people of Caucasian descent in the United States, Miss Dunham's comparatively light brown skin was a threatening reminder of slavery. Peggy Phelan has observed: 'Since race is thought to be "carried" by blood and the history of slavery for African-American women is also the history of rape, the belief that one is "purely" black or white is difficult to sustain' (Phelan 1993: 7).[3] Miss Dunham was of mixed race and her husband, John Pratt, who was company designer, was white. In the United States, the admittedly overt eroticism of a few of her pieces surely aroused so much critical concern because it hinted at the spectre of miscegenation and loss of racial distinctness. If there is hardly any mention of sexuality in English reviews of her work in 1948, this should not just be attributed to English reserve. At that time her African features were not directly threatening to racially based notions of English national identity. In the United States, however, there was a 'Negro problem'. 'Immigration' was not yet a problem in Europe, though sadly it would shortly arouse extreme opinions.

Nevertheless when The Sitter Out said that Miss Dunham and her company believed in 'the value of *their* own culture, arts and traditions' (my emphasis) he was implying that their work presented some sort of essence of African identity. Far from being essentialist, Miss Dunham had a sophisticated understanding of cultural adaptation and change. Her work performatively demonstrated the creolisation of African and European cultural forms in the Americas. The ballet *L'Ag'Ya* is set in the eighteenth-century at Vauclin, a small fishing village in Martinique. In the third scene, to quote Buckle, 'The people of Vauclin assemble to dance the Mazouk and the Beguine. They wear clothes imitated from the court of Louis XVI' (Buckle 1949: 42). The village women wore costumes that derived from French fashion, particularly the elaborate head dresses, to perform a Creole Mazurka, the result of adaptation by the slaves of the social dances of their French owners. The chain came round full circle when *L'Ag'Ya* influenced Paris fashions. A clipping from a newspaper fashion column notes the Dunham company's influence on the new season's hats – particularly checked cotton sun hats with wide straw brims, and the use of knotted kerchiefs.[4]

Pieces like *Barrelhouse* (1938) and *Flaming Youth 1927* (1944) showed modern African American city dwellers, not the pure dance of happy African natives. The front page of the *Sphere* (1948) had photographs of Miss Dunham lecturing to the Royal Anthropological Institute at University College, London.

> She took as her subject the occurrence of cults among peoples whose connection with their traditional culture had been lost. She instanced the popularity of such cults as the Abyssinians, The Temple of Israel, and Father Divine as examples of compensation for the oppression of the Negroes in the United States.
>
> (*Sphere* 1948)

In other words, she lectured about the forerunners of the Rastafarians and the Nation of Islam. As well as showing what people of African descent had to be proud of, Miss Dunham also tried to show the problems of deracination. Her performances were likewise lessons in the history and sociology of modern African American culture.

The 'Gala Noir' on the opening night of *Caribbean Rhapsody* at the Théatre de Paris, 25 November 1946 was attended by the President of the Republic, several ministers, Jean Paul Sartre, Jean Cocteau, Jean Marais, Mistinguette, Josephine Baker, and many other celebrities. More than one newspaper compared it with the *Revue Negre* which was Josephine Baker's Paris premiere nearly a quarter of a century before. The souvenir programme even included colour lithographs of Dunham by Paul Colin and Miguel De Covarrubias, both of whom were closely associated with Baker in the 1920s. Whereas London critics saw her work as 'negro ballet', in Paris some called it experimental theatre. In a lengthy, poetic review, Jean Barreyre wrote:

> How to speak of these bare foot dancers whose docile bodies shudder with an almost imperceptible tremulation, a hidden tropical disease, and who leap and somersault in the fury of their joy or fear. These are excellent artists and are undoubtedly capable of astonishing technical feats.
>
> (Barreyre 1948)

More so than in England, Parisians welcomed Miss Dunham, not least because she spoke some French. She recalls that reporters were so desperate to interview her that they used to hide under her dressing table and as she was touching up her make-up between pieces, disembodied voices would ask her questions.[5]

Intellectuals play a much more important role in public life in France than they do in Britain or the United States. Cécile Mauriac reported that Miss Dunham was sad because Jean-Paul Sartre, the author of *Dirty Hands*, would not shake hands with black hands (Mauriac 1948). Sartre had gone to the show but had not, as Miss Dunham had hoped, come to meet her afterwards. While she was in Paris, Miss Dunham met a number of artists and intellectuals including one or two who were close to Sartre. Her acquaintances in Paris ranged from Charlie Chaplin to Franz Fanon. She met Roger Caillois, who wrote a foreword for the souvenir programme of her 1952 season at the Théatre des Champs Elysées. She got to know Claude Lévi-Strauss who later wrote the introduction to the French edition of *Dances of Haiti*, published in 1957. More so than Sartre, these two men had a strong influence on the subsequent development of structuralist and post-structuralist theory. Caillois, who had been an associate of Georges Battaille, and whose essay 'Mimicry and legendary psychaesthenia' was cited by Jacques Lacan in his psychoanalytic essay on the mirror stage, wrote about Miss Dunham's dances of possession. As a prominent anti-fascist campaigner before the war, Caillois had fled France for South America, returning in 1945. In his essay he writes about the dances of possession he had witnessed during Brazilian Candomblé and Cuban Santaria rituals. Cuban and Brazilian cult adherents, he wrote, were 'favoured, more or less from birth, with a profound ability to follow rhythms' (Caillois 1951). They were unable to resist going into a trance, while modern western people, however enraptured, could never, Caillois believed, become possessed. The goal of modern art, he said, was to experience intoxication while holding onto part of that drunkenness. Miss Dunham's achievement, he argued, was not only to be able to draw through rhythm on joys and celebrations, sacred and profound emotions, but also to give them a structure: 'It is her glory to show so well a serendipitous alchemy which is made up of marvels of knowledge and instinct' (ibid.).

Miss Dunham has fond memories of meetings with Claude Lévi-Strauss, commenting that he had no difficulty understanding the connection between her art and her anthropology. This must have helped heal the wound of Herskovits's disapproval. Discussing her insights into the functioning of voodoo cults, Lévi-Strauss observed that social behaviours such as possession which in modern western society are generally taken as signs of mental derangement could, in another sociological context, be factors of collective cohesion and spiritual enrichment:

> This fact provokes serious thought about certain restrictions placed in our civilization during its development which are perhaps the price unconsciously paid for deriving other advantages. The mass confusion of the twentieth century, expressed partially by this growing vogue of ethnographic research, is that we no longer can discern very well these advantages or their value.
>
> (1983: xvii)

Like Caillois, Lévi-Strauss was identifying cultural and spiritual values in African-derived dance and music traditions with which modern western society had lost touch. This was in some ways what an earlier generation of avant-garde artists and intellectuals had sought in the performances of Josephine Baker (see Burt 1996), though Lévi-Strauss states it more clearly and with a more self-critical, intellectual rigour.

The other important group of intellectuals whom Miss Dunham met in Paris were the French-speaking black poets and politicians of Léopold Sédar Senghor's circle. Lévi-Strauss's and Caillois's melancholy admissions of 'loss' contrast with the more positive notion of negritude. Aimé Césaire, who first coined the term, praised those qualities which distinguish people of African descent from 'civilized' western people: 'Heia for those who have never invented anything / for those who never explored anything / for those who never tamed anything / for those who give themselves up to the essence of all things / ignorant of surfaces but struck by the movement of all things / free of the desire to tame but familiar with the play of the world' (Césaire 1969: 75). By implicitly critiquing western modernity and colonial imperialism, Césaire poetically imagined a quality of negritude to which Africans and people of African descent had access. Negritude drew both on the affirmative example of the Harlem Renaissance and the shockingly visceral style of contemporary French surrealist literature.

Miss Dunham later described her company as a 'floating island of negritude' (Clark 1983: 19). Senghor famously said that black people should integrate, not be integrated, a sentiment with which Miss Dunham agreed. In her 1969 book *Island Possessed*, Miss Dunham cites Senghor's later definition of negritude as 'unité pluraliste', which she said 'remains the ideal of humanists today' (Dunham [1969] 1994: 4). 'For myself', she wrote, 'I insist upon the meaning of negritude as the effort to create a community of men, who happen to be black but must belong to the world around them, no matter what kind of colour' (ibid.). She wrote this while working in Dakar as cultural adviser to Senghor, then President of the newly independent Senegal. As well as helping establish the Senegalese National Ballet, she helped organize the First International Festival of Negro Arts in 1966. A model of folkloric ballet she initiated in *L'Ag'Ya* was thereby disseminated to the national dance companies of many newly independent African nations.

In 1949, while staying in Italy between engagements on their tour, Miss Dunham first met the ageing art historian Bernard Berenson at his famous villa, *I Tati*, outside Florence. Recent biographies of Berenson have revealed that when in the early 1900s he wrote his ground-breaking studies of the Florentine Renaissance, he became secretly involved with the art dealer Sir George Duveen (Samuels 1979, 1987; Simpson 1987). He authenticated paintings that Duveen sold and then received from Duveen a cut in the profits. David Rosand argues that at the end of his life, when Dunham knew him, Berenson was a deeply disappointed man. He felt he was merely a connoisseur who had never written the serious, philosophical study of aesthetics and art history that he envisaged

(Rosand 1987). Dunham too had the feeling that, abandoning the university for the theatre, she had never done the serious academic work she ought to have done. And it was Berenson who encouraged her to start writing again. She sent him each chapter of her next book, *A Touch of Innocence* (1959), as she finished writing it on tour. In Berenson and in Senghor's circle Dunham therefore found solutions to intellectual problems that she had been fighting with for years but not been able to find help with in the United States.

The reviews of the Paris season in 1951 were mixed. Some critics unfavourably compared her new programme of largely South American work with *Caribbean Rhapsody*. It had opened with a gala attended by all the South American Ambassadors. During the 1939–45 war, the United States government had used the arts as one weapon in a campaign to encourage South American states to align themselves with the United States rather than Germany, Italy, and Spain. Seen in this context, Miss Dunham's 1951 programme took a liberal internationalist stance by emphasizing cultural and humanistic values that all in the Americas shared. In the 1950s, the United States used cultural diplomacy to try to counter Russian influence in Europe. The French communist party had been deeply involved in the French Resistance and remained strong in France after the war. Many artists and writers, including Picasso and Sartre, were communists. The ballet *Southlands* was made in Santiago, Chile, where it was first performed in January 1950. It was only presented once more, during her third Paris season in 1953. Constance Vallis Hill has written at length about the piece and the circumstances of its performances (Hill 1994). Miss Dunham said she presented it in Paris because she felt she must have something new to show audiences. In Santiago, the US embassy told all the newspapers not to review *Southlands* – all newsprint came from the United States so there was some implicit control over the content of the newspapers. The communist paper refused to comply. When three years later Miss Dunham announced she would perform *Southlands* in Paris, the French communist paper *L'Humanité* was full of praise for her. In the context of US foreign policy, this was the worst possible outcome, and, as Hill demonstrates, Miss Dunham was made to suffer for it.

Miss Dunham was no hardline black activist. The Katherine Dunham Dance School in New York was racially mixed which, as Miss Dunham told Buckle, was 'controversial among the whites and not a medium of cultural propaganda for the Negroes' (1948b: 6). *Southlands* was more than just an agit-prop ballet. It told the story of a black man who rejected the sexual advances of a white woman. She therefore turned on him and falsely accused him of raping her, leading to his lynching. The last scene showed the victim's body carried through the ghetto. As it passed a smoky café, gamblers' cards fell to the ground and a youth threw his knife into the floor boards, slowly pulled it out, and ruthlessly kept on throwing it (cutting up the dance floor, much to the theatre manager's horror) until the curtain fell. It had the edgy atmosphere of one of Marlon Brando's films

– Brando having briefly attended the Dunham school. It had the angst that Alvin Ailey would later evoke in *Blues Suite* (1959) and Eleo Pomare would create in *Blues for the Jungle* (1966). However, neither artist and no New York critic ever saw *Southlands*. Miss Dunham's reputation as a choreographer might have been different if they had. Becoming a legend, she lost touch with the dance scene.

The fact that Miss Dunham spent so little time in New York after 1948, closing her school in 1954, cut her off from the way modern dance developed there during the 1950s. But would she have made *Southlands* if she hadn't been to Paris? The story of her decision to show it there despite the US embassy's warnings gains another dimension when one realizes that its audience must have included Césaire, Fanon, and Senghor. Her European tours in the late 1940s and early 1950s were very important for Miss Dunham. She received affirmation and a level of support from both black and white intellectuals in Europe that she had not found in the United States. An examination of this period suggests that Miss Dunham's contribution not only to the development of modern dance in Europe and Africa but also to the development of the concept of negritude has not been sufficiently acknowledged.

Acknowledgements

I am grateful to Miss Dunham for talking at length to me about her memories of her first visits to London and Paris. This research was in part made possible by a grant from the British Arts and Humanities Research Board for a research trip to New York. I also wish to acknowledge the help of S. Ifeh Barnes, and the librarians at the Jerome Robbins Dance Collection at the New York Public Library.

Notes

1 Deren's third completed film, *Study in Choreography for the Camera* (1945), was made in collaboration with Talley Beatty, who by that time was working largely independently from Dunham.

2 The term modern dance wasn't used in England at the time. English exponents of the work of Laban and Wigman euphemistically spoke of 'Central European dance' in order to try to disavow any troubling association with Nazi Germany. The Martha Graham Company first performed in London in 1954.

3 This comes in a discussion of Adrian Piper's work.

4 Unidentified English newspaper clipping in the company's scrapbook in the New York Public Library.

5 Interview with Miss Dunham, June 12 2002.

Bibliography

Barreyre, J. (1948) *Opéra*, 183, 1 Décembre, in Katherine Dunham Company *Scrapbooks: 1937–49*, New York Public Library.

Beckford, R. (1979) *Katherine Dunham: A Biography*, London: Marcel Dekker.

Buckle, R. (1948a) 'Ballet', *Observer*, 6 June: 2.

—— (1948b) 'Profile: Katherine Dunham', *Observer*, 12 September: 6.

—— (1949) *Katherine Dunham, Her Dancers, Singers, Musicians*, London: Ballet Publications.

Burt, R. (1996) *Alien Bodies: Representations of Modernity, 'Race', and Nation in Early Modern Dance*, London: Routledge.

—— (2001) 'Katherine Dunham's *Rites de Passage*: Censorship and Sexuality', in D. Fisher-Hornung and A. Goeller (eds), *EmBODYing Liberation*, Münster: Lit Verlag.

Caillois, R. (1951) 'Foreword' in Katherine Dunham Dance Company, *Souvenir Programme*, Paris: Théatre des Champs-Elysées.

Césaire, A. (1969) *Return to My Native Land*, Harmondsworth: Penguin.

Clark, Vévé (1983) 'Dunham's Tropical Revue', *Caribe*, Special double issue 7(1 and 2): 14–20.

Dancing Times (1948) 'The Sitter Out', July: 526.

Dunham, K. (1959) *A Touch of Innocence*, New York, NY: Harcourt Brace.

—— ([1946] 1983) *Dances of Haiti*, Los Angeles, Calif.: Center for Afro-American Studies, University of California.

—— ([1969] 1994) *Island Possessed*, Chicago, Ill. and London: University of Chicago Press.

—— (2002) Interview with the author, New York, 12 June.

Gennep, A. van. (1960) *The Rites of Passage*, London: Routledge and Kegan Paul.

Hill, C. V. (1994) 'Katherine Dunham's *Southlands*: Protest in the Face of Repression', *Dance Research Journal*, 26(2): 1–10.

Lévi-Strauss, C. (1983) 'Foreword to the French Edition', trans. Jeanelle Stovall, in K. Dunham, *Dances of Haiti*, Los Angeles, Calif.: University of California Press.

Lloyd, M. ([1949] 1974) *The Borzoi Book of Modern Dance*, New York, NY: Dance Horizons.

Mauriac, C. (1948) Untitled article, *Ici Paris Hebdo*, undated, in Katherine Dunham Company *Scrapbooks: 1937–49*, New York Public Library.

Phelan, P. (1993) *Unmarked: The Politics of Performance*, New York, NY and London: Routledge.

Phillips, M. and Phillips, T. (1998) *Windrush: The Irresistible Rise of Multi-Racial Britain*, London: Harper Collins.

Pierre, D. B. (1947) 'Katherine Dunham: Cool Scientist or Sultry Performer?', *Dance Magazine*, May: 11.

Reynolds News (1948) 'Sex and Magic Not to be Missed', no date, in Katherine Dunham Company *Scrapbooks: 1937–49*, New York Public Library.

Rosand, D. (1987) '*Bernard Berenson, The Making of a Legend* (book review)', *New Republic*, 197: 35–41.

Samuels, E. (1979) *Bernard Berenson: The Making of a Connoisseur*, Cambridge, Mass.: Belknap Press.

—— (1987) *Bernard Berenson, The Making of a Legend*, Cambridge, Mass.: Belknap Press.

Simpson, C. (1987) *Artful Partners: Bernard Berenson and Joseph Duveen*, Basingstoke: Macmillan.

Sphere (1948) 16 October, in Katherine Dunham Company *Scrapbooks: 1937–49*, New York Public Library.

Tierney, T. (1983) *Isadora Duncan, Martha Graham and Other Stars of the Modern Dance: Paper Dolls in Full Color*, New York: Dover.

Chapter 10

Marion Kant

GERMAN DANCE AND MODERNITY

Don't Mention the Nazis

IMAGINE YOU ARE SITTING in an archive and you come across some documents – piles of dusty material, yellowed paper with rusty marks of paperclips, some sheets slightly torn and worn at the edges, all with that unmistakable musty smell of age – and you read that some of your admired heroes of modern dance were caught up in the unpleasant politics of the Nazi system.

You are puzzled; these papers do not fit the story you were told all along. You did not know that Rudolf von Laban or Mary Wigman had anything at all in common with one of the worst political regimes of European history. You did not know that they were fellow travellers of Nazi cultural politics. You did not know that they not only took advantage of the system but openly supported it. You do not like what you see. What do you do next? Tick the correct answer.

- ☐ You change the subject and find something nicer to research.
- ☐ You tear up the evidence so it disappears and nobody else finds it.
- ☐ You discard the evidence as inconsequential and thus negligible.
- ☐ You break down in tears and seek therapy.
- ☐ You become angry with the archive for keeping damaging files.
- ☐ You sit down and think.

Rudolf von Laban has been considered the 'father' of modern German dance, an artistic movement that provided the ideas and structures for a fundamentally new and historically different dance in Europe. Laban saw himself as both a reformer and a revolutionary. Because our notions of 'modernity' rely heavily on the concepts developed in the early twentieth century, we hesitate to query the motives or actions of the founding fathers and mothers of that beloved art. We prefer to interpret them in a positive way and like to see the departure from tradition and history as an essentially progressive movement.

What happens if we do question the lives and works of those who created the new dance? What happens when we examine history and do not like the results of our examination? These questions raise many problems about the way we direct our research and the assumptions we use to write that research up.

The twentieth century was a violent age; Eric Hobsbawm called his history of the 'short twentieth century' the *Age of Extremes* (1994). Europe, and Germany in particular, suffered under deep social and economic divisions that led to the establishment of the most extreme of political regimes in 1933: Nazism. How did artists such as dancers, choreographers, teachers; how did Rudolf von Laban or Mary Wigman cope with the vicissitudes of life in Germany? How did they react to a growing radicalisation in Germany? How did they face Nazism? Are the politics of the 1930s reflected in their dances and choreographies?

Though the questions seem innocent enough, the answers have deeply divided the dance community. To come back to our multiple choice suggestions: there are people who would prefer to eliminate the questions – and the documentary material. Then there are people who do not like the questions but have answers ready, answers that aim at protecting dancers and choreographers under all circumstances. The threatening questions are avoided by finding an acceptable story that makes further inquiries undesirable. Yet what is so threatening about those questions? Why has there been such hesitance to face them?

The uses of history

Historical inquiry offers a particular strategy to answer those questions. But history is not something simple. Volumes and volumes have been written to suggest and analyse what history is about and how to study it. Hence history can be written in many ways – chronologically or categorically/analytically, describing 'micro history' or tracing 'macro developments'. Yet, however it is written, the concept of 'time' is one of the defining categories. What happens in a certain period of time, how things and people develop over time, what changes they undergo and what relationships they enter, how societies are formed, how and why they sometimes disappear, etc., are questions a historian might ask. In history, events or people of the past are taken, looked at and put into a context – a political, economic, social, cultural, psychological and/or institutional context. This context is necessarily defined by using present knowledge. After all, we know what happened next; the people we study did not. Historical inquiry uses documents of the past – sources – to construct or reconstruct or deconstruct (every one of these verbs already indicates a principal attitude towards history) the past reality of a three-dimensional historical situation.

The documentary sources are one important starting point of historical research. But they are not sufficient in themselves. Some kinds of models are needed to organise our sources. Otherwise they are just disconnected bits and make no sense at all. Here we enter tricky ground because the application of any and every model implies epistemological (that is, how knowledge is created) consequences. Models, informed by philosophies and theoretical ideas, are necessary not only to transform the three dimensions of historical reality into thoughts and words but also to offer a mould, which will give a comprehensible form to the thoughts. Models say much about the background, the very general way of thinking of any historian. These models also determine the direction of the examination, what will be emphasised, what left out because it does not suit the argument or fit into the mould. The choice of methods, the choice of models, will shape the process of thinking about an argument and will guide the research and the organisation of the research material.

Just as it is necessary to choose a theoretical frame, it is also necessary to be conscious of this process and the choices made. The relationship between models, methods and historical research is complicated and requires experience, flexibility and intuition, a feeling for the period and the people. In principle, any theoretical framework could be used to organise historical documentation. But not all theories can help to understand the material and not all theories are suitable for every historical research project. There exists a correlation between theory/model and sources. Both have to be evaluated and tested constantly for their mutual suitability. A model or a theory can, of course, be forced onto historical material. Yet the outcome would be a poor and one-sided image of the reality. 'Theory' fashions have not helped this complex process; for example postmodern theories, drawn from the sensibilities of the mid- to late twentieth century can often be anachronistic when imposed mechanically on earlier periods. As much as some theories have been overused, others are underused. Jürgen Habermas and his theory of 'Öffentlichkeit' – the public sphere, or Noam Chomsky's theories on language development and language skills have hardly made an appearance in dance studies, though they offer alternative ways of looking at the public role of dance as expressive art (Habermas) or of considering whether there are deep structures of meaning in bodily expression as there appear to be in language (Chomsky). Whatever theory or model is applied, however, it should disappear into the historical investigation and not dominate the resulting text or narrative. It should fuse with evidence in an elegant synthesis.

Once the theoretical framework is chosen, the historian begins the research process (locating sources, visiting archives, reading primary sources, collecting other evidence, filing documents and other evidence); next comes the writing and publishing process, and then finally the process of discussing, presenting and defending the version of the past that has emerged. None of these stages are mechanical nor are they completely separate from each other. Thought goes into filing as much as into writing. Documents are never self-evident. They need to be decoded, deciphered, understood and reassembled within a context or milieu, which the historian creates. Writing down arguments within a historical context, composing a 'text', is a very personal process and the above mentioned choice of methods is a subjective matter as well as an objective necessity.

German modern dance as a historical research topic

Let us develop some arguments concerning German dance in the 1920s and 1930s, which can serve as guidelines or hypotheses. In the course of research the hypotheses will be modified and constantly assessed for their value, helpfulness and correctness. Specific questions, like those above, turn into hypotheses to trigger the research and act as constant reminders of important strands of ideas that need to be followed. They serve as threads to construct traceable and cohesive narratives.

The first argument proposed as a working hypothesis is that Laban and Wigman were great artists and therefore they deserve a special kind of protection. As dance belongs to the higher sphere of art, it cannot be contaminated by tedious and disagreeable realities like politics. Dance has to be measured only against itself and its aesthetic advances. The artistic invention of dancers or choreographers is above critical inquiry and there is no need to question either the person or the work of art. Laban's and Wigman's ideas and original innovations have initiated an entirely new way of creating and teaching dance. That is proof enough of their superior status. They deserve our admiration. Any questionable political alliances they might have entered can be discarded as insignificant for their work. Investigation should therefore illuminate their contribution in dance history by adding further detailed understanding of their artistic achievement.

Here is an argument that contradicts the one just stated: Laban and Wigman absorbed and contributed to a certain kind of German thought of the early twentieth century. Both can be considered to have belonged to a nationally orientated and conservative movement, which embraced racist as well as occult notions. This current of thought was part and parcel of what later became the Nazi state, the Third Reich. By the 1920s Laban had made and represented a particular kind of modernity. His entire opus on dance embodied modern notions. Yet his modernity hated and fought many of the equally modern representations and aspects of western capitalist bourgeois society. Laban did not participate accidentally in the Nazi regime; his theory of dance and community disposed him to arrive at the same *völkisch* [untranslatable, but roughly 'racist'] ideas as the Nazis. Similarly, Wigman's dances reflected the need for a strictly hierarchical structure of society with a chosen leader; a society which also depended heavily on national identity. Laban, like other famous German dancers, might not have initiated the political process of nazification in Germany but he contributed to the making of a German society ready for the Nazis.

Laban and Wigman stood at the forefront of the radical new changes in dance aesthetics and dance management. They and the other dancers profited personally and artistically from the new structures. Their aesthetic propositions reflect the greater ideas of their time.

Choice of hypothesis

How did I arrive at this argument? There are always personal reasons in any choice of subject, certain topics which attract the researcher. In my case I was intrigued by the 'missing period' in the history of modern dance in Germany. I found that the years from 1933 to 1945 seemed to be absent from the written accounts of German dance. The years of the Third Reich were either left blank or compressed into prefabricated apologies. There were cryptic statements about the suffering of artists/musicians/dancers and the suppression of their work. Yet the evidence was never supplied.

My research began by questioning the standard formulas about German art and dance in the Nazi period. I began by looking at all the arts in Germany from 1933 to 1945 and found that dance had been left out. At most the histories stated that German dance, and its dancers, were 'forbidden' and had been silenced by the political regime. Modern dance and modern dancers, it was asserted, had not been visibly connected to the political or cultural structures of Nazism.

The next step was to examine how some of the leading representatives had actually lived and worked during the period I had chosen. I found that the majority had not emigrated but had remained in Germany. This fact was interesting and, when compared to the fate of the other arts, of singular importance. Since some of the most famous German modern dancers had chosen to remain in Nazi Germany, their relationship to the regime must have been different from that of the writers, painters, musicians or those dancers who were forced to leave. If they stayed and collaborated with the Nazis, that raised a new question about the aesthetic and moral values in their art. That, in turn, raised the question of the social involvement of the artists, the political context of the creation of art and the integrity of the artists under a brutal regime. It also involved the analysis of ideological and philosophical tendencies of the early twentieth century and their evolution during the 1910s and 1920s.

Laban came into my research naturally; he was one of the outstanding figures in dance history of the twentieth century, not only in Germany. If I was looking at the leading representatives of German dance I had to find out where and how the 'father' of modern dance, the inventor and master of the movement, was placed in this particular regime. I had to find out who he was and what made him act the way I thought he had.

I can summarise and say that my approach was to deconstruct the dominant and authoritative perception and to construct my version of this period in history. In the beginning I applied a deductive method; I took a particular situation and applied the results of general historical research of this period. Historical inquiry helped me to analyse the situation of the arts and their histories during Nazism in Germany – I could compare dance with the broader picture given. Then I used an inductive method and conducted research that might generate a deeper understanding of what drove the German dance movement into Nazism.

As time was one important category in history I had to ask whether German dance had always been part of the Nazi system or what it had been before the Nazis came to power. I had to find out the differences or similarities and follow changes that occurred. Above all I had to search for the ideological bases and theories of this movement. So, from a specific example, I arrived at a general notion and attempted to verify these arguments.

The documentation in the various archives substantiated my theoretical arguments. Every chronology I created seemed to prove the arguments useful and confirmed ever more that the questions I had asked and the theses I had constructed at the beginning of my research were fruitful. Thus, I assumed that they were 'correct' and would make it feasible for me to 'write' about a particular part of German history and the history of German dance.

On the one hand there are the ideas, the theoretical framework, the assumptions within a historical frame, but on the other hand this frame has to be filled with substance, with historical data, with 'evidence', with something that will make this period come to life.

As an example of Laban's position in Germany I shall present a document from the files of the Bundesarchiv [the Federal German Archive] in Berlin from 1935 (see Appendix). It was written by Rudolf von Laban, who at that time headed the Deutsche Tanzbühne, the German Dance Theatre. Addressed to Herr von Keudell, a bureaucrat in the Ministry for Popular Enlightenment and Propaganda, the memorandum answered a query, which the top bureaucrats of several ministries, including the Ministry for the Interior, as well as the Police Force, had posed. On 11 February 1935 Laban offered a definition of what constituted German dance. The letter was signed by Laban with 'Heil Hitler!', the Nazi salute. The date of February 1935, the address to the Ministry of Popular Enlightenment and Propaganda with its Minister Joseph Goebbels, Hitler's devoted propagandist, and the closing formula give important general information. They help identify the circumstances and give a greater picture of the time. We are now aware that we are looking at a letter written in Nazi

Germany to a highly influential government agency. We also learn that the memorandum is a reference to a letter from the Ministry to Laban. Without knowing exactly what his status was at that time we could conclude that he must have been of some importance otherwise the Ministry would not have turned to him in a vital matter: the definition of something German.

Laban's explanation offered three main arguments for the identification of German dances – geography, 'racial essence' and social usage. 'German' was defined by what had been danced in the 'various German regions from olden times in traditional manner', and had been incorporated into German customs. He perceived dance as part of a heritage in which foreign influences had been stripped off and thus made into German cultural assets. German soil and land had embraced these alien inventions and turned them into something they had not been before. Laban created a mythical historical evolution in which these dances, like migratory tribes, had travelled to German areas over the centuries. Though such dances had once upon a time arrived on German soil as borrowed assets, they had passed so deeply into the 'flesh and blood of the German population that one could safely call them German dances, art forms, which arose from German ways of life'. The 'nature of movement' and 'movement forms', which 'originate in, and represent, the German spirit', he concluded, would further inform definitions of 'German' dance. Laban accepted waltzes, or 'turning dances' and 'running dances' as 'German' dances.

In his second argument Laban went to the heart of the matter. He turned from external factors to internal matters, to the 'way to move' and the 'form of movement'. For Laban, 'racial criteria' characterised dance movements, in particular 'rhythm' but also 'body posture' and the 'way the extremities' are used. The 'racial criteria' determined the 'essence of German expression' as much as they were a result of them. This 'essence' in the end distinguished 'German' dance from any other movement form.

In historical research one document cannot tell a whole story. The definition of 'German' in dance formed part of a wider debate on the nature of the new racial state. Sometimes the researcher knows that context before she gets to the archive; in an ideal world she should always command the general information before taking up the detailed evidence. In reality our knowledge is always imperfect. Let us go on to see what we can read in the document by guessing at what must be happening.

It is clear from the text that Laban had trouble defining precisely what constituted the 'German' element in dance; his statements appear vague. Therefore he needed to identify 'racial characteristics', which he did by separating the 'German' from the 'non-German'. With these opposite categories Laban constructed a theory that recognised what 'German' was not. Here again the letter conceals important information. If we are not familiar with positions of German ideology and the turn towards racial philosophy we cannot recognise that Laban simply copied a method applied by one of Hitler's demagogues, Alfred Rosenberg, in his book *The Myth of the Twentieth Century* (1982). One of Rosenberg's constructions introduced opposing groups of ideas or terms. He defined 'German' as the opposite of 'Alien'/'Foreign'/'un-German' – Jewish. Once the construct was in place, it was easy to build a hierarchy and justify whatever one wanted to be 'German'. 'German' represented the positive, which had to be protected and rescued from the negative, which was threatening and had to be eliminated. Laban adopted exactly this method when he wrote that clarification would be achieved by 'reflection on that which is not German in dance'.

The memorandum shows that Laban was familiar with and adopted Nazi terminology and racial theory. It also reveals that he accepted Rosenberg's polarisation of good and evil – 'German' and 'un-German'. He set an arbitrarily defined 'German' characteristic against an equally arbitrary 'un-German' feature. Within this hierarchy of dances Laban – like Rosenberg – proved that 'German' dances were better, racially superior, of higher quality. The next step, and this the Nazis had made clear in their party programmes right from the beginning, was the eradication of the 'un-German', even 'un-German' dance – because it was inferior. Laban's role was to underpin theoretically the Nazi desire to cleanse the dance scene in Germany.

Laban found a third distinction by examining the social usage of dances. He suggested that folk dance should no longer be separated from social dance because social dances had in fact become so popular that they already were a form of folk dance. The idea that folk dance would disappear and be replaced by a particular kind of social dance had been established in many of his writings, his teaching programmes and not least in the creation of the movement choir scheme. Again, the letter does not tell us about the 1920s and Laban's achievements in reorganising the German dance scene. This is the 'context' that has to be developed in order to understand the memorandum of 1935. Laban had hoped that his movement choirs would prove to be the future form of social dance, a united and unifying folk/community socialising through movement. In 1926 he promoted social dance as he saw it as a positive morale for the white race (Laban 1926). Shortly after that, in 1928 he sketched the basic body movement of the white race on which the new dance could build. As he wrote, 'The picture, which we have of the most natural movement for the white race, is roughly the sideward movement' (Laban 1928).

Laban designed his own new social dance as a merger of folk dance and art dance, which reflected the true rhythms of life of the 'master' race. The popular dances of the era, Charleston, Black Bottom, Swing, though, he rejected as 'degeneration'.

The memorandum that Laban composed gave the Nazi administration an apparently scholarly justification for the prohibition of jazz and swing dance in both musical and dance entertainment. Written by the most influential dance theoretician and practitioner it added a particular kind of weight to the decision-making process. Laban provided the state prohibition of swing and jazz as 'Nigger- and Jew dance' with a pseudo-scientific basis. His definition became a valuable means of orientation throughout the debate about prohibiting 'un-German' dance practices.

There is no evidence in the document that Laban was under any pressure by the civil servants in the Ministry of Propaganda. The document shows that he collaborated keenly in the creation of a Nazi dance theory. If artists willingly created the intellectual foundations for Nazi cultural policy, they could be utilised by the administration, the police force or the SS to evaluate dances, to ban or encourage them or to employ them in propaganda.

To read the document with full comprehension, the historian would need a background in the previous period, the so-called Weimar Republic, 1919–33. Two broad cultural debates of those years shaped Laban's notion of modernity and the invention of a new dance: one concerned the clash between 'community' (*Gemeinschaft*) and 'society' (*Gesellschaft*). The former was organic, face-to-face, based on village and small town; the latter artificial, mechanical, urban, non-natural. Laban passionately advocated the former. The other great debate concerned the concepts of culture and civilisation. In order to analyse a letter or memorandum, written by Laban in 1935, the historian has to be familiar with these discourses. Inevitably, she will take sides. Whether she prefers to use the positions and arguments of German philosophers Martin Heidegger or Georg Gadamer, both tainted with Nazist ideas themselves, to justify Laban's decision or, for instance, those of the Marxist philosopher Walter Benjamin, who provides different tools to critique Laban's beliefs, is up to her. The choice, though, will inform and guide her inquiry.

Now the next step is yours. You become the historian. Read the document printed in the Appendix in the light of what I have offered you as background. Ask yourself the following questions:

- Does the document 'prove' that Laban was a Nazi?
- Does it suggest that he was forced to work with the Ministry?
- Do you see evidence that he regarded art as above the politics of his time?
- Should you revise your attitude to German modern dance because of this evidence?
- Should you make no judgement until you have seen more evidence or constructed your own context for the Nazi period?

However you answer them, by asking them you become a real historian, for, after all, history is not the past but thinking about the past.

Appendix

(50.01/237)
Deutsche Tanzbühne

To: Reich Ministry for Pop. Enl. and Prop.
Attention: Herr von Keudell
11 February 1935
Ref: in reply to your letter of 29.1.1935, herewith my interpretation of the concept "German Dance"
Heil Hitler!
(signed) Laban
Deutsche Tanzbühne

The categorisation of a dance form as "German dance" can be justified from many points of view. In the first place there are to be sure those dances, which from the remote past have been danced in various German regions in traditional forms, which we can certainly call German dances. Here there are certainly mutually borrowed elements from the dances of neighbouring peoples. A whole array of folk dance steps are cultivated in the same ways in Holland, England, Poland, Czechoslovakia, Austria, Switzerland and Northern Italy as well as in Germany (Polka, Mazurka, many counter dances). It cannot be established if one or the other of these peoples first developed the relevant dance steps and dance forms, but they have penetrated so deeply into the flesh and blood of the German people that they can confidently be termed German dances. The waltz is certainly a German dance. Indeed it can be called the typical form of dance movement of the German *Volk.*

This brings me to the second point of view, from which the concept "German Dance" is to be assessed. Here we deal with the *type of movement* and the *form of movement,* which corresponds to and arises from essential German features. Here it can only be briefly remarked that racial characteristics stamp themselves in the movements, especially in the rhythm, in the posture of the body and the use of the body parts.

Reflection on that which is not German in dance will most quickly lead to clarification. Certain Spanish or Hungarian or indeed certain definitely Slavic bodily movements and rhythms are so foreign to the essence of German expressive and cultural sensibilities that they could never be taken over and moulded into German forms of dance. This applies to exotic forms of movement of more distant races such as Negroes, Indians, Mongols etc.

To be sure, there are sometimes occasions when something native will be adapted from a foreign stimulus, which we can observe both in the Middle Ages and in modern times. For example, at the time of the Crusades both peasant and aristocratic forms of our own racial dances evolved from the *Moriscos* (Moor's dances) and more recently the so-called German tango grew out of Iberian dance rhythms and Anglo-German social dances from Negroid running and hopping dances. How far such transformations, often third hand, of dance structures can be considered German dance types depends doubtless on they way they are performed and used.

There is here a third point of view. One can assess dances according to their social and societal use as either foreign or home grown. There are courtly dances, which are historically undoubtedly of foreign origin, such as the minuet. Although they reflect a foreign choreographic origin, and in spite of the fact that they reflect entirely courtly customs, they have in certain transformations had an impact on peasant dancing. Thus today social dances have by their very wide use become themselves folk dances. It is even questionable today and for the foreseeable future, if the distinction between folk dance and social dance is really tenable and where the boundaries are to be drawn.

In conclusion it can be said that today waltzes and running dances from the area of so-called social dancing can be certainly accepted as German dances, in so far as they are performed in the German way and to music, which corresponds to the sensibilities of the German Volk. An interpretation of the concept "German Art Dance", that is, the various representational forms of dance, must be approached in much the same way from similar points of view.

(*A note handwritten by the Minister Rat von Keudell is appended to this memo, as follows: It is probably still premature to provide a fixed definition. What can be said is that "today waltzes and running dances from the area of so-called social dancing can be certainly accepted as German dances, in so far as they are performed in the German way and to music, which corresponds to the sensibilities of the German Volk."*)

Bibliography

Guilbert, L. (2000) *Danser avec le IIIe Reich. Les Danseurs Modernes sous le Nazisme*. Paris: Éditions Complexes.

Hermand, J. (1992) *Old Dreams of a New Reich: Volkish Utopias and National Socialism*, Bloomington, Ind.: Indiana University Press.

Hobsbawm, E. (1994) *Age of Extremes. The Short Twentieth Century 1914–1991*, London: Michael Joseph.

Karina, L. and Kant, M. (2003) *Hitler's Dancers. German Modern Dance and the Third Reich*, Oxford and New York, NY: Berghahn Books.

Koegler, H. (1974) 'In the Shadow of the Swastika: Dance in Germany 1927–1936', *Dance Perspectives*, 57: 3–48.

Laban, R. von (1926) Notizen zur Vorlesung, März/April, Halensee, NRCD Laban Archive, Dance in General E (L) 20, MS. 7.

—— (1928) Vortrag in der Berliner Universität 1, April, NRCD Laban Archive, Dance in General E (L) 20, MS. 7.

Launay, I. (1996) *A la Recherche d'une Danse Moderne. Etude sur les Ecrits de Rudolf Laban et de Mary Wigman*, Paris: Chiron.

Levinson, A. (1929) 'The Modern Dance in Germany', *Theater Arts Monthly*, 2, February: 143–55.

Long, R. C. W. (ed.) (1993) *German Expressionism: Documents from the End of the Wilhelmine Empire to the Rise of National Socialism*, New York, NY: G. K. Hall.

Manning, S. A. (1993) *Ecstasy and the Demon: Feminism and Nationalism in the Dances of Mary Wigman*, Berkeley, Calif.: University of California Press.

Mosse, G. L. (ed.) (1966a) *Nazi Culture. Intellectual, Cultural, and Social Life in the Third Reich*, trans. Salvatore Attanasio and others, New York, NY: Grosset and Dunlap.

—— (1966b) *The Crisis of German Ideology: Intellectual Origins of the Third Reich*, London: Weidenfeld and Nicolson.

Noakes, J. and Pridham, G. (eds) (1974) *Documents on Nazism, 1919–1945*, New York, NY: Viking Press.

Rosenberg, Alfred (1982) *The Myth of the Twentieth Century: An Evaluation of the Spiritual-Intellectual Confrontations of our Age*, trans. Vivian Bird, New York, NY: Noontide Press.

Steinweis, A. E. (1993) *Art, Ideology and Economics in Nazi-Germany: The Reich Chambers of Music, Theatre and the Visual Arts*, Chapel Hill, NC: University of North Carolina Press.

Chapter 11

Larraine Nicholas

DANCING IN THE MARGINS?
British Modern Dance in the 1940s and 1950s

IN 1934, JEANNETTE RUTHERSTON reviewed the burgeoning British modern dance scene in the *Dancing Times*, explaining the lineage of dancers and teachers working in Britain according to their training with Rudolf Laban, Mary Wigman or Gertrud Bodenwieser (Rutherston 1934). In spite of the latent possibilities, Rutherston was aware that the roots of central European modern dance were deeply implanted in the experiences and temperaments of foreign lands and that crossing the divide of national identity was always going to be a problem. The following years further complicated this with the political realities of 1930s Europe, the rise of Hitler and fascism and World War II, but a decade or so later, as Britain emerged from war into the late 1940s, it was still possible to see the outlines of the European dance lineages Rutherston had described and to feel the potential for modern dance to put down native roots.

The 1930s' contingent of European modern dance in Britain comprised both dancers returning home after training abroad and foreign refugees from Nazism. Among the former was Leslie Burrowes, a student of Wigman, who returned to London in Autumn 1931, becoming an influential teacher and recitalist. Among the latter, the most celebrated grouping was around Kurt Jooss. In 1934, following his flight from Essen and the international success of his anti-war work *The Green Table* (1932), he was provided with a base for his company, Ballets Jooss, and the school he directed with Sigurd Leeder at Dartington Hall in Devon, under the patronage of Leonard and Dorothy Elmhirst. Rudolf Laban himself arrived at Dartington in 1938, making it an important enclave of émigré European modern dance.

However, the following decades did not result in the European styles of modern dance taking on a central role in British theatre. Jooss and Leeder returned to mainland Europe and Laban's name became synonymous with the application of his theories to creative movement for schoolchildren (Modern Educational Dance), so that by the early 1960s a critic would declare:

> Now that the Central European tradition of expressionist dance has virtually dried up, practically everything that is of interest in non-classical, non-ethnic theatrical dancing has it roots in America.
>
> (Barnes 1961: 29)

This summarizes the growing perception of the relative theatrical value of European and American modern dance. It is certainly possible to disagree with the conclusion implicit in the 'drying up' metaphor, since modern dance was firmly implanted in schools, teacher training colleges and drama colleges, a process begun in the 1930s. A theatre critic such as Clive Barnes would find these facts of marginal significance. However, his metaphor is an effective reminder that the past studied in dance history should be one of processes and not just of the productions and events which appear to be 'landmarks'. The process of change in the position of modern dance in Britain during the 1940s and 1950s has received little historical scrutiny to date. Although major accounts have focused on the central figures of the genre of the stature of Laban and Jooss, including their British careers, there has yet to be a comprehensive survey of British modern dance as a continuing tradition, in the manner of Jacqueline Robinson's account of modern dance in France, 1920–70 (1997). The result of this neglect has been a gap in the records which could be interpreted as 'nothing going on' in modern dance in Britain before the importation of the Graham technique from America in the 1960s. In fact there was a whole range of activity, educational and theatrical, amateur and professional. Although all these areas were interlinked through individuals who worked across them, theatrical performance was the standard by which modern dance was judged in contemporary accounts, and therefore is the focus of this short survey.

What was modern dance in the 1940s and 1950s? As Jack Anderson (1997) has suggested, modern dance is almost undefinable, but there are recurring characteristics – the emphasis on the personal and unique, the rejection of classical ballet as form and aesthetic[1] and engagement with the twentieth-century world. In these terms, Britain was not a blank slate before the 'central Europeans' arrived. The 'free' dancers of the turn of the century, in particular Isadora Duncan and Maud Allan, had generated a similar British movement of 'Hellenic' dancers among whom Margaret Morris was the most radical, developing from 1910 onwards in an astounding number of diverse theatrical, educational and therapeutic areas. In some ways Morris is comparable to Rudolf Laban in that both attempted to find and build upon the natural laws of movement; their work encompassed dance for both amateurs and professionals; they envisioned a wide application for their movement theories, and both developed systems of notation.

A major difference is that Morris codified a technique and system of exercises arranged in progressive levels.[2] Some of the British dancers who later trained in central European styles, for example Leslie Burrowes and Jack Skinner (a later member of Ballets Jooss) were originally her students. During the 1940s and 1950s, Morris was one of the individuals attempting to establish dance companies and repertoires using a non-balletic vocabulary and encoding the work with a specifically British, or in this case Scottish, identity.

It is important to remember how little the British public knew of dance developments in America at the beginning of this period. The early postwar years brought American ballet companies to Britain, but modern concert dance remained a largely unknown area. Martha Graham had her first London season in 1954, to the bemusement of traditional critics.[3] Perhaps the shock was all the greater because there had already been an influx of American musicals bringing a popularized notion of modern dance with the work of modern choreographers such as Helen Tamiris and Hanya Holm, as well as others who crossed ballet/modern genres such as Agnes de Mille and Jerome Robbins. This version of modern dance, with all that it said of a vigorous, 'go ahead', postwar world dominated by America, in culture as in politics, was a contributing factor which gradually coloured public and critical standards of what modern dance should offer.

Jooss, Leeder and Laban

This period begins with the years of World War II, 1939–1945, which were especially difficult for the émigrés. In 1940, Jooss and Leeder were interned in camps as 'enemy aliens'. The school at Dartington closed down; the Ballets Jooss, which had embarked on tour without its director, was marooned and subsequently disbanded in the US in 1942. It was the intervention of Maynard Keynes, dance-lover, economic adviser to the government, and now Chairman of CEMA (the Council for the Encouragement of Music and the Arts, the antecedent of the Arts Council), which allowed the company and school to reassemble at Cambridge. Isolation from the rest of Europe and the political will to promote the arts for the benefit of the population offered opportunities to modern dance as to ballet. From 1943 to 1945 Ballets Jooss toured Britain under the auspices of CEMA, making a visible contribution to the war effort.

By 1945, Jooss's profile was such that a number of British dance writers of the postwar period (e.g. Coton 1946; Storey 1948) placed him in the continuum of those great reformers of ballet as a coherent dramatic form, Jean-Georges Noverre and Michel Fokine. In his 1946 book, *The New Ballet*, Coton projected an image of Jooss almost as the saviour of ballet as a genre. By 1945, however, there were problems within the company. It was difficult to keep the repertoire of some twelve works fresh, especially when wartime conditions necessitated a group of dancers, not all of whom had received consistent exposure to the Jooss–Leeder technique and ideology (Stöckemann 2001: 315). The repertoire was still weighted towards the pre-war works with the oldest, and arguably finest, dating from 1932.

Ballets Jooss continued to be associated with the Arts Council (created in 1946), but the subsidy ceased in March 1947 on the grounds that it had resumed its international touring schedule rather than the predominantly British one; the company closed down in August of that year. Jooss himself went to work in Chile before returning to the Folkwangschule at Essen. When he brought his Essen-based company to London in 1953, shortly before it was disbanded yet again, there was an uneasy feeling among some writers that, in spite of some new works, the repertoire spoke of old concerns, 'stamped with the leaden hopelessness and cynicism that we associate with the period between the wars' (Pratt 1953: 5). Modern dancers continued to face similar criticism throughout the 1950s.

Although Jooss left Britain, his long-time collaborator, Sigurd Leeder, opened his own studio in London in 1947. The Jooss–Leeder School had been geographically rather isolated at Dartington Hall and failed to attract large numbers of British students. Leeder's teaching was firmly grounded in Laban's spatial and dynamic theories but his training method was a highly individual one, developed through dance studies embodying particular principles, which were gradually built up in successive classes (Hutchinson Guest 1985). This was to be the most professionally orientated British studio of the period, offering full-time diploma courses as well as classes for amateurs. Leeder was also a talented artist and designer and brought these subjects into the curriculum of a broadly conceived dance education.

Since Dartington days there had been a Studio Group envisaged as a halfway house between graduating and a professional career. The postwar Sigurd Leeder Studio Group was composed of staff, graduates and students, who gave showcase performances of their choreography, often in the intimate surroundings of the studio. In 1957, when the Studio Group celebrated ten years of the school in London, a critic declared of Leeder:

> His is the only [modern dance] group which possesses dancers with a sound technique, and although the group is not without its minor defects, it is the only one which has a fully professional standard of production.

However, the critic concluded that 'he has not transformed the face of English dance, or even attempted to' (Mason 1957: 41). This perception hardly gives credit to the influence of Leeder on the careers of individuals such as Eileen

Cropley, Jane Winearls, Ludmila Mlada and Colin Paterick who were noticed to be fine performers or choreographers. It was not until 1959, when the school moved to Morley College, that the Studio Group could be seen in a better theatrical setting in Emma Cons Hall. The comments above suggest disappointment at the scale of the work: there was clearly not to be a major new modern dance company arising here. In 1959 Leeder left the school under the directorship of Simone Michelle and June Kemp, going to work in Chile, and then Herisau, Switzerland, which became the centre of his activities from 1964.[4]

Modern dance was simultaneously developing along different lines around Rudolf Laban. During the war, accompanied by Lisa Ullmann, a teacher from the pre-war Jooss–Leeder School, Laban worked on the various aspects of his movement theory, including industrial movement studies and the development of dance as a creative school discipline. The Art of Movement Studio was set up in Manchester in 1946, under the direction of Lisa Ullmann, but with Laban taking an active part. The Studio had a multi-disciplinary ethos. Students might take off in a variety of directions – the stage, therapy, teaching, notation or movement analysis work – but as time went on, Ministry of Education approval being received in 1948, the requirements of school teachers came to dominate the curriculum. Teacher training attracted grant-aided students and the most significant support for Ullmann and Laban came from individuals in the education establishment who saw the development of Modern Educational Dance as a component of the reformed, child-centred educational system.[5] Nevertheless, in the late 1940s there was still an active notion that a British-trained modern dance company could emanate from the Art of Movement Studio.

Dancers working: companies, platforms, recitals

After the demise of Ballets Jooss, dancers were faced with the need to find work, in the absence of another company or a strong modern dance recital culture. Some (for example Rolf Alexander, Noelle de Mosa, Jack Skinner) danced for a while in the American musicals such as *Oklahoma!*, *Brigadoon*, and *Annie Get Your Gun*, which were a feature of the British stage from 1947. Throughout the 1950s, the musical stage (including opera), film and television continued to offer the main opportunities for dancers with an exclusively modern dance training to dance professionally but we should not assume that this was always a 'second best' experience for them. Working dancers did not necessarily see themselves as embodying the ideology of modern dance as high art; for one thing, being a 'modern' dancer was sometimes the result of circumstances such as making a late start. Mixing with dancers from different backgrounds, including American trained dancers in the musicals, was stimulating and encouraged a widening of skills. In her memoirs, the Wigman and Jooss–Leeder-trained dancer

Joy Bolton-Carter remembers this as a time when 'classical dancers were eager to acquire a modern technique, and vice versa' (Skinner 1999: 58). For modern dancers this was also a matter of necessity, since they frequently found that their training had not created the physical instrument needed for a professional dancer in the commercial theatre.

Considering the history of Ballets Jooss in Britain, it is inevitable that the model of a repertory company should remain an attractive one for modern dancers. In addition, the Arts Council of Great Britain was shaping public perceptions, with its emphasis on supporting what it considered to be the nation's 'power houses' of culture, Covent Garden's resident ballet company being at the pinnacle of a hierarchy. Little else in dance was subsidized. At the Art of Movement Studio in Manchester, a company developed under the direction of Hettie Loman, a student and then a member of staff. This group became the British Dance Theatre, with Loman as the main choreographer.

It is easy to detect the significance of the company's title and its appeal to the notion of a native shoot from the old central European stock, and even to the hierarchical model of companies as promoted by the Arts Council. The title also has something of the tone of nationalism encouraged by preparations for the Festival of Britain in 1951, which galvanized the nation to project a positive image of its achievements in arts, sciences and technology. It seems that Laban hoped to set up a larger professional group, or enlarge the existing company, for a Festival of Britain tour of 'an artistic spectacle characterising the development of this new art in the spirit of his country', but this project came to nothing.[6] In the summer of 1950, Laban decided that the British Dance Theatre was no longer financially viable as part of the Studio. The company then split off as an independent, professional dance company based in London. A school, the Dance Theatre Studio, was also opened. In the heady days when British ballet was expanding, it seemed that modern dance could do the same. The British Dance Theatre toured nationally during 1950 and 1951. There was even a television transmission on 18 September 1950 (Rowson Davis 1996: 45–50), but after the summer of 1951 bookings became harder to obtain, so that performances continued on a less regular basis.[7]

Hettie Loman, like Jooss, was committed to themes addressing the human condition, including anti-war and social themes, with her choreography marked by a strong sense of the dramatic use of Laban's dynamics and space harmony in delineating character. In common with the reaction to Jooss and other groups (and indeed to Graham in 1954), themes such as the psychological effect of concentration camp survival in *Once I Had Laughter* (1949) elicited press comments on the gloomy subject matter.[8] Perhaps this is not surprising for critics more used to reviewing ballet, but behind these comments are more fundamental questions. Was modern dance moving on? Could the new generation demonstrate a break from the past? As young Britons, members of the

British Dance Theatre felt they were pioneers in adapting the central European style to British taste and that the themes of their more serious works were not less valid but more so in the postwar nuclear age.

In Glasgow, where she had been based since 1939, Margaret Morris also launched a professional company, the Celtic Ballet of Scotland, in 1947. The choreography utilized both her own technique and Scottish country and Highland dance movements. Many of her works had Scottish national themes such as *Skye Boat Song*, and the identity of the company was reinforced by much use of kilts and tartans as stage costumes, and also as offstage uniforms on foreign tours. The Celtic Ballet was invited to perform at Jacob's Pillow Dance Festival in the US in 1954; this was followed by an American tour (Carrell and Hastie 1985).

The company model was also utilized to challenge the assumed inflexible opposition between ballet and modern dance. In 1946 the Wigman-trained dancer, Ernest Berk, joined forces with a ballet teacher and choreographer, Nesta Brooking, to create a company called Dance Theatre. For this company Berk made a work which was entered in the competition of the Archives Internationales de la Danse in 1947, and received a special award. *Trilustrum* was about three periods in the life of a British family before, during and after World War II. Following the competition, Dance Theatre completed a short season in London and an Arts Council booking in Manchester before disbanding for financial reasons. The programme showed this convergence between the two techniques, not only through Berk's *Trilustrum* in a style said to combine elements of modern dance and ballet (Hall 1950: 148), but also by including pieces from the modern dance recital repertoire of Ernest Berk and his wife Lotte Berk, a ballet by Nesta Brooking, and a lecture demonstration on the training of a ballet dancer, including classical excerpts.

In another example of this kind of convergence, The New-Ballet Company was formed by dancer Antoinette Wijnberg and musician Patrick Harvey. Both had been at the Jooss–Leeder School at Dartington in the 1930s and Wijnberg had more recently trained and performed in Spanish dancing. The interest of this short-lived company – it existed for only a few weeks in 1952 – is in the way it was positioned through its repertory with ballets by Frank Staff and Walter Gore in the same programme as a modern dance work by Sigurd Leeder, *Story of a Man*. This was an allegorical piece, showing a man's journey through life (Barnes 1953: 14). Wijnberg herself contributed *A Touch of the Sun*, said to show the influence of both Spanish and modern dance genres. Both modern dance and ballet, as the company name implies, were seen to be needful of new choreography. Critics welcomed this approach at a time when there was disquiet about the increase in classical ballet revivals and a perceived decrease in financing new choreography.

Attempts to create professional dance companies, wholly or partially in modern dance idioms, belong to the late 1940s and early 1950s.[9] The later prospects for companies seem to have been much less favourable, although in Scotland Margaret Morris continued with the hope of a permanent company, relaunching it in 1960 as the Scottish National Ballet.[10] The British Dance Theatre continued to give performances on a less regular basis but the symbolic title was relinquished in 1958 when Loman renamed her company the Hettie Loman Dance Theatre.

Modern dance continued in educational establishments, in numerous studios and in recitals given by soloists and groups. In London, for example, as well as the Sigurd Leeder School of Dance and the school associated with the British Dance Theatre, there were other studios including those of the Vienna-trained teachers Lilian Harmel and Hilde Holger, which contributed to the dance culture. Recitals were an important signal of independence and creativity for dancers who might otherwise be earning a living through teaching and/or the commercial theatre. As well as performances in small venues, modern dance in the educational sector provided a network which could offer performance opportunities. For example, Geraldine Stephenson, who trained and subsequently taught at the Art of Movement Studio in Manchester, was encouraged by Laban to develop a solo recital programme, mainly of character studies, which she took to colleges as well as arts societies. She secured a television transmission in 1951 and the director, Christian Simpson, made use of what were then experimental camera techniques to convey the nightmarish quality of *The Dream* to which Stephenson had also composed and recorded an equally experimental piano, percussion and sound score, described as 'wails and hisses, horrible howls and ticking noises' (Brunelleschi 1951: 49; Rowson Davis 1996: 73–4). Ernest Berk was also a frequent recitalist, sometimes with Lotte Berk and later with a group of students. His work was distinguished by a wide sense of theatricality which encompassed pure dance, mime, mask work and percussion and electronic musical compositions.

Without a dance department or dance advisory panel, there was no Arts Council strategy for development in the art form and no voices of concern in favour of a diversity embracing modern dance. Apart from the regular clients – Sadler's Wells Ballet, Sadler's Wells Theatre Ballet (together becoming the Royal Ballet in 1956), and Ballet Rambert – support for other companies was sporadic until the late 1950s. This also made the Arts Council vulnerable to criticism that it was neglectful of the provinces and 'theatreless' towns. One way in which it tried to counter this complaint was to manage small-scale tours of musicians, dancers etc. These provided limited opportunities for small companies and recitalists to obtain subsidized work. Two dancers who had been students of Gertrud Bodenwieser in Vienna, and members of her company in Australia, based themselves in Europe from 1947. Evelyn Ippen and Bettina Vernon, performing as a duo named Ballet for Two, worked frequently on the Arts Council circuit. Their light and varied repertoire and flowing style, danced to Strauss, Dvorák, Schubert and Brahms, proved successful for small-scale touring, especially with the exotic title *Dancers from Vienna*. In another example, the Scottish Committee of the Arts Council made a grant of £200 to the Celtic Ballet, for its visit to Jacob's Pillow Festival in 1954; clearly there was an issue of nationalism to be addressed here. Such examples of subsidy arose, however, as a reaction to an immediate situation, rather than as the result of a strategy for dance.

In an effort to establish a supportive organization for modern dancers, Hettie Loman and Sally Archbutt of the British Dance Theatre set up the Contemporary Dance Theatre Centre at Toynbee Hall in 1954. In adopting this name, they were consciously attempting to define their work in terms of the present, in order to counter criticisms that modern dance was old-fashioned, locked in a pre-war style. In fact, the term 'contemporary dance' began to be used from the mid-1940s, Ballets Jooss being advertised as 'the contemporary dance theatre' and the term gained currency as synonymous with modern dance during the 1950s.[11]

The intention behind the Contemporary Dance Theatre Centre was to provide a platform for modern dance from Britain and abroad. During 1954 there were nine performances but after this the momentum slowed, partly because the premises were lost. The Contemporary Dance Theatre Centre was undoubtedly a scheme of potential, although some of the original objectives, for a choreographic competition, for lectures, and to stimulate collaboration between the arts, were not achieved and may not have been attempted. In addition to the British Dance Theatre, dancers from a cross-section of modern dance backgrounds were presented: Ernest and Lotte Berk, Leslie Burrowes,[12] Peggy Rowlands (a student of Burrowes and Wigman), Geraldine Stephenson, Ludmila Mlada, Colin Paterick and Jane Winearls with her group The Little Company. Among the foreign dancers were former Jooss soloist Lisa Czobel and her partner Alexander von Swaine and, just before Martha Graham's first disappointing season in London in 1954, the American modern dancer and choreographer Eleanor King, formerly a dancer with Doris Humphrey and Charles Weidman.

The Related Arts Centre was another platform organization, formed in the late 1950s. One of the groups performing under its auspices was formed by John Broome, who had a mixed background in ballet and Jooss–Leeder technique. During the late 1950s and early 1960s he was rather a maverick on the dance scene, making works which integrated dancers and actors in stylized movement dramas. Another related Arts Centre concert appears to have foundered in the tiny and inadequate theatre, but a report conveys the variety of the work being shown – a group *Abstract Dance* by Hilde Holger, solos from Lilian Harmel and Ludmila Mlada, Jane Winearls' dance-drama *Salle d'Attente* and a choreographic study of three aspects of a woman's character, *Lylia*, by Colin Paterick (Mason 1959: 30–1).

Choreographers might also come together to mount a performance, such as the recital named 'Six Choreographers' in July 1959. The programme included a movement drama critical of various elements of society, *The Blind People*, by John Broome. There were other group dances by Leeder and the performance gave Jane Winearls an opportunity to show a revised version of *Salle d'Attente*. Eileen Cropley showed some solos choreographed to Stravinsky's music (Franks 1959: 546).

The model of the repertory modern dance company had been found financially and artistically impossible to sustain, but by the late 1950s there was a steady stream of activity by small groups and solo recitals. Ventures such as platforms, recitals and group performances succeeded in keeping modern concert dance before the public throughout the 1950s and beyond. Comments in the dance press were very often uncomplimentary, even from A.V. Coton who, although he remained a supporter of modern dance, did not hesitate to voice his disapproval of outdated, poorly conceptualized choreography and weak technique (1959: 6). There were expectations that modern dance should be constantly breaking new ground in themes, choreography and technique and yet it can be argued that British culture in the 1950s was not yet ready to support any kind of iconoclasm. This was observed by the British dancer resident in America, David Vaughan, when he returned for a visit in 1956. In comparison to the scene in the US, he found all branches of British theatre dance – ballet, modern dance and musical theatre – in a rut (Vaughan 1956).

If, after the optimistic years, modern dance moved into the margins of theatre dance activity as defined by the critics, warranting few column inches, at least these were lively margins which were well-populated with like-minded dancers and teachers.

Continuities

Did dance acquire a British identity? The most obvious affirmation that it did so is that, by the end of the 1950s, there was an active British generation of dancers trained in or influenced by this tradition. It could also be argued that the alliance between modern dance and education was a well-established British phenomenon. The Hellenic pioneers, including Margaret Morris, were deeply interested in education and the personal development of the adult amateur. Sigurd Leeder's teaching method, with its concern with the education of the whole personality of the dancer, harmonized well with established British interests. Lisa Ullmann and Laban made their own contribution with the development of Modern Educational Dance.

Time does not come to a full stop just because a historian claims to see a period begin or end. Dancers, teachers and choreographers of the 1940s and

1950s continued to work into the next decade, interacting with new developments. Some of the dancers who seized the opportunities offered in the 1960s had already been fully involved in the modern dance performance culture of the 1950s. For example, Eileen Cropley, whose dancing and choreography have already been mentioned, later studied at the Martha Graham School in New York and danced in Paul Taylor's company (Bannerman and Nicholas 2000).

There is also something very valuable in the continued practice of a coherent aesthetic and method, in spite of the fluctuations of fashion. It remains available as a refreshing resource, like a varied gene pool. There is no more potent symbol of this, and of the longevity of the European tradition in Britain, than the former Bodenwieser dancer, Hilde Holger. She opened a studio in London in 1949, where she taught until her death in 2001. She influenced successive generations of British dancers, no more so than in recent years with the reawakening of interest in the Tanztheater tradition.

Notes

1 There was, nevertheless, a general use in Britain of the word 'ballet' by modern dance practitioners to indicate theatrical dance technique (e.g. 'modern ballet') or a dance work intended for theatrical performance.
2 The other important founders of 'free dance' styles in Britain were Madge Atkinson (Natural Movement) and Ruby Ginner (Revived Greek Dance).
3 For example, Cyril Beaumont (*Sunday Times*, 7 March, 1954: 8) found she expressed 'a being mentally wracked' which he could not relate to his own understanding of what ballet was about. Other, younger critics, like Richard Buckle (*Observer*, 7 March, 1954: 11), Peter Williams and Clive Barnes (*Dance and Dancers*, April, 1954: 12–13) expressed a much more positive response.
4 The London school finally closed in 1967.
5 The Art of Movement Studio moved to Addlestone, Surrey, in 1953. In 1975, under the directorship of Marion North, it moved into London as the Laban Centre for Movement and Dance (now the Laban Centre London) with a new emphasis on theatre dance training.
6 National Resource Centre for Dance: Lisa Ullmann Archive, Box 037, Fol. 01, item 2b, p. 1, *Modern Ballet Performances at the Festival of Britain 1951*.
7 At the time of the television transmission the company members were Sally Archbutt, Joan Carrington, Ronnie Curran, Warren Lamb, Valerie Preston and Meggie Tudor. Curran later performed with Jooss. Lamb and Preston (later Preston-Dunlop) have since made considerable contributions to dance and movement scholarship.

8 A number of Loman's works, including *Born of Desire* (1948), and *Once I Had Laughter* (1949) are available in Kinetography Laban scores, published by Croydon Dance Theatre.
9 I have not included Berto Pasuka's company, Les Ballets Nègres, in this survey. It existed from 1946 to 1952, a highly successful British repertory company performing in an African dance idiom. Recent research suggests that Fernau Hall (1950) may have overemphasized the modern dance contribution made by Ernest Berk to their first productions.
10 The company foundered after a tour cut short for financial reasons.
11 It is also significant that the British Dance Theatre sometimes performed under the name of the British Contemporary Dance Theatre in the mid-1950s.
12 Performing under her married name of Leslie Goossens.

Bibliography

Anderson, J. (1997) *Art Without Boundaries: The World of Modern Dance*, London: Dance Books.

Bannerman, H. and Nicholas, L. (2000) 'The Graham Explosion in Britain: Evolution or Revolution?', *Dance History: The Teaching and Learning of Dance History*, Conference Proceedings of the European Association of Dance Historians, Twickenham: EADH.

Barnes, C. (1953) 'New ballets', *Dance and Dancers*, 4, 1, January: 12–15.

—— (1959) 'Six choreographers', *Dance and Dancers*, 10, 9, September: 27.

—— (1961) 'It always reigns on Sundays', *Dance and Dancers*, 12, 6, June: 28–30.

Brunelleschi, E. (1951) 'Television Ballet: *The Dream*', *Ballet*, 11, 7, August: 49.

Carrell, C. and Hastie, J. (eds) (1985) *Margaret Morris: Drawings and Designs and the Glasgow Years*, Glasgow: Third Eye Centre and the International Association of Margaret Morris Movement.

Coton, A. V. (1946) *The New Ballet: Kurt Jooss and His Work*, London: Dennis Dobson.

Coton, A. V. (1959) 'London Ballet Month', *Ballet Today*, 10, 4, May: 6.

Franks, A. H. (1959) 'New Dance Works', *Dancing Times*, XLIX, 587, August: 546.

Hall, F. (1950) *Modern English Ballet: An Interpretation*, London: Andrew Melrose.

Hutchinson Guest, A. (1985) 'Sigurd Leeder: Images for the Dancer', *Ballett International*, 8, 10: 14–20.

Mason, E. C. (1957) 'Sigurd Leeder Studio Group: 10th Anniversary Festival Programme', *Dance and Dancers*, 8, 9, September: 41.

—— (1959) 'An Evening of Modern Dance', *Dance and Dancers*, 10, 1, January: 30–1.

Pratt, D. (1953) 'Ballets Jooss at Sadler's Wells', *Ballet Today*, 6, 4, May: 5.

Robinson, J. (1997) *Modern Dance in France: An Adventure 1920–1970*, trans. C. Dale, Amsterdam: Harwood Academic Publishers.

Rowson Davis, J. (1996) 'Ballet on British Television: Christian Simpson, Producer, 1949–1959 – divine or diabolic?', *Dance Chronicle*, 19, 1: 17–92.

Rutherston, J. (1934) 'The Central European Dance in England', *Dancing Times*, 291, December: 313–16.

Skinner, J. (1999) *Over the Hill with a Magic Carpet*, Haddenham, Cambridgeshire: Fern House.

Stöckemann, P. (2001) *Etwas ganz Neues muss nun entstehen: Kurt Jooss und das Tanztheater*, München: Kieser.

Storey, A. (1948) 'Three Men: Kurt Jooss', in *Arabesques*, London: Newman Wolsey.

Vaughan, D. (1956) 'Transatlantic View: 5', *Dance and Dancers*, 7, 10, October: 13, 27.

Chapter 12

Beth Genné

"DANCIN' IN THE STREET"
Street Dancing on Film and Video from Fred Astaire to Michael Jackson

THE BIRTH OF SOUND FILM also saw the birth of a new site for dance – and with it a new dance genre. The "street dance", as I will call it, takes film dance off the stage, out of the ballroom and into the everyday life of the city street. The street dance also resulted in a reconceptualization of film dance as directors and choreographers began to realize that the camera as well as the dancer could be choreographed to create a new kind of dance–cinema. And, of course, the genre is transformed over time in response to the changing social and political climate of America's street life.

Established by Fred Astaire with Hermes Pan in the 1930s and developed by Gene Kelly with Stanley Donen and Vincente Minnelli in the 1940s and early 1950s, the street genre continued through the 1960s, most notably in Jerome Robbins's choreography for the film *West Side Story*. In the second half of the twentieth century, the street dance moved, for the most part, to video as dancers like Michael and Janet Jackson and their choreographers and directors took the form in new directions to fit the concerns of contemporary audiences and the changing urban environment.

The street dance has roots in the early 1930s in films of René Clair, Ernst Lubitsch and Rouben Mamoulian. In Mamoulian's landmark musical *Love Me Tonight* (1932), Maurice Chevalier, a carefree young tailor, strolls to work through the busy streets of his *quartier*. His walk is engagingly rhythmic and he salutes his neighbors in song. He's not exactly *dancing* but he is awfully close, and his music and movement poeticize early morning workaday Paris.

Fred Astaire also turned walking into a form of dance. George Gershwin, inspired by his elegant but carefree style, wrote music to accompany Astaire's shipboard stroll with Rogers in the "walking the dog" sequence in *Shall We*

Dance (1937). It is also Fred Astaire who really begins to *dance* in the street in *Damsel in Distress* (1937) when he performs amidst a traffic-filled London thoroughfare for an audience of delighted pedestrians and hops a moving bus for a finale.

But long before Astaire was filming his street dances in London-recreated studio lots, African American dancers were dancing on real urban streets. From New York to Philadelphia to Kansas City, jazz tap dancers were developing their art on busy street corners and in urban alleyways. As dancer Sandman Sims and others tell it, city streets had become open air dance schools where young and old dancers could meet, challenge and learn from each other (Nierenberg 1979). Certain street corners in Philadelphia were known for their exceptional dancers. Though these dances did not enter mainstream films, the lucky pedestrians who stopped to gape at them undoubtedly witnessed some of the greatest dancing of the era.

In another part of Pennsylvania, on the streets of Pittsburgh, Gene Kelly would learn from these marvelous dancers and from Astaire. Kelly would definitively establish the street dance genre in films, from the dockland streets of Brooklyn in *Cover Girl* (1944) to the rain-washed streets of Hollywood in *Singin' in the Rain* (1953). In his first major street dance in *Cover Girl*, Kelly, Rita Hayworth and Phil Silvers transform Brooklyn streets with their antics. The bright, confident tone of Jerome Kern's song "Make Way for Tomorrow" musically reflects Ira Gershwin's lyrics, with their clever internal rhymes expressing the three friends' optimism just as the dance reflects their youthful enthusiasm and camaraderie (see Kimball 1993: 310). They begin in a small, dockyard Brooklyn restaurant then continue outdoors, comandeering street paraphernalia to dance with. Silvers makes cymbals of dustbin lids, Kelly drums on a bucket and Hayworth uses a breadstick as an imaginary flute. Silvers rhythmically bails out an imaginary boat which Hayworth and Kelly row vigorously. A passing policeman twirling his nightstick puts a temporary stop to the fun, but the trio explode again into dance when they turn the corner out of his view. Passers-by join the fun: a milkman participates in a spirited reel, the neighborhood drunk's staggering steps unsteadily counterpoint the dancers. The policeman's reappearance forces a finale to this early Kelly street dance and they tiptoe indoors to the woozy applause of the drunk.

"Make Way for Tomorrow" establishes an iconography that will recur in whole or in part in many street dances to come: an urban or suburban street, choreography based on variants of walking; skipping and running steps or children's street games and the transformation of ordinary street objects such as stairs, curbs, gutters and lamp posts into dancing partners. Part of the street dance, too, are passers-by who may, like the milkman, enter into the dance, or like the drunk form a delighted audience. The policeman will reappear too, most notably in "Singin' in the Rain". He helps to emphasize the idea of the dancers as *enfants terribles* who, in response to music and their own high spirits, temporarily become children in an adult world, flouting convention by transforming the street into a musical playground.

Kelly also uses the long narrow street shape, to reconceptualize his dance space and explore the possibilities of the cinematic medium by choreographing for the camera as well as the dancers. He uses the moving camera and editing not only to record but enhance the dance. In the street dance in *Damsel in Distress* Astaire uses the camera mostly to document his movements. The street becomes a stage; the camera takes the position of the audience in a theatre. We view Astaire from the front and the camera remains relatively stationary in front of him, moving only slightly so that in Arlene Croce's words 'one has the impression of watching every moment from an ideally placed seat in a theatre' (1972: 126). But although many of Astaire's dances were conceptualized with the stage–audience relationship in mind, Astaire didn't always use the full-frontal format and these exceptions would become models for Kelly and his colleague Stanley Donen. In another section of *Damsel in Distress*, "Things are Looking Up", Astaire is tracked by a moving camera as he walk dances Joan Fontaine down a wooded path. In *Carefree* (1938), the moving camera follows a procession of dancers from a country-club dance floor along a curving path as they try out "The Yam". These are the precedents that Kelly and his colleagues Stanley Donen and Vincente Minnelli would follow, explore and develop for their dance on film (Genné 1984: 170–207).

Around the same time as *Cover Girl*, Minnelli's choreography for the camera in the dance sequences in *Meet Me in St Louis* (1944) and for Fred Astaire and Lucille Bremer in *The Ziegfeld Follies* (1944) and *Yolanda and the Thief* (1945) would also prove that the dance and the choreographed moving camera could be extraordinary partners. Minnelli was particularly interested in the possibilities of what was called the boom camera: a camera mounted on wheels and attached to a crane, allowing the camera to move in height as well as on the ground. Minnelli working with Kelly would bring an exciting new dimension to dances manipulating the boom camera in ever more daring ways (Genné 1984: 234–62).

A good example is the street dance "'S Wonderful" in *An American in Paris*, directed by Vincente Minnelli and choreographed by Gene Kelly. By the time of *An American in Paris*, Minnelli's skill with the boom had become something of a legend among film makers and technicians. Only a handful of directors and their camera operators had mastered the technique of using it effectively. Directors too often used boom shots gratuitously, employing them solely for their breathtaking effect with no real relationship to the dramatic action. Walter Strohm, head of MGM's production department, notes this as he pays tribute to Minnelli's virtuoso use of the boom:

> Minnelli loved to be on the boom and was very astute in using it, although it's a time consuming and costly thing because you could take a whole day just to rehearse and shoot one boom shot.
>
> Sometimes he did a whole day's work in one shot, which is rather interesting. Some days he would be on the boom all day rehearsing, riding it, and, when the end of the day came they would make the shot and that would be the whole scene. Well, there are very few directors you could allow to do that because they are not capable of visualizing and timing boom shots. They become very awkward and mechanical, and you become conscious of the boom and not the action. Booms are deadly to most directors. In fact, we had a rule – people hated it, but we had to have it because everybody wasn't Minnelli and everybody didn't know how to use the boom – so directors couldn't use the boom without my okay . . . But, with Minnelli, some of his great boom shots were classic. I just used to love to watch his boom shots. The one he did on "'S Wonderful" with Gene is just a classic.
>
> (Strohm, in Knox 1973: 109)

The boom shot to which Strohm refers is the final shot of the "'S Wonderful" street dance sequence. Kelly and Georges Guetary start the song seated in a sidewalk café then stroll rhythmically down the street. The camera, on a level with them, parallels their movement, gliding precisely in tempo, pausing briefly while Kelly dances and Guetary sings to an audience of pedestrians. The song is a compendium of slang superlatives that climaxes as each singer outdoes the other in finding the adjective that describes the emotional "high" he feels for the girl he loves, moving chromatically up the scale with every new adjective.

Kelly's choreography and Minnelli's boom camera work parallel this crescendo of emotion, music, and lyric. The singers move in opposite directions down the street, shouting to be heard over the people and traffic as Minnelli's camera glides back and up to capture them. The pull-back of the camera, precisely coordinated with the music, becomes a visual metaphor for the crescendo of sound and emotion that conclude the song. The camera's highest point coincides with the song's final note, then hangs in the air as people in the street are carefully positioned to form, in color and compositional arrangement, a dynamic diagonal across the screen. At either end of this the two singers stand, applauding their impromptu performance.

Following Kelly's experiences with Minnelli in *An American in Paris*, Kelly and Donen's moving boom camera achieves a new level of fluidity and expansiveness, demonstrated in the most famous street dance in all films. "Singin' in the Rain" incorporates almost every Kelly convention: a "street" dance, it expresses the hero's euphoric response to falling in love and it makes use of a dance vocabulary of typical Kelly vernacular movements. "Singin' in the Rain" is also a kind of children's dance. Kelly performs a set of variations on the theme of playing in the rain as, drenched and euphoric, he abandons all sense of decorum and dances in the driving rain. He uses his umbrella as a dancer's prop rather than protection as he balances on the curb, dances under a downspout and, for a finale, stomps and splashes ecstatically in the street's deepest puddle. The appearance of a policeman, like his counterpart in *Cover Girl*, puts an end to his musical games.

The song starts quietly. At first, the camera simply glides in front of Kelly as he strolls towards it. It becomes more active, however, after the dancer abandons himself to the rain, shuts his umbrella, and begins to sing. When Kelly suddenly vaults a lamp post in his excitement, the camera (equally suddenly and exhilaratingly) pulls back and up, then swoops in to capture, in close-up, his euphoric smile as he dismounts and leans drunkenly against the post. This camera gesture is repeated a few steps further down the street when he opens his arms in an invitation to the heavens to soak him, and the camera responds by swooping low over his upturned face. At the emotional and musical climax of the dance, the camera sweeps exhilaratingly back, up, and around as Kelly catapults off the sidewalk and, using his open umbrella as a sail, traces a circle on the street while brass and percussion forcefully state the song.[1] The final camera gesture we have seen at the end of "'S Wonderful" in *An American In Paris*, but here it parallels (equally effectively) a *diminuendo*: the camera pulls back and up slowly to give us a full view of the final poetic moment – the black-slickered policeman watching Kelly skip off down the street (Genné 1984: 375). Kelly pauses briefly to hand his closed umbrella to a passer-by who is hunched over to protect himself from the downpour. He opens the umbrella, then hurriedly moves on as Kelly, drenched and happy, skips off.

In addition to the reconceptualization of the relationship of camera work and dance, the street dance genre was ideally suited to the new, "ordinary" American that Kelly portrays in *Cover Girl* and would develop throughout his career. The street dance was the perfect answer to Kelly's wish to create a new kind of dance with which ordinary working-class Americans could identify. "Dance for the common man" was a phrase the young Kelly used a lot when describing his ideals to his friends, the playwright Dick Dwenger and his future wife Betsy Blair.[2] Kelly's ideas about the social role of dance were honed during his years as a student at the University of Pittsburgh and continued in New York where he participated excitedly in groups of socially minded intellectuals and artists like William Saroyan in whose play, *The Time of Your Life* (1939), Kelly first appeared as the down and out dancer Harry the Hoofer. These utopian ideals were in line with the increased social consciousness reflected throughout American arts and letters beginning in the 1930s in response to the great depression. Kelly's interest in the "common man" was also a part of the burgeoning interest in developing a new and specifically American subject and style for dance, an interest he shared with fellow choreographers working at the same time such as Ruth Page, Martha Graham, George Balanchine, Eugene Loring, Lew Christiansen, Doris Humphrey and Charles Weidman and others whom he knew and admired (Genné 2001: 87).

Following *The Time of Your Life*, Kelly made a tremendous impact on Broadway playing a new American character type for musicals in Rodgers and Hart's *Pal Joey* (1940). Street smart, cocky, depression-hardened Joey was diametrically opposed to the idealistic romantic juveniles on Broadway or the dapper, off-handedly elegant American type modeled by Fred Astaire. Kelly's stocky, compact frame suited this character and the street choreography he would later devise for himself – choreography he infuses with a distinctively aggressive energy that differs radically from Astaire's casual, seemingly effortless dancing nonchalance. Kelly's body was ideal for his vision of dance: it is a body with which a worker can identify and he looks right in shirt and pants. "Put me in a tuxedo," Kelly once remarked, "and I look like a truck driver going to Mass on Sunday."[3]

The choreography that Kelly devises for his street dances is more overtly based on ordinary gesture than is Astaire's complex, multi-layered choreography or the intricate elegant patterning of jazz tappers like John Bubbles or the Nicholas Brothers. To be sure, Astaire and jazz tap dancers often began their dances with a simple walk, which is basically a street gesture, but that walk would soon develop into a complex, multi-layered series of rhythmic foot movements. Kelly's "walk" is simple, down-to-earth and purposeful and he combines it with a repertory of movements derived from the children's street games he played in the streets of Pittsburgh. These are movements with which any urban American can identify: teetering on the curb, vaulting fire hydrants, skipping along the sidewalk, swinging on lamp posts, splashing in the gutter, roller skating. In *Living in a Big Way* (1945), for example, Kelly leads a group of kids over a construction site balancing on beams and swinging on rafters. In *It's Always Fair Weather* (1955), Kelly glides through the streets on roller skates captured by a swift moving camera. In *On the Town*, Kelly and Donen use brilliant jump cut editing wed to music and the actors' movements to transform an out-of-town sightseer's exuberant, wide-eyed, and bewildered walking tour into a kind of dance. (Kelly and Donen's editing for this sequence would have a tremendous impact not only on future musicals, but on French new wave film making, and you can also see influences in Richard Lester's editing for the Beatles' musicals *A Hard Day's Night* and *Help!* (Delameter 1981: 460)).

Kelly saw a strong link between his choreography and sports, especially urban "street" sports. Sports movements give his dances the "vernacular" flavor that so suit his character type and the street dance itself (Genné 1996: 644). Kelly said that when he was "groping for an American style",

> the closest thing I could get was how American men moved in the field of sports . . . If you were raised in a poor neighborhood you don't grow up with a tennis racquet or golf club in your hand . . . Soccer is a poor man's sport because you don't have to have anything but newspaper to kick around . . .[4]

Kelly doesn't mention it but the most basic "poor kid's street sport" is simple competition: Who can vault the highest over the fire hydrant? Who is most agile at curb balancing? Who can jump off the curb and swing with impunity into the forbidden territory of that street your mother won't let you cross? Who can get away with stunts without incurring the wrath of the cop on the beat? In "Singin' in the Rain" and in other street dances, Kelly turns this urban child's sport into art and proves he is the very best kid on the block.

But urban streets have changed. In most of Kelly's street dances, the city is benign and his use of street props is playful. He stops short of disrupting the passers-by and vandalizing the objects on the street. The street dances that follow, in line with growing class unrest and the developing drug culture, increasingly portray American streets as places of danger rather than delight. In *On the Town* (1949), New York and its citizens are bright and cheerful. We don't see vagrants or drug sellers and the policemen are stern but benevolent. However, in two instances Kelly departs from this benign model. The Alter Ego dance in *Cover Girl* and the drunk dances in *It's Always Fair Weather* become more threatening and the dances are used to express the dark side of human nature: anger, jealousy and despair. In the Alter Ego dance Kelly works over his complex and conflicting feelings of jealousy by dancing down a deserted, rundown street with a transparent image of himself (the "alter ego"). The dance ends when Kelly angrily shatters the plate glass window of an empty store front to destroy his reflected image. In *It's Always Fair Weather* (1955) three soldiers, panicked at facing their new lives at the end of World War II, reel drunkenly down 3rd Avenue, commandeer a taxi, shake up its driver and dance noisily with garbage can lids in a forbidding street shadowed by the elevated tracks.

Six years after *It's Always Fair Weather* the film version of *West Side Story* (1961) made its debut. In it Jerome Robbins adapts and expands Kelly's cinematic street dance traditions using a brilliantly choreographed mobile camera on a crane and exciting rhythmic cutting to enhance the dance's excitement. But now the street dancers dance to demonstrate their domination of the city streets they skim across and the fire hydrants they leap over. Gang warfare and racial tension are transformed into dance. The passers-by look upon them with fear and despair rather than delight as they disrupt traffic and steal street vendors' wares to fight their enemies. The littered rundown streets, with their broken windows and graffiti-defaced walls, reveal a society at war with itself and the distinctive energy that Kelly used to portray enthusiasm and joy in "Make Way for Tomorrow" and "Singin' in the Rain" is now transformed into something darker: a combination of anger and alienation. The policemen who break up *West Side Story*'s dance–fight are anything but benevolent: they threaten the boys and use them as pawns in a race war, offering to help the white gang, the Jets, clean up their rivals, the Puerto Rican Sharks.

By 1960 the terms "juvenile delinquency" and "street gang" warfare had become buzz phrases in the American media. New York increasingly came to be seen as a frightening and dangerous place. My research has shown that the rise of popular interest in the subject of urban teenage gangs is dramatic. A search of *New York Times* articles from 1870 to the present under the key words "juvenile delinquency", "street gangs" or indeed any combination of a word and gangs reveals relatively few articles on the subject between 1929 and 1945. After that articles about street gangs increase steadily, peaking in the late 1950s and early 1960s. A search of the *Reader's Guide to Periodical Literature* covers a wider range of popular magazines and reveals a similar trend.

The decline of the film musical as a form also contributed to the temporary disappearance of the street dance in movies. There were exceptions. Bob Fosse carries on the Astaire–Kelly–Robbins tradition with his own distinctive accent in *Sweet Charity* (1968). But the most popular street dance of the era takes place not in America, but in Austria. Julie Andrews leads her troupe of children through the sunny streets of Salzburg and the surrounding countryside, singing "Do Re Mi" in *The Sound of Music* (1965). "Do Re Mi" also owes a lot to the walking tour opening of *On the Town*, but its roots are also in *West Side Story*. Robert Wise, who also directed *West Side Story*, directed *The Sound of Music*. It was Wise who conceived the opening sequence of the former leading into Robbins's dance in which a camera moving above the city streets leads us from the tip of Manhattan to the upper west side. He duplicates that idea in the opening of *The Sound of Music*, but we've left the littered streets of New York for a more pastoral landscape: the green and majestic mountains of Austria.

Saturday Night Fever, the big hit of 1977, gave the street dance new life. John Travolta is a direct descendant of Maurice Chevalier in *Love Me Tonight*, taking us on a rhythmical walking tour of his urban neighborhood. His director, John Badham, employs a new variation for dance with his tracking camera. It glides along the sidewalks on a level with Travolta's feet pulling us along in tempo just ahead of the young dancer. Travolta's walk and the music of the Bee Gees captures the distinctive temper of this young character and his time, just as Rodgers did for Chevalier in *Love Me Tonight* and Gershwin for the elegant Astaire and Rogers in *Shall We Dance?*

Around this time, the film street dance also received another powerful infusion from the 'real' streets where African American hip hop culture and the various forms of street dancing it engendered (B-Boy dancing resulting in breakdance, popping, locking and other forms) would give street dances a new look (see Banes 1994: 126–58). The immensely popular *Flashdance* (1983) brought breakdancing into mainstream films such as *Wild Style* (1982) and *Beat Street* (1984). Mostly, however, movie street dances in the second half of the century come in the form of *homages* (tributes) to the earlier ones and they are few and far between. In 1967 French new wave director Jacques Demy paid tribute to Gene Kelly in *Les Demoiselles de Rochefort* in which Kelly, as choreographer and star, reprises the street dance form in the French port town of Rochefort. In Martin Scorsese's *New York, New York* we catch a glimpse of a sailor and his girl dancing under the elevated tracks. Billy Crystal and Woody Allen "quote" the romantic quay side dance "Our Love is Here to Stay", from *An American in Paris*, in their films *Forget Paris* and *Everybody Says I Love You*. And Baz Luhrman, who seems to be the director most interested in reviving the musical film, has his dancers perform above the street under a glittering sign in *Strictly Ballroom*.

In the latter part of the twentieth century the street dance moves to another visual medium, that of video/dvd. Again the immediate influence is African American hip hop culture, but the roots of video dance in African American jazz dance and in the Astaire–Kelly–Robbins street dances are still visible. Michael Jackson and his choreographers and directors build on the camera movement and editing innovations of his film musical predecessors, adding new tools from the computer age. In Jackson's early videos *Thriller* (1983) and *Beat It* (1984), choreographer Michael Peters, an admirer of Jerome Robbins, draws directly on his own experience as a dancer in *West Side Story*. The gang dances in *Bad* (directed by Martin Scorsese and choreography by Gregg Burge and Jeffrey Daniels) are not too distant relatives of the *West Side Story* dances, in particular "Cool", danced in an underground garage. In *Bad* the dancers dance *under* the streets in the New York subways.

Reflecting an urban culture where children carry uzis and kill over designer clothing, Michael Jackson's street dances get progressively more surreal and frightening. Even love dances are scary. In *Thriller*, a chorus of the dancing dead led by a Zombie-like Jackson, captured by the moving camera of director Michael Landis, transforms an after-the-movie stroll into an unforgettable experience for Jackson's terrified date. In *The Way You Make Me Feel* (1987), choreographed by Vincent Paterson, Jackson dances through the streets singing of the same euphoric feelings as Kelly in *Singin' in the Rain*, but the streets through which he dances are run down and grafitti-littered as are the eerie surrealistic city scapes of *Billie Jean*. Urban poverty is brought up close and personal. And Kelly's childlike games and innocent enthusiasm are transformed into dancing with a real edge. Jackson aggressively taunts his would-be lover and his openly erotic gestures have an undertone of anger. The finale of *The Way You*

Make Me Feel resonates with *Singin' in the Rain*'s waterlogged ending. This time a fire hydrant explodes in the heat of the summer: the arc of glimmering water is as beautiful as the backlit rain in Kelly's street dance. And the Place de La Concorde sequence in *An American in Paris* is a direct ancestor of this moment when the girl finally succumbs to Jackson's wooing and we see them embrace in silhouette against a tapestry of vapor clouds. But the image is also a reminder, albeit unconscious, of those hot summer days when the poor migrate to the streets to get relief and have to vandalize city property to do so. (Think of Spike Lee's *Do the Right Thing* which similarly evokes a hot summer night.)

In the street dance section of Jackson's "Black or White" race issues are directly addressed, as they are in *West Side Story*, but this time on a global scale. Jackson dances with a classical Indian dancer on a busy highway and moves to various locations around the globe where his choreography reflects a variety of folk forms. Both Kelly and Astaire are referenced in this video: in one street scene, Jackson combines an elegant hands-in-his-pocket nonchalance with intricate footwork that has roots in Astaire's moves although they are used along with crotch-grabbing gestures Astaire wouldn't consider. Kelly's final window smashing gesture in the Alter Ego sequence and Astaire's drunk dance in *The Sky's the Limit* (1943) are also in the background of this dance but without the clear dramatic motivation. Jackson vandalizes a car, resulting in an extended and violent glass-shattering sequence that concludes with the heaving of a barrel through a plate glass window that duplicates the climactic gesture of the Alter Ego dance. He follows this with a very dark take on Kelly's ecstatic splashing at the end of the "Singin' in the Rain" street dance.

It is no secret that Jackson idolized Astaire. He and his sister, Janet Jackson, grew up on the "street dance" musicals of the first half of the century. Janet Jackson pays direct homage to these roots and to other of her African American dance predecessors in her video, *It's Alright*. And, as in her brother's work, digital imagery is added to the arsenal of tools used to enhance the scope and drama of the dance. In *It's Alright*, The Nicholas Brothers, Cyd Charisse, and Cab Calloway appear with Jackson and Heavy D as they dance through the busy city streets, captured by a choreographed and extremely mobile camera which sweeps over the streets on a level with the dancer and, at times, hovers in the air above them.

The popularity of the street dance shows no signs of waning and we can expect that there will be dancing in the streets way into the twenty-first century. There is a lot more to be said about video street dancing since Michael Jackson, but that will have to be left to another article. In the meantime, it is clear that the dance genre that grew up in the movies has now found a home in video and on dvd. It seems likely to continue so long as we have streets to walk on and to dance through.

Notes

1 The grandest camera gesture of the entire sequence relates to the climactic gesture in the courtship dance "You Were Meant for Me" (and also to a gesture in the "Olivera Street" sequence in *Anchors Aweigh*.
2 Beth Genné interview with Betsy Blair, London, 1998. Some of the material on Gene Kelly in this section has been published in my article on Kelly in *Envisioning Dance on Film and Video* (Genné 2002).
3 Gene Kelly interviewed by John Russell Taylor, National Film Theatre, London, May 20, 1980.
4 Gene Kelly interviewed by Marilyn Hunt, Los Angeles, 1975.

Bibliography

Banes, S. (1994) *Writing Dancing in the Age of Postmodernism*, Hanover and London: Wesleyan University Press.

Croce, A. (1972) *The Fred Astaire and Ginger Rogers Book*, New York, NY: Galahad.

Delameter, J. (1981) *Dance in the Hollywood Musical*, Ann Arbor, Mich: UMI Research Press.

Genné, B. (1984) *The Film Musicals of Vincente Minnelli and the Team of Gene Kelly and Stanley Donen (1944–1958)*, University of Michigan doctoral dissertation, Ann Arbor: University Microfilms.

—— (1996) "Gene Kelly", *Dancing Times*, April: 643–9.

—— (2001) "'Freedom Incarnate': Jerome Robbins, Gene Kelly and The Dancing Sailor as an American Icon in World War II", *Dance Chronicle*, 24, 1: 83–103.

—— (2002) "Dancin' in the Rain: Gene Kelly and Musical Films", in J. Mitoma (ed.) *Envisioning Dance on Film and Video*, London: Routledge.

Kimball, R. (ed.) (1993) *The Complete Lyrics of Ira Gershwin*, New York, NY: Knopf.

Knox, D. (1973) *The Magic Factory: How MGM Made "An American in Paris"*, New York, NY: Praeger.

Mueller, J. (1985) *Astaire Dancing*, New York, NY: Knopf.

Nierenberg, G. T. (1979) *No Maps on My Taps* (film).

Chapter 13

Ananya Chatterjee

CONTESTATIONS
Constructing a Historical Narrative for Odissi

Problems with historiography

IN WORKING WITH DANCE histories of non-western cultures, I have learnt well the inadequacy of existing models of historiography, and widespread notions of their apparently "universal" applicability. Indeed, projects of constructing historical narratives are, everywhere, more often than not, subsumed under western, Europeanist models of historicizing, dominated by organizing modes such as modernity, development, and other post-Enlightenment structures of linearity and coherence that have come to be legitimizing factors in any understanding of history. This has made such projects suspect to scholars working from other locations, both geopolitically and discursively, and from perspectives of oppositional politics. Scholars of the subaltern studies group, in particular, urge reconceptualizations of history as a contested narrative, where supposed "facts", documented in texts privileged as sources of "truth", grapple with human memories and dreams, engage with oral histories and incomplete memories. In contesting the thematization of "history" in accordance with grand Europeanist paradigms, such scholarship points to the grand theories of civilization, and power plays inherent in them, which tend to masquerade as "history". However, the disciplinary institutionalization of history in modern times in accordance with the specific norms of linear chronology and the thematic concerns of European modernity has meant that those who do not, or perhaps cannot, produce such narratives often get petrified in some notion of ahistoricity and timelessness.

These ideas have become particularly valuable to me as I have researched the few historical accounts of Indian dance, all of them written in current times, retrospectively. The lack of historical texts about performance practices from the past is of course natural in contexts dominated by direct bodily and oral modes of transmission, which raise questions about the need for documenting developments in cultural practices in the manner of historical texts. It also draws attention to the kind of validation that accrues to embodied practices through textualization and to the logocentric imperative that has come to be our legacy from the west. At any rate, while Indian dance has seldom been texted in detail according to chronologically developmental histories, a study of the cultural and political upheavals and policy making over the last century make obvious that the dancing body has been at the center of much national debate and deliberation. Here, I am specifically referring to the forms of concert dance that were revived in the first half of the twentieth century, and upheld as representing the "classical" traditions of Indian dance. It is from this time – interlinked with the development of nationalism and the constitution of the independent Indian nation-state, and post-colonial politics thereafter – that I find it interesting to work through timed and complex tracings of developments in these dance forms. For such endeavours often point to how these forms mark and immediately cover the site of a series of ruptures, attempting to project a continuity of "tradition" and establishing a strict code of "classicism". They also compel recognition of the infinitely detailed suture that enables the authority of classicism, while we cannot help noticing the slippages in negotiations, and the dancing bodies that fell through the cracks.

Talking origins

Here, I want to reflect on some of the issues that have played a major role in the constitution of Odissi as a classical dance form. My comments emerge from the endeavour to write an appreciation of my guru, Sanjukta Panigrahi, who died suddenly on June 24, 1997, of breast cancer, at age 53. As my research progressed, I found that the emotional journey of this tribute, with a clear pathway, had become wedged in the midst of a contested terrain. I finally realized that there was no way I could write a history of Sanjukta Panigrahi's life without immediately writing about the development of Odissi, and involving the lives and work of several others in that field.

Scholars have argued that the state of Orissa, in the eastern part of India, presents some of the earliest evidence of dance in India.[1] They refer to various sculptural and literary sources, such as the images of dancing women found in the caves of Khandagiri and Udaygiri, dating back to 100 BC, to argue that by the first century BC, dance and music flourished in the region currently known as Orissa. Moreover, talking about the major dance forms of his time, the sage Bharata, author of the *Natyashastra*, the earliest and highly influential scripture of performance, written between the second and fifth centuries, mentions the Odra-Magadhi style practiced primarily in the regions that constitute current-day Orissa. Previously known as *Odra Nrutya*, Odissi was named as such in 1955 at the suggestion of poet, playwright, and musicologist, Kalicharan Patnaik, signaling a clear regional and cultural specificity: Odissi is the dance form that emerges from the state of Orissa.

The impulse of much of the scholarship tracing the origins of Odissi to emphasize its ancientness, and to claim that it is one of the earliest Indian dance forms, is largely wrapped up with the story of the revival and constitution of Bharatanatyam as the paradigmatic "classical" dance form in India in the 1940s, a project intimately linked with nationalist politics, and the foundation of India as an independent nation-state. Most of the early dance forms that had flourished in India obviously underwent change through time, and no doubt suffered severely during foreign invasions. The most erosion, however, seems to have happened during the period of British colonization, largely because of the huge shift in the principles and philosophy of governance. For these "classical" dance forms had been practiced, for the most part, in temples, as an offering to the deity, and the dancing women who were attached to the temple for this service were supported by royal patronage. This was a system that depended for its survival on the general Hindu belief in the spiritual and creative energy of dance. While Muslim rulers often attacked and ransacked the temples, particularly in northern India, impacting the freedoms enjoyed by the dancing women, there were some benevolent rulers who supported these systems. They also continued to encourage the practice that had developed later, under the Hindu kings, of performances at court, before select audiences of connoisseurs.

These women, generally known as *devadasis*, were married to the resident deity of the temple at an early age and they served their lord through various means, one of the most prestigious among which was singing and dancing before his image. Married to a divine partner, and blessed as forever-brides, these women found themselves paradoxically both at the center and margin of the socio-cultural nexus in which they lived and worked. Because they signaled auspiciousness, no temple ceremony was ever complete without their presence. At the same time, because ultimately they came to serve their lord through his representatives on earth – the king, members of the royalty, and high priests – and thus often enjoyed sexual agency, they were outside of a social organization where women were recognized primarily in terms of their familial relationships. At any rate, dependent on royal patronage for support, the system deteriorated rapidly once the British Raj came into power.[2] Not only did the colonial government withdraw all support to temples; it also pronounced moral outrage at the sensuousness of the dances. The *Bengal District Gazetteer* of 1878 reported the words of an indignant British civil servant, William Ward Hunter (1872) regarding the dancers of the Jagannath temple at Puri, Orissa:

> Indecent ceremonies disgraced the ritual, and dancing-girls with rolling eyes put the modest worshipper to the blush . . . The baser features of a worship which aims at a sensuous realization of God appears in a band of prostitutes who sing before the image . . . In the pillared halls, a choir of dancing-girls enliven the idols' repast by their airy gyrations.
>
> (Quoted in Patnaik 1990: 71)

The colonial government's withdrawal of any support to the temples left the *devadasi*s without any income. These women, who could hardly find their way back into a more-or-less strictly regulated social system, were often forced to earn their living through prostitution. Moreover, hounded by daily worries of survival, it was hardly possible for them to continue to practice their art with the kind of attention and dedication that had earlier characterized their practice. Their dance gained prominence only years later, during the cultural revivalist movement of the 1940s, when the cultural leaders of modern India insisted on "reviving" these dance forms as part of the project of reconstructing India's grand culture, a project influenced by the western orientalist scholars of the nineteenth century. This movement began in the South, with the reconstitution of the vernacular *sadir nac* as the classical Bharatanatyam. The long-drawn-out anti-*nautch* campaign that was central to this process of restoration was led on the one hand by social activist Muthulakshmi Reddy, herself a descendant from a *devadasi* family, denouncing the moral outrage of the system, and on the other hand by cultural leaders such as E. Krishna Iyer and Rukmini Devi, who argued that the dance at least be saved. Dislodged from the practices of the *devadasi*s, the dance was reborn when, in 1947, after a long-drawn-out anti-*nautch* struggle, it became illegal to dance in the temple.[3] Concomitantly, the secular government of independent India announced its support of the classical dance traditions in their reincarnations as concert stage forms. Rukmini Devi, guided by her friend and mentor Annie Besant, leader of the Theosophical Society, meanwhile "cleansed" the dance of its associations with prostitution by shifting the foundational emotion from *sringara*, the erotic mood to *bhakti*, the devotional mood. This reconstitution gained validation through Rukmini Devi's vehicular institution, the Kalakshetra College of Dance and Music, established in Madras in 1936, as a concert dance form, angular in its lines, sharp in its energy, and predominantly an expression of spirituality.

These developments deeply affected the rest of the dance forms. First of all, *sadir*'s renaming as Bharatanatyam had its own symbolic weight. Supposedly it reflects the amalgamation of *bhava* (emotion), *raga* (musicality), and *tala* (rhythm), *bha-ra-ta*, at the confluence of which the dance is located. However, its simultaneous if less-acknowledged claiming of affiliation to Bharata, the author of the *Natyashastra*, suggesting its adherence to the standards of "classicism" outlined in that scripture, as well as to *Bharat*, one of the indigenous names for India, implying its status as national dance form of India, are hard to miss. Moreover, the un-negotiated transfer of dance forms from the temple and court to the proscenium stage left many questions unresolved, causing problematic erasures. For instance, the dance forms that were generally described as *margi*, a term which probably referred to their organization in terms of a specific aesthetic – the term *marg* meaning developmental pathway – were inaccurately translated as "classical". Other styles locally strung together more as a series of pieces or social dances, and referred to as *desi*, translating more or less incompletely as vernacular, were classified as "folk". The different levels of formality, varying organization and goals of the plethora of cultural practices in India, reflected in loose groupings of these forms as *desi* or *margi*, were reified and hardened with the mistranslation of the above descriptors as "classical" and "folk", with their inevitable implications of high and low art.

Now because Bharatanatyam was the first to claim its "classical" status, it effectively set a clear model for how "classicism" might be interpreted, with the corollary that the claim of classicism and the demonstration of organization according to a uniform code as outlined by Bharata in the *Natyashastra* were proven validation of classical "authenticity".[4] The organization of the Bharatanatyam repertoire in a specific format to suit the new needs of a stage recital, in fact like a journey through "a great temple", was also an important model. This left dancers and advocates of several other dance forms, in particular Odissi, Kuchipudi, and Mohini Attam, in a quandary, for while they felt strongly that these forms had their aesthetic and regional specificities, they also recognized the necessary uniformity of any notion of "classicism", and that, in order to support their claims to classicism, they would have to work with the already established model. The "classical" claim is thus complicated: while it accurately reflects the long, if interrupted, histories of these forms and their complexity, it is also based on grand narratives about elite art and a singular aesthetic framework. Moreover, logistically, this descriptor immediately signaled higher prestige, more resources, and greater opportunities for the field. I want to flag this troubled desire for "classicism" and the struggle to move away from the conflicted history of the temple dancers and their sexual politics as vital directions in the developmental pathway of contemporary Odissi.

The problem of sensuality

The appointment of *maharis* – the *devadasis* of Orissa – for essential temple rituals dates at least as far back as the ninth century AD. That dancing at temples continued to be customary through the rule of different dynasties, whatever the branch of Hinduism they followed, is obvious by the plenitude of sculptures of dancing women on temple walls, as well as the regular presence of the *natamandap* or dance hall in temples constructed at different times. The system was in effect till the establishment of British rule, though it began to decline during the sixteenth century due to changing attitudes about women dancing. At the beginning of the twentieth century, the few remaining *mahari*s were in penury; their art had degenerated due to lack of support and practice, and they were demoralized and felt that the legacy they carried was now devalued.[5] All evidence about the *mahari* dance style suggests that it was distinctly sensuous and graceful, and in fact highly erotic.

At any rate, another branch of this dance style had meanwhile begun to be practiced, by young boys who dressed in drag: the *gotipua* dancers. It probably came into existence around the seventeenth century, evolving rapidly with the establishment of the *akhada*s, or gymnasiums, by King Ramachandradeva, to encourage physical training and preparation as warriors in case of need at the time of foreign attacks. The *akhada*s became important sites for the training of *gotipua* dancers as well as other cultural activities and performances, and by the nineteenth century there were several professional *gotipua* groups in existence, largely supported by local *zamindar*s or small feudal landlords. Importantly, however, the *gotipua*s never performed inside the temples, and their style was different from that of the *mahari*s. One of the important elements of the *gotipua* style and a central part of its repertoire is the *bandha nrutya*, a uniquely acrobatic and intricate movement style, requiring a high level of suppleness and flexibility. The typical markers of the *mahari* dance style, the rounded lines, the overt sensuality, the displaced hip marked by the *bengapatti*, the heavy silver belt tied around the hip, are here overshadowed by the *gotipua* insistence on a much more acrobatic and linear style, characterized by jumps and extensions.[6] Interestingly, several of the current gurus of Odissi, largely responsible for its reconstruction in the twentieth century, were trained as *gotipua*s.

There is continuous evidence then that erotica was a central part of Odissi dance and music. This is particularly true during the period of Shaivite rulers of Orissa, and also when Tantrism was popular.[7] Vaishnavism, which ultimately came to have the biggest influence on the development of Odissi, partly supported this tradition through its belief in music and dance as modes of worship and the faith in *sakhibhava*, where the devotee, regardless of her/his sex, is always in a feminine positionality in relation to divinity, worshipping god through performances of love and adoration. However, allegedly it was also under the influence of later Vaishnavism that the dancing of women was disfavored and *gotipua* dancing was encouraged. The poets whose songs and poems were performed by the dancers wrote lyrics that were sensuous, articulating spiritual longing through the fullness of human sexual encounters. In the poet Jayadeva's songs, for instance, which are a central part of the abhinaya or expressional repertoire of Odissi, metaphors of sexual union, physical intimacy, and pleasure, often initiated by the woman, are articulated as part of the urgency of the human soul's longing for divine contact. The rich physicality of this poetry, the matching sensuousness of the dance form marked uniquely by torso movements, displaced hip line, and rounded curvilinearity, the full articulation of female sexuality, and the belief in the utter unison of bodily and spiritual desire is remarkable here.

However, these *abhinaya* pieces, a central part in the *mahari* repertoire, signify differently on the contemporary stage where Odissi is performed primarily by women: here, dance is no longer contexted in an overt religious framework, but is much more a performance event that is ticketed and marketed in the secular and fiercely competitive cultural circuit; here the dancers are professionals, dancing at least as much expressions of personal artistic excellence as ritualized spiritual articulations. This seems to be at the root of one of the central controversies in Odissi today. For when Odissi was reconstructed in the 1940s and 1950s and these songs were choreographed by leading gurus, it seems that some of the erotic physicality inherent in the style was subdued in order to emphasize the spirituality. Indeed, it seems that the performance of sexual desire and sensual pleasure drew critiques about the "vulgarity" of the form, which in turn led to questions about its classicism, where supposedly passion is interpreted through a physicality sublimated in spirituality.[8]

Issues of the legitimacy of hip movement, as well as the appropriate degree of deflection of the pelvis to one side or another in *abhanga* and *tribhangi* positions, have become important questions in the Odissi technique precisely because of the allegiance to an image of classicism that was largely dictated by modern Bharatanatyam.[9] Classicism is also, of course, wedded to notions of uniformity, and manifested, in the context of Indian dance, through representations of *angasuddhi* or purity of line, and *saustabha* or appropriateness. My guru repeatedly taught me, for instance, never to overstep the line of classical restraint (*ouchitya*) and "taint" the classical purity of Odissi with folk-style exaggeration and excess. Thus, though notions of line and degree are not new in Indian dance, their interpretation and tethering to certain kinds of movements are part of the modern construction of the neoclassical. Further, because the slur of sexual excesses of the temple dancers could not be allowed to touch the dance that women from upper and middle classes were now embodying, apparently in an effort to uphold "tradition", performances of sexuality or sensuality had to be kept within the clear demarcations of classicism. The project of the reconstruction of Odissi is constrained and troubled by such debates about "appropriateness", instigated by the usurpation of a viable model of classicism by modern Bharatanatyam. And the sculptors of modern Odissi have had the difficult task of having simultaneously to resist its structural and formal dominance, while carefully watching the parameters of classicism established by it.

Claims of classicism

This long-standing anxiety over the dominance of Bharatanatyam was no doubt compounded by the fact that, while accomplished dancers from Orissa, such as my guru, Minati Misra, Priyambada Mohanty, Kumkum Mohanty, and others, had worked hard to learn and perfect the form and make a name for it outside of Orissa at a time when it was barely acceptable for women from "respectable" families, particularly in Orissa, to take up dancing as a profession, a great deal of attention had come to Odissi when already established Bharatanatyam dancers such as Indrani Rehman, Sonal Mansingh, and Yamini Krishnamurthy took it up. Indeed, Odissi was first performed outside of Orissa in 1951, when Sanjukta Panigrahi performed in Kolkata's New Empire Theatre as child artiste. However, it was the performance of Priyambada Mohanty and Dhiren Patnaik at the Inter-university Youth Festival in Delhi in 1954 that drew serious attention to the form, largely because it happened in the national capital, and also perhaps because this time it was performed by older dancers in a competitive forum. In the audience was Charles Fabri, art enthusiast and critic for *The Statesman*. His subsequent writings about Odissi, highly responsible for bringing national attention to it, illuminate some of the anxieties about classicism and questions about "authenticity" that continued to haunt Odissi for a while. Fabri (1972: 2) writes that when he first hailed Odissi as a "classical" dance form after witnessing Mohanty and Patnaik's performance in Delhi, he had met with much incredulity on the part of people that such a form existed.

That this had become part of a larger debate was obvious even in 1958, when Odissi's inclusion at the All-India Dance Seminar organized by the Sangeet Natak Akademi in Delhi was interpreted by some as a final recognition of its status as a classical dance of India.[10] Yet, as late as 1968, the question of the recognition of Odissi as an independent form was still being debated when Guru Kelucharan Mahapatra was nominated for the prestigious national award from the government of India for his contribution to the development of Odissi. Earlier, of course, Odissi had been only grudgingly recognized as a variety of Bharatanatyam, and Rukmini Devi's (Arundale 1957) statements that ". . . Bharata Natya includes all forms of dances and dance dramas which are in accordance with the Shastra as laid down by the great sage Bharata" (p. 16) and that Odissi was a "variation" of Bharatanatyam, had added further weight to this contention.[11] What is also obvious here is the underlying nationalist agenda of building a cultural framework that demonstrated the government's favored theme of unity-in-diversity that was supposed to be part of age-old "tradition". The situation seems to have been further exacerbated by debates about the kind of relationship these forms had, immediately indicating temporal precedence. Noting the similarities yet differences between the two forms, Fabri ([1960] 1972: n.p.) writes that

> these differences consist in Odissi being the simpler, chaster, more straightforward dance, concentrating on beautiful postures, charming gestures, and sensuous bends rather than on a detailed hand and finger explanation (*hasta-lakshana*) of the sung texts, as in Bharata Natya.

His discussion is permeated with descriptions of Odissi as "unspoilt", "ancient" and "primitive", terminology that in general betrays a conflation of binaries like primitive–modern, sensual–intellectual, simple–complex, as well as problematic deployments of terms like "purity" and "chastity".

Such repeated enunciations from those considered at the helm of the cultural–artistic field suggest that the project of constructing a lineage of Indian classical dance was becoming enmeshed in the problematic terms of the reified and linear trajectory of western modernity, with its typical conflation of categories of primitive, primal, and primeval.

The project of reconstruction

It is in the light of these complicated politics that one must look at the famous Jayantika project that was inaugurated in 1957. Troubled by the controversy that surrounded the development of Odissi and the difficulties around its recognition as classical art, the prime gurus of Odissi, primarily Kelucharan Mahapatra, Mayadhar Raut, Dayanidhi Das, and Debaprasad Das, worked together to codify the style. They were joined in this by dance scholar Dhiren Patnaik, who had been awarded a national scholarship by the Department of Culture in 1955, to research the origins and development of Odissi, and Kalicharan Patnaik, scholar of Odissi culture. Sanjukta Panigrahi, who, in the meantime, had been sent to Kalakshetra to train in Bharatanatyam with a scholarship from the state government, and Mayadhar Raut, studying Kathakali at Kalakshetra with a similar award, returned every summer to work intensely with the gurus and scholars on this project. It was through them that knowledge about the systematization of style, the categorization of movements of different parts of the body, the establishment of parameters of *angasudhhi* that typified the institutionalization of Bharatanatyam at Kalakshetra, entered the Jayantika process as well, providing a blueprint for the classicization of Odissi.

So far the gurus had worked with some very basic and tacit consensus on matters of style, which meant that there had been a lot of room for personal interpretation and idiosyncratic structuring. Now, with questions of origin and authenticity being debated, matters of style became embedded in the clamoring rhetoric of "retrieval". Jayantika began a process whereby most of the Oriya names for foot positions and hand gestures and other movement elements were replaced by an 'even' Sanskrit nomenclature, and a fully articulated movement grammar was established, drawing on the *Natyashastra* and other texts of classical performance. Moreover, this process was intensified, elaborated upon, and finalized with the publication of the *Odissi Dance Pathfinder*, volumes I (1988) and II (1995), illustrated manuals for instruction in the Odissi style, by the Odissi Research Center in Bhubaneshwar, directed by eminent disciple of Guru Kelucharan Mohapatra, Kumkum Mohanty. The uniformity thus achieved established a common movement grammar for Odissi and formalized its technical base. Moreover, the process of Sanskritization validated the projected narrative of recuperation of an age-old tradition that had continued through time, disrupted unfortunately due to foreign invasions, colonial rule, and the sexual degradation of the *maharis*; successfully dislodged anxieties about reconstruction that inevitably brought up questions about "authenticity"; and made formulaic matters of "stylistic purity" (Mohanty 1988: i) and training, those inevitable markers of classical style.

Finally, and most importantly, this uniformity, projected as issuing from a clearly locatable origin in the ancient past, also made opaque the very project of reconstruction and modern choreography by the gurus, such that the rupture in the continuity of the dance, its disturbed and disjointed history, could be folded under a remarkable suture, and such that neo-classical Odissi would seem logically continuous with the dance form that Bharata had described as Odra-Magadhi. Also, at Jayantika, the order of repertoire was fixed to better suit the needs of evening-length concert events in the proscenium theater and discrepancies in costume design were evened out. From successive designs of this new stitched costume, which replaced the wrapped sari, it seems that the attempt was to emphasize closely the lines of the dancer's body in a way that would optimize the sculpturesque style of Odissi, while still maintaining general notions of "respectability". For instance, the initially uncovered short blouse worn by the women, covered thereafter with the semi-transparent scarf tied diagonally across the chest, is finally replaced by a scarf of the same thicker material as the sari.

However, even during Jayantika, disagreements arose among the gurus about the dominance of the *gotipua* style through the foregrounding of certain elements of technical virtuosity and the increasing pace of execution. Guru Debaprasad Das, though trained in the *gotipua* style, was insistent in support for "tradition" which he identified with the Tantric aspect of the style and with the legacy of the *maharis*. He resented the influence of external standards drawn from other classical forms, and argued that this diminished the earthy vitality of Odissi; he was critical of the "cleansing" of the form whereby all "folk" elements were weeded out, arguing that all of these various styles were part of the typical flavor of Odissi; he also disliked the diminishing of the typical local cultural specificity of Odissi through the process of Sanskritization, preferring Oriya lyrics to

Sanskrit ones even in *abhinaya* items. While Guru Kelucharan's is acknowledgedly the most widely practiced style today, it is important to remember the multiplicity of styles that continue to comprise the body of Odissi dance even today.[12]

Re-mark-able ventriloquisms

In conclusion, I want to remember that much of these conflicting debates about aesthetic forms were occurring in the mid-century, when the ambiguities, paradoxes, and tensions of the typical conditions of postcoloniality were at their sharpest. In such a cultural field, still smarting from the implication of lack, and laboring to prove its "ancient" and distinct artistic heritage, power belonged to those who could articulate their claims with clarity and in terms of an established legitimacy. It is hardly accidental that Bharatanatyam's coming to acquire the status of a national dance form is linked to a highly public debate, one end of which rested with Rukmini Devi, Brahmin, highly educated, someone who was highly conversant in English, and could brilliantly position her claims before national and international audiences. None of the gurus of Odissi, however, hailing from middle- to working-class families, could lay claim to this skill.

This is compounded by the fact that, while the gurus certainly worked to energize the form when it was virtually unknown and disseminate it through training students, the form came into sharp limelight primarily when a specific group of women dancers entered into the scene. For instance, Guru Kelucharan Mahapatra came to be known, initially, largely through the brilliant performances, national awards, and international tours of disciples such as Sanjukta Panigrahi and, later, of Sonal Mansingh, already famed as a Bharatnatyam dancer. Guru Debaprasad Das shot into fame through his association with famous Bharatanatyam dancer Indrani Rehman, who was by then living in New York. The untiring work of a most senior guru, Pankanj Charan Das, for the cause of Odissi, also came into the limelight through his disciples, such as well-known exponents of Bharatanatyam, Yamini Krishnamurthy and Ritha Devi, the latter also being settled in New York. All of these women, from upper-class and middle-class families, educated, most often Brahmin women, were able to effectively mobilize the movement for the "revival" of Odissi through their immaculate performances, which tapped into all resources of modern staging, such as effective lighting and publicity, and were accompanied by clear program notes in English. They were able to initiate diverse audiences into this different aesthetic framework and create various entry points for them into the dance through their live spoken and practical introductions to pieces, particularly *abhinaya* numbers, and communicate with international audiences through the newly devised genre of lecture demonstrations and through interviews, much of which was in English. While the gurus also performed, the proscenium stage of modern India was most welcoming to women from these upper castes and classes who could fulfill their expected roles as the guardians of "tradition". Finally, by a terrible irony, those whose voices were completely erased in this series of re-presentations of an "authentic" classical dance form, were the *maharis*, whose displacement through the foregrounding of the *gotipua* tradition and the legacy of male gurus is doubled, with the prominence gained by contemporary female dancers, whose dance is based on very different premises. Gender and sexuality function here in a composite relationship with class, to maneuver social and economic leverage. Furthermore, the validity and strength of claims made in this field are attendant strongly on fluency in English, which underscores the ability to speak across diverse local languages in a postcolonial society, and to act as cultural ambassadors in international events.

It is my hope that through these reflections on the various issues that I suggest mark the ground and terms on which the currently practiced forms of Odissi were shaped, I have been able to communicate the complex and slippery negotiations involved in what Richard Schechner (1985) has called the "reinvention of tradition". I have tried to suggest that, contrary to Schechner's argument, these wounds of past tears, despite meticulously undertaken projects of suture, do not necessarily heal: the graft continues to show, the jagged edges of disjunction show themselves, often in our dancing bodies, revealing power plays and human hands at work in the construction of the overarching categories of national identity: those of culture and tradition.

Notes

1 Interviews and conversations with Guru Kelucharan Mahapatra, Sanjukta Panigrahi, Raghunath Panigrahi, Dr Kapila Vatsyayan, Dr Sunil Kothari, Dhiren Patnaik, Sharon Lowen, Ramli Ibrahim, Bhagirathi Das, and many other dancers and students of Odissi have contributed vitally to the development of this research.

2 I have referred here to arguments made by scholars such as Amrit Srinivasan, Saskia Kersenboom-Story, Frederique Marglin and, most recently, Avanthi Meduri.

3 *Nautch*, a term that came into being in the colonial era, is the British mispronunciation of the local vernacular *naach*, meaning dance. Initially, the term *nautch*-girl was used to refer to traveling entertainers, but the term ultimately came to refer to all dancers.

4 Comments to this effect were in fact made by Rukmini Devi at her Presidential address given during the Annual Conference of Music and Dance of Tamil Isai Sangam, Madras, 1975.

5 In the film "Given to Dance: Orissa's Dance Tradition", directed by Ron Hess, for instance, Parasmani Mahari says "Our hearts are saddened but what can we do? . . . Just one person cannot sustain the service . . ."

6 According to Dhiren Dash (1981), an authoritative scholar in this field, ". . . except the fact that the present Odissi Nrutya is mainly being taken up by girls as of the custom of *Mahari* dance, there seems to be no other point where the present Odissi Nrutya matches with the tradition of the *Mahari* Nrutya" (p. 97).

7 Tantrism is a less popular branch of Hinduism where physical union between the male and female devotees is a means of arousing powerful energies that can then be channeled towards spiritual enlightenment. It is based on the philosophy of coupling Shiva and Shakti forces in energizing, sustaining, and preserving creation.

8 Illeana Citaristi, chronicling the life and times of Guru Kelucharan Mahapatra, writes about Rukmini Devi's comments on the "vulgarity" of the Odissi presentation during a seminar in 1967. Citaristi (2001) notes that Rukmini Devi's comments were published in the press, where she expressed "her opinion that such explicit allusions of an erotic nature should not be portrayed in dance" (pp. 120–1).

9 The *tribhangi* position, unique to Odissi, is a threefold position, with bends at the neck, the waist, and the knees, with the majority of the weight being placed on the back foot. In the *abhanga* position, which is found in other styles, but is used extensively in Odissi, the weight of the body is shifted largely to one foot, with the feet still placed parallel and next to each other.

10 The government of independent India established a centralized institute of performing arts, dance, music, and theater, the National Sangeet Natak Akademi, in 1952, to support the development and propagation of these art forms, and to "preserve traditions".

11 The term "shastra" means scripture, and refers generally to "classical" texts.

12 Relatively recent developments in Odissi would suggest, however, that now that the dance form is enshrined in classicism, there is a movement gathering force that is pushing for choreographing to Oriya lyrics, the typical tonality of Oriya music, and for heightening the specific local aesthetic.

Bibliography

Arundale, Rukmini Devi (1957) "Bharata Natyam", *Kala Vikash Kendra Journal*, pp. 15–20.

Citaristi, Illeana (2001) *The Making of a Guru*, Delhi: Manohar.

Dash, Dhiren (1981) "This . . . Odissi Dance", *Kala Vikash Kendra Journal*, pp. 87–100.

—— (1990) *Odissi Dance*, Bhubaneshwar: Orissa Sangeet Natak Akademi.

Fabri, Charles ([1960] 1972) "Introduction to Odissi Dance", *Marg*, Mumbai; Marg Publications (1960), reprinted in and cited from *Kala Vikash Kendra Journal* (1972), pp. 1–5.

Hess, Ron (1988) *Given to Dance: Orissa's Dance Tradition*, Madison, Wis.: University of Wisconsin.

Mohanty, Kumkum (1988) Foreword, *Odissi Dance Pathfinder*, volume 1, Bhubaneshwar: Odissi Research Center.

Mohanty, Kumkum (1995) *Odissi Dance Pathfinder*, volume 2, Bhubaneshwar: Odissi Research Center.

Patnaik, Dhiren (1990) *Odissi Dance*, Bhubaneshwar: Orissa Sangeet Natak Akademi.

Schechner, Richard (1985) *Theater and Anthropology*, Philadelphia, Pa.: University of Pennsylvania Press.

Chapter 14

Alastair Macaulay

MATTHEW BOURNE, DANCE HISTORY AND *SWAN LAKE*

The choreographer Matthew Bourne only began formal dance education at the age of 22. Then, in 1982, he began as a student in the three-year BA (Hons) Degree in Dance Theatre at the Laban Centre for Movement and Dance. Though he was an enthusiastic and hard-working student on all aspects of the course, he has said on record that, for him as a choreographer, the most important part of the course was Dance History. I was his Dance History teacher. It happens that, in Bourne's very first term, I taught nineteenth-century ballet history; and so he was at once plunged into the context and composition and meanings of *La Sylphide*, *Swan Lake*, and *The Nutcracker* – all of which he went on to re-choreograph during the 1990s. 'The two Freds' – Astaire and Ashton – were areas of twentieth-century dance history I taught with particular love; Bourne has said in recent years that they are his two favourite choreographers. When he took Dance History as his optional subject during Part Two of his course, his special study was on Astaire's choreography.

In the years that followed, we remained friends, even though occasionally I said, or (as a critic) wrote, the wrong thing. For example, while Bourne was preparing his 1995 *Swan Lake*, I found myself telling him the remark once made by the dance critic David Vaughan: 'The worst *Swan Lake* is the one you are watching.' But Bourne's *Swan Lake* was a huge success – it has won numerous awards on both sides of the Atlantic, and, by 2000, it had been performed more often than the traditional Swan Lake has been performed at the Royal Opera House, Covent Garden – and attracted a very wide-ranging audience, many of whom were attending dance for the first time.

In 1998, Walter Donahue of Faber and Faber approached Bourne with the idea of a book of interviews. Bourne in turn approached me to ask if I would like to conduct and edit the interviews. From the book that emerged as a result,

Matthew Bourne and his Adventures in Motion Pictures (Faber and Faber, 2000) I have reassembled various portions of our interviews to show how Bourne's *Swan Lake* drew from aspects of his interest in dance history and in earlier choreography.

MATTHEW BOURNE:
I think now that, in my teens, I was very into self-education, without knowing it. In 1979, when I was 19, I saw my first ballet: *Swan Lake*. I wonder now: what made me go? To Covent Garden; then to Sadler's Wells. I know that I went on my own. I think that I thought it was about time I saw a ballet: to see if I might like it. With most things, no one encouraged me to do it; I did it myself. And I read things because I felt 'I've not read that author – and I should do.'
What impressed me most was its seriousness as dance. I'd seen Fred and Ginger handling serious emotion in dance, I'd heard serious music in musicals, too, but until ballet I hadn't encountered a whole genre that seemed to make dance, and dancing to music, something serious as a matter of course. It was the impact of that which gave it an erotic quality, because it was seriously sexual and sensual. I had never found that kind of appeal in the stars and musicals and showbiz I'd been following up to that time.

ALASTAIR MACAULAY:
So what had Swan Lake *been to you before you made your own? When was the first time you ever saw* Swan Lake *on stage?*

MB:
The way I've remembered it for years is that I first saw the Scottish Ballet production, Peter Darrell's production. It was at Sadler's Wells in 1979, and I'm on record as saying it was not only my first *Swan Lake* but also the first ballet I ever saw. I've just discovered that it wasn't! But we'll come to that.

AM:
That Darrell production is a drug-dream retelling of Swan Lake; *it has a fairly tormented, psychological drama. The swan scenes are opium-induced hallucinations in the Prince's mind.*

MB:
Yes, but I thought this was *Swan Lake*; that all *Swan Lakes* would be along these lines. I didn't know then that Darrell's treatment of the story was something new. And my memory is that, because I loved the piece so much – I'd never seen a full-length dance piece before – I very quickly followed it up by seeing it again

that summer, at Covent Garden. This time it was the National Ballet of Canada doing the Erik Bruhn production with Karen Kain. During these conversations with you, however, I've discovered that I must have seen the Canadian production first! It came to Covent Garden early in August that year. The Scottish production came to Sadler's Wells about a fortnight later. This tells you something about my memory.

AM:
Bruhn's Canadian version is also a psycho-drama.

MB:
I don't remember it well. I just remember the swans, which made a greater impression with a bigger ballet company on a bigger stage than in the Scottish production. I was surprised at how fast they moved; I wasn't expecting that! I do remember thinking, after the second *Swan Lake* in a fortnight, 'This is really different!' I had thought it would be the same. I had thought *Swan Lake* was *Swan Lake*.

AM:
And now, almost twenty years later, someone is probably thinking that your Swan Lake *is the one and only* Swan Lake . . .

MB:
That's literally true, I've discovered! Especially with young audiences.

AM:
You're on record as saying that the two choreographers you most admire are the two Freds: Astaire and Ashton. Is that true?

MB:
Yes, it still is true. I grew up watching Fred Astaire with my parents, but the moment when suddenly I realized he was a major choreographer came when I watched a whole programme of Astaire–Rogers dance duets in the old Everyman Cinema in Hampstead, in 1979. Then, the next year, I caught *La Fille mal Gardée* at Covent Garden, fell in love with that, and started to catch whatever Ashton I could from then on.

AM:
'Fred' Ashton put one obvious Astaire quotation – the 'Oompah Trot', which he had seen Fred Astaire doing on stage with his sister Adele, and which Astaire does with Gracie Allen in the movie Damsel in Distress *– into his own 1948 ballet* Cinderella. *He and Robert*

Helpmann did it, as the two Ugly Sisters, in their duet with the oranges, hilariously; and it remains in the choreography for the two Ugly Sisters today. Do you find yourself consciously quoting Astaire movies when you choreograph?

MB:
Yes, many times! The *pas de deux* in Act Two of my *Cinderella* starts, absolutely, with the Astaire–Rogers idea I've been talking about: they just walk, then they elaborate on the walk, and then that builds into a dance. The sort of things I tend to notice in Astaire, for possible use of my own, are certainly not his tap numbers: certainly not in terms of their steps. But I do take definite ideas from the duets. Not just Fred and Ginger actually, but also Fred with, for example, Cyd Charisse. 'Dancing in the Dark' from *The Band Wagon* is one that I watch again and again to remind me of something that's very simple but beautiful. I've used Astaire exits a few times. I particularly love the exit at the end of 'Let's Face the Music and Dance' – but, though I've tried more than once to put it in my work, it doesn't really work on stage. I know – I was still trying to bring that off at the end of the Spanish dance in *Swan Lake*! But, in rehearsal, it didn't work. So we changed it.
I think that the more you watch great choreography, the more you learn from it. I was lucky enough then to be seeing a fair amount of works regularly in the theatre, seeing things again and again. And that's how they sink in.

AM:
Were you interested in dance history before you began the BA course in 1982?

MB:
Yes. I'd started to be interested about two years before. I'd begun to read a lot of dance biographies: Buckle's *Nijinsky* and *Diaghilev*, Taper's *Balanchine* . . . And books about the early Royal Ballet – the Vic–Wells Ballet, then the Sadler's Wells Ballet – and about Robert Helpmann and Margot Fonteyn. You see, whatever dance I'd be watching at the time, that would trigger me onto reading anything about it I could lay my hands on.

AM:
Do you think, though, that dance history is generally of use to a would-be choreographer? Would you recommend it?

MB:
I would think that some study of dance history should be a necessity for a choreographer of classical ballet: in that genre, with such a tradition and such a legacy and such a repertory, to know where you're coming from is particularly important. But I also think that any choreographer should be interested in what's

gone before. Plenty of modern-dance people feel that there's no point in learning about the long-distant past and, in particular, about the ballet past. No doubt, dance history could be made to seem irrelevant to current dance practice. But, to me, it seemed very relevant. I found that a formal study of history gave me a wider sense of dance practice. Even learning about long-dead ballerinas and long-extinct ballets interested me – because I was learning more about how dances and dancers had worked. As a choreographer, that knowledge can widen your options. It liberates you to hear how famous dances were made; to look at the great choreographers not as icons but as artists-in-the-making and at the great masterpieces not as shrines but as works-in-progress; to get deeper into their methods.

History for me was just a very good way of learning more about dance values and about choreography. People are so busy being contemporary and being innovative that they don't see how the past can be useful. Yet it can be a revelation. It allows you to develop your own way.

AM:

You yourself nickname your first four full-length works – Nutcracker, Highland Fling, Swan Lake, Cinderella *– 'classics', because they use the scores and (to some extent) the scenarios of ballet 'classics'. In fact, in your very first term at the Laban Centre, we concentrated on Romanticism and the nineteenth-century ballet repertory: the 'classics', as they're widely known.* La Sylphide *(the basis for your* Highland Fling*),* Swan Lake, *and* The Nutcracker *were all discussed in some detail. The whole idea of Romanticism in its full political and social context was a wonderful way in which to make dance students see the excitement of history. And it was good to make them see how much there is to say about each of these old ballet warhorses, when they're taken seriously. Was dance history the only area where you were encouraged to consider narrative seriously? Particularly in modern dance, particularly in the early 1980s, narrative was very unfashionable; it was regarded as impure, outmoded.*

MB:

In general, yes. Also you showed us a variety of important dance works on video, and some of those made a lasting impression. So, for example, when I made *Spitfire* in 1988, I used one grouping idea from Balanchine's *Serenade*: now, that was a work I had only seen because you showed it to us.

I'll tell you what was very interesting to me. The other day, when we were looking through old photos of nineteenth-century and of early twentieth-century dance history for this book, I thought: 'I must look at these more again now.' I remember being so inspired by even just pictures of older works, by seeing how highly designed a lot of the choreography seems to have been, in both ballet and contemporary work. I think that, earlier on, I was using so many of those images in my mind. I could do with an influx of that again – to go back to looking at pieces that I loved and watched years ago. I feel that I learnt the most about choreography and theatre in those years, when I was regularly watching a lot of other people's work, a lot of good and great choreography.

AM:
As you know, you weren't the first person to choreograph male swans. But the idea of reversing the gender of both the ballerina role and the corps de ballet made an especial impression. Yet the seeds are already there in historic Romanticism. The 1832 La Sylphide *– the prototype for innumerable Romantic/classical ballets that followed throughout the nineteenth and twentieth centuries – was itself a gender-reversal of Nodier's story* Trilby, *in which a male spirit lures a Scots croftswoman. In* La Sylphide, *a mortal male sleeps while, from the open window, the sylph vision of his dreams hovers about his chair; in 1910, Mikhail Fokine reversed the genders back again in* Le Spectre de la Rose, *when he had Nijinsky arrive, through the window, as the androgynous vision of romance dreamt by the young girl asleep in her armchair.*

MB:
At one stage, I had toyed with the idea of dancing the role of the sylph myself in what later became *Highland Fling*. And, the moment I dropped that idea, I began to think of *Swan Lake* with male swans.

AM:
Did you straightaway think of a male protagonist in the double role of Swan Lake *– as both 'the White Swan' Odette and 'the Black Swan' Odile, as the roles are known in most versions?*

MB:
I don't think that came straight away, no. My immediate idea was of a *corps* of male swans.

AM:
And a male Prince. So straight away it becomes a sexual drama to some degree in your mind?

MB:
Yes. That was something that probably interested me from the first: the sexual issues within *Swan Lake*. Still, the more I went along, the more I found other things in it. I found that it could be seen, and interpreted, in different ways; and, when we were making it, I made it a little more open for interpretation.

AM:
The idea of the male dream object: how conscious was that to you from Nijinsky's role in Le Spectre de la Rose*?*

MB:
I don't think it was conscious. You see, I was also thinking of other Nijinsky roles, especially the Faun, who isn't a dream object – although that kind of image can certainly fill your dreams. Unconsciously, though, perhaps there is a connection. When I first thought of doing *Swan Lake*, I wasn't thinking of Adam Cooper or of anyone from the ballet world. But I certainly used to glorify – though I don't now – dancers in his field, ballet. I would see them as little gods or goddesses.

AM:
During the early 1980s, I know that you saw the Royal Ballet staging of Swan Lake *produced by its then artistic director Norman Morrice, quite a number of times. This new/old production, very traditional in outline and developed from the company's own previous productions, was set in the mediaeval Age of Chivalry: which is – you'll forgive my saying this – where Tchaikovsky intended it. It was full of major classical choreography, albeit by five different choreographers (Marius Petipa, Lev Ivanov, Ninette de Valois, Frederick Ashton, Rudolf Nureyev). In particular, you were able now to watch and rewatch much of the choreography made by Petipa and Ivanov for the 1895 St Petersburg production of* Swan Lake *– the text that is generally called the 'traditional'* Swan Lake. *How did this production strike you, after your first two* Swan Lakes?

MB:
Ballet is so strange and exciting when you first see it that you remember few specific details afterwards. Yes, those first two productions I'd seen had been more psychological; yes, I do remember the Prince smoking opium in the Darrell production; and, yes, I was aware of differences between each production. But I think I may also have made connections between them that weren't intended. Because of the Darrell, I think I always saw the Prince in the Royal Ballet's *Swan Lake* as a more complex figure than he actually was in that production. He always intrigued me. I know in that particular Royal Ballet production there wasn't a lot to go on – I have the official 1980 video, with Makarova and Dowell in the lead roles, so I can check out my memories – but, through the music, you can feel more. To me, that character was quite complex. After all, he turns down one batch of women his mother puts before him in Act One; then he turns down another batch in Act Three, more emphatically. With some ballet dancers in the role, I couldn't help giggling. But I had no sense of disappointment in that production; I was excited by it. I may have projected onto it psychological ideas from the Darrell production; if so, they enriched it for me. I wasn't analysing things much; I just absorbed.

AM:
Now, that Royal production, however traditional in appearance, had supplementary choreography by Frederick Ashton, by Ninette de Valois, and by Nureyev. The whole fourth

act was by Ashton. Then, in 1987, when you were still a frequent ballet-goer at Covent Garden, the Royal Ballet brought in a new production, which returned completely to the 1895 St Petersburg musical text, and to a great degree to the 1895 choreographic text too – though there's always dispute about a great many details. On the other hand, this production – by the company's new artistic director Anthony Dowell and designed by Yolanda Sonnabend – updated the ballet to the nineteenth century.

MB:
Yes; and, though it's interesting to see the original choreography, that production never made as strong an impression on me. The designs and the choreography aren't really in the same world as each other.
There are ways of doing *Swan Lake* well, and ways of messing it up. If you look at the video of the 1964 Nureyev production in Vienna, with Fonteyn dancing, it plays around with the music in a dreadful way. To me, that's unacceptable. And, you know, Act Four never felt to me, in any production, so substantial that it merited an intermission before it – the second, or even sometimes the third interval of the evening – not even with Ashton. So, when it came to my production, I always knew I wanted it to run straight on from Act Three. In fact, when you go back to the music Tchaikovsky wrote for Act Four, it's a very short act anyway. I was very much aware when we began to plan our *Swan Lake* that it would coincide with the centenary of the 1895 production.

AM:
The traditional Swan Lake *has Rothbart the sorcerer presiding, in the guise of an owl, as an evil genius over the Swan scenes. The music's most famous theme is connected to his fateful power over Odette. I like Rothbart in the traditional version, and yet the fact that you omit him strikes me as maybe the most brilliant feature of your production. What led you to cut Rothbart out?*

MB:
I felt that he wasn't relevant to the story I was telling. I didn't want anything to be explained by magic, and I feel that that's what he was there for. Above all, I didn't want that three-way relationship – Prince, Swan, Rothbart – in the Swan scenes. I just wanted the simplicity of the Prince and the swans without something else controlling it. After all, it's in his mind. So it didn't seem appropriate to have anyone else involved.

AM:
So there is a Romantic, unbridgeable gap between the Swan and the Prince in your Swan Lake, *as in the traditional one. But that gap isn't created by Rothbart's power in your version, it's created by the block, the repression, in the Prince's own mind. He can't fully grasp the Swan, be at one with it, for reasons that are entirely in his own mind.*

MB:
Yes, that's right.

AM:
To what degree are all your shows about sexual longing? The 'Shallow Brown' dream in Town and Country, *the emotion that Clara has for her Nutcracker hero, the adulterous desire that James has for one female after another (primarily the Sylph) in* Highland Fling, *the Prince's feeling for the Swan, and the longing that Cinderella and the Pilot have for each other: these are all striking stage visions of sexual desire.*

MB:
I always see that as the basis of a good story. The longing is the interesting thing. That, and the journey of getting together or not.

AM:
I would say that, very often in your work, it is also a longing for beauty. At several points in your shows, there is a moment of either the shock of beauty or the shock of sexual allure: in fact, a moment when the recognition of beauty becomes the recognition of sexual desire. For example, when Clara suddenly sees the bare-torsoed Nutcracker along with – by implication – the whole of the male sex.

MB:
I think that's true. I think those feelings are something that I feel a lot of people share, so I'm aware of the impact they will have on a viewer. Yes, it's true, at that moment in *Nutcracker* and at the moment when the Swan first enters, I want the audience to feel the same impact as the character in the piece. I want them to be slightly overwhelmed by the beauty of what I'm showing, to feel its excitement.
I consciously wanted to make *Swan Lake* about a man – very much a man, who happened to be a prince as well – who had trouble expressing himself and couldn't, for whatever reason, be who he wanted to be. He was also a needy person: that was the centre of it. And the swan was a symbol, a symbol of what he needed – rather than some tragic figure who's been magically transformed into something else – I didn't feel it needed that. Once the decision was made that the swan was in the imagination of the prince and then projected on to a real person in Act Three, then it made sense that other things were not relevant then to our story.

AM:
When you were researching it – thinking about the music – you read, or reread, Roland John Wiley's 1985 book Tchaikovsky's Ballets?

MB:
Yes, I read it.

AM:
One of the points he makes about the 1877 score is that there is an inner family (my word, not his) of Swan Lake *music. Much of the music – by reason of either melody or orchestration or tonality – is connected to Odette, the swans, Rothbart, or Prince Siegfried. In the lakeside acts, Acts Two and Four, this is hardly surprising. Some of the music in Acts One and Three, by contrast, has little or no connection with this family, and therefore was surely designed simply as divertissement music. I don't know whether you were inspired by Wiley, or if his book gave you confidence in your own instincts. But, as soon as I first saw your* Swan Lake *in 1995, I was amazed to see that, in Acts One and Three, you distinguish dramatically between this 'family' and 'non-family' music.*

MB:
I can't say that I consciously absorbed that point from him. He doesn't make that point forcefully; and I wasn't thinking hard of my textual decisions when I read his book. I would say that I made my choices from musical instinct. Still, it's possible that my instinct may have been subconsciously guided by having read Wiley; I don't know. But textual decisions certainly became very important to me. Wiley finds a fair deal of merit in the 1895 St Peterburg musical text of *Swan Lake* that Drigo arranged after Tchaikovsky's death, doesn't he? I've often loved it in the theatre, but in preparing my version, both David Lloyd-Jones, our musical director, and I made it a rule to eliminate all Drigo's musical arrangements and to return to Tchaikovsky's own. The one passage where that seemed very hard to bring off at first was the Swan *pas de deux* in Act Two: Tchaikovsky's 1877 original suddenly shatters the mood with an upbeat allegro ending. When I tried choreographing that, all of us kept bursting into laughter in the rehearsal room. Finally, however, we found that Tchaikovsky himself had come with a quiet diminuendo ending in his *'Swan Lake' Suite*; and that was what we used.
I've forgotten some of the research I did, whereas I remember quite a lot about the research Scott Ambler and I did into royalty; Scott was to play the Prince. We did a lot of reading around all the princes and monarchs of this century and last: virtually anything relevant that we could get our hands on. So the Prince in our *Swan Lake* is an amalgamation of characteristics of different kings and princes. The one thing they all seemed to have in common – the royal men we chose to research – was that they all seemed very unsuitable for the job that they were born into; that they were not complete people. The actual job seemed to make them worse. We used the nervous twitches and the stammering of various kings. George VI was quite an inspiration: he was so unsuited to public life.

AM:
Any foreign ones?

MB:
Ludwig of Bavaria, of course, because he was so obsessed with swans. In fact, he seemed too obvious a link. Still, we did read books about him, and a certain amount of him went into it. We really might have gone more for the Ludwig connection. But we were aware that he had been used as the Prince in some previous production of *Swan Lake*. Was it John Neumeier's? Not one I'd seen. But the idea had already been used.

AM:
How early did you conceive Act One beginning right back in the Prince's childhood?

MB:
Quite early on. It emerged from my concern that the hero should be more complex; that his feeling for the Swan should not be only something sexual. I wanted to show him in innocence early on as a child, with the vision of the swan – so that it was a vision that was there from childhood, but was also something that took on new meanings for him as he got older, something that he desired, wanted to emulate. Our first *Swan Lake* poster, or logo, made before we ever choreographed it, was of a naked young man kneeling with a swan folding its neck around his – a young male version of the famous photos of Pavlova embracing her pet swan at Ivy House. But in our version it's altogether more intimate. I think also it helped to show that he was a troubled child, having nightmares, alone in this great big bed – this tiny boy who's surrounded by adults all the time.

AM:
What Swan movements did you already have in mind before you started rehearsals?

MB:
I wanted that Nijinsky-type use of the arms crossed over the head – as in the photographs of *Spectre* or *Narcisse*. It has nothing to do with swans in particular. It just has a draping, hanging flow to it, that position. In *Town and Country* (1991), during 'Shallow Brown', there's a bit where the chorus group comes on shuffling with their arms like that. There are some tree images that are a bit like that, like blossom on trees. I like having the hands very relaxed, just hanging. Either that or very cleanly with fingers all together. I don't like the spikily separated fingers you often see in ballet. I'm always getting people to close their fingers if they're taking a strong position: clean lines. So the arms draped over the head does reappear quite a lot in my work. It feels sensual to me, and sexy as well, because it's about touching your own body, which is another thing that I like to use

onstage. In *Swan Lake*, there's a bit where the swans wrap their bodies. Like taking a T-shirt off: that type of movement.

AM:
Did you also find yourself fascinated by the photographs of, say, Fonteyn in The Firebird *and* Ondine, *where she is again wrapping the arms and hands around the head and torso in very picturesque ways?*

MB:
I love those pictures; and I also think that *Firebird* was going through my mind in *Swan Lake*. I was probably thinking of bird-like pieces that I'd seen. That *Firebird* image of shielding the face is in there somewhere.

AM:
Once you'd made the two major decisions about your lakeside scenes that there would be no Rothbart and that the swans would be male, the general outline of Act Two seems to have fallen into place. A few of your choreographic motifs and patterns are adapted from Ivanov's choreography in the 1895 version, and in general you use the 1895 ordering of the score.

MB:
When it came to making the movement, we began with the swans. We wanted to put some ungainly things in, you see: we didn't want it to look all beautiful and serene. Because, when swans are out of the water, they're very awkward, and slightly turned-in. So, within the swan choreography, there are two contrasting elements. Sometimes they scrunch up, sometimes they open out again. To a certain extent, we were remembering the traditional ballet. But we were trying to get away from flapping wings all the time. Obviously you can't get entirely away from that in *Swan Lake*, but we wanted to find some variations on that: with birdlike head movements and twitches. There also came a point when we decided to make the swans creature-like as well as bird-like at times. Also semi-human.

AM:
In your notebooks for Swan Lake, *there's a section just called 'Ideas', in which – before rehearsals, I think – you've put down your conceptions for each of the four acts. But you've also added other ideas – especially movement ideas – during the early rehearsals. Here are some notes for Act Two. 'Notes for swan motifs. Head nestling.'*

MB:
That's very much out of the traditional *Swan Lake*, isn't it? But then it's what real swans do.

AM:
You've mentioned the traditional Swan Lake. *What other choreography was in your mind at this period?*

MB:
I did have a feeling of Nijinsky's *Faune* in my mind for it. The general look of the costume, the intensity of the eyes, the two-dimensional feel to a lot of the movement. Particularly earlier on, when we started, I had the pictures of *Faune* in my mind for the atmosphere of what we were trying to create.
Also I felt an early modern dance influence. At this stage, Jose Limon was in my mind. I had done a lot of Limon classes at one time, and I took class for a few weeks with the Limon company in New York in about '88, '89. What I remember is the feeling of the movement. Those classes are very long, about two hours, starting with barrework and centrework, and then with movement based in Limon repertory. I enjoyed that style very much. Also, for *Swan Lake*, I was looking through all the photos of Denishawn group pieces from the 1920s, trying to get ideas about group designs.

AM:
In the coda, you capture the music's competitive spirit. In the traditional Swan Lake, *the way in which the ballerina does her thirty-two fouette turns over a drastic change in the music is always horridly unmusical.*

MB:
I definitely stole one thing there. The way the Swan lifts the Queen over his hoisted leg over a series of tables: Fred and Ginger do that in the 'Yam' in their film *Carefree*. I'd always wanted to put that in somewhere!

Chapter 15

André Lepecki

CONCEPT AND PRESENCE

The Contemporary European Dance Scene

TO UNDERSTAND THE CURRENT TRENDS in the European dance scene is to wander through a historical path that traverses both sides of the Atlantic. Such wandering maps a choreographic ground that refuses stability. This chapter addresses some of the main aspects and most recent developments in European dance – from the early 1990s to the present – in order to propose an understanding of contemporary European dance's unstable ground. This unstable ground does not at all denote weakness or a lack of foundations: rather it presents itself as both sign and basis for a necessary rethinking of certain formal and ontological parameters set by modern dance in the beginning of the twentieth century. Some time in the early 1990s, it became transparent for a whole generation of choreographers and dancers that those parameters, notably the isomorphism between dance and movement, and the emphasis on dance's autonomy with regard to the verbal, had set up an ontological and political trap for dance. The current scene critiques those parameters and identifies the contours of the trap. Does this critique repeat yet another moment like so many others in the history of twentieth-century dance when choreographers announced yet another radical "rupture" with the past? Those moments of rejection have repeated and reinforced the dynamics of modernist ideology.[1] Think of Isadora Duncan's and Martha Graham's oppositional stances in regards to classical ballet; or Merce Cunningham's refusal of expressionistic dance; or Yvonne Rainer's writings against compositional and technical aspects in both modern and classical dances. I believe the rethinking currently taking place in Europe is informed by a different project and a different stance with regard to the past. Rather than rehearsing a modernist rupture with the past, contemporary European choreography sees the past as a common ground, as the surface it is inevitably destined to wander on. This wandering happens both as a restepping of known paths and as a stumbling upon the unexpected reconfigurations of what might have been there.[2] For what contemporary European dance perceives as unbearable are the modernist imperatives, still so prevalent in dance criticism and marketing, of asserting an absolute (and absurd) division between artistic disciplines, and of considering historical time as teleologically linear. The consequence of these two imperatives is the imposing of yet another problematic division: that between artists on one side, and agents responsible for producing and controlling the discourse on art on the other (critics, theoreticians, programmers). Such imperatives and divisions presuppose a historical ground that must be kept flat, clean of debris and brightly open towards the clear horizon of the future as the house of the forever new.

Since the early 1990s, a variety of choreographers coming from diverse training backgrounds, different social and national contexts, conflicting aesthetic lineages, and sometimes dissonant political views have dedicated themselves to explore the role of dance within the broader realms of art and of society. I believe that presently this common vision has reached a certain critical mass, a certain momentum and a certain specificity that allows it to be qualified as an artistic movement. This movement does not yet have a name, and perhaps it is important (and even essential to its project) that it remains nameless. However, this nameless movement certainly has faces, whose names are well known: the French Jérôme Bel, Xavier le Roy and Boris Charmatz, the Spanish La Ribot, the Germans Thomas Lehmen, Sasha Walz, Felix Ruckert and Tom Plischke, the Portuguese Vera Mantero, João Fiadeiro and Miguel Pereira, the Belgium-based North American Meg Stuart, the Belgian Christine deSmedt and the British Jonathan Burrows are just some of the most prominent of those names.

In October of 2001, Jérôme Bel, La Ribot, Xavier le Roy, and critic Christophe Wavelet organized a meeting in Vienna, to propose and discuss a *Manifesto for a European Performance Policy*.[3] The *Manifesto* was signed by many of the names listed above and by many others. At a certain point, it reads: "We consider the borders between disciplines, categories and nations to be fluid, dynamic and osmotic . . . We consider dialogue, thinking, research and making as equal constituents of our labour." What the *Manifesto* makes clear is that European dance's unstable ground is a common ground stretching across disciplines, whether aesthetic, theoretical or performative. Thus, despite the many national differences within the European dance scene, and despite the many (and very strong) authorial voices in the scene, it is possible at this point to identify a sort of coherent vision and practice within those differences. First, this vision thoroughly acknowledges the impact of the experimental tradition brought by performance art in the 1960s and 1970s to contemporary art at large. It also acknowledges and is informed by the propositions put forth in the visual arts by minimalism and conceptual art. Such grounding of contemporary European dance on minimalism, conceptual art, and performance art marks an interesting (and perhaps surprising) development of what had been, throughout the 1980s and the early 1990s, the consensual mode in European dance: *tanztheater* and its variations. This essay proposes an interpretation of this move of dance from a theatrical paradigm to a performance paradigm as a necessary political move and as a radical recasting of dance. This move is articulated already in the opening paragraph of the *Manifesto*. Note how the Manifesto opens by recasting the very nature and essence of choreographic work by acknowledging precisely how this work stands on an open surface of events, artistic currents, topologies, signifiers, historical movements and contemporary trends.

> Our practices can be described by a range of terminology, depending on the different cultural contexts in which we operate. Our practices can be called: "performance art", "live art", "happenings", "events", "body art", "contemporary dance/theatre", "experimental dance", "new dance", "multimedia performance", "site specific", "body installation", "physical theatre", "laboratory", "conceptual dance", "independance", "postcolonial dance/performance", "street dance", "urban dance", "dance theatre", "dance performance" – to name but a few . . .

The very possibility of open and endless naming suggests that the truth of the work resides in its performance rather than in its accommodation to previously fixed, established, hermetically sealed aesthetic and disciplinary boundaries. Moreover, what becomes quite clear from the names listed to describe contemporary European dance practices is that these names define a very specific semantic field for this dance. It is a field where the visual arts, performance art, political art, meet performance theory and institute a mode of creation truly trans-disciplinary.

It is impossible to honor and address in the space of this chapter each of these choreographers' rich, important and provoking work. Thus, I will restrict myself to outlining the artistic and political context that frames their emergence and their impact. To trace an "artistic and political context" is to propose neither a narrative of direct descent nor the identification of genealogical, direct lineages between past choreographers and contemporary ones. Much of dance history has been caught in the webs of self-contained narratives of family feuds and lines of transmission. Rather, I would like to make it clear that I am indeed mapping a common ground of concerns, a ground that has been stepped on and explored before by previous generations of dancers, performers, visual artists, performance artists and choreographers whose bodies, weight and impacts defined the grooves of the terrain where contemporary European dance currently strolls and stumbles on. By mapping and accepting this common ground, by extending it across time and space, the past loses its ephemeral gloss and becomes literally alive at the present moment – whenever one moves on it.

In order to escape generalization I will draw my examples mainly from the work of three major names in contemporary European choreography: Jérôme Bel, Vera Mantero and La Ribot. The proposals that these three choreographers/performers/dancers have been developing since the beginning of their careers (late 1980s for Mantero and La Ribot, early 1990s for Bel) exemplify this broader European movement. A provisional listing of those characteristics would include: a distrust of representation, a suspicion of virtuosity as an end, the reduction of unessential props and scenic elements, an insistence on the dancer's presence, a deep dialogue with the visual arts and with performance art, a politics informed by a critique of visuality, and a deep dialogue with performance theory. The most important element behind all these aspects would be: an absolute lack of interest in defining whether the work falls within the ontological, formal or ideological parameters of something called, or recognized as, "dance."

This provisional list of some main characteristics in contemporary European dance leads us directly to two major events in western theatrical dance, events that since the second half of the twentieth century have destined the shape of the dance that concerns this chapter. It leads us first to the experiments at Judson Church in New York in the 1960s by pioneers such as Steve Paxton, Trisha Brown and Yvonne Rainer. Then it takes us to the compositional and political shift proposed by German choreographer Pina Bausch, when, some time between 1976 and 1977, she decided to ask her dancers questions, rather than to propose movement as the compositional point of departure for her pieces. These two crucial moments in the history of contemporary dance are separated by geography and time. If, when seen as isolated incidents, each of those events qualify as massive tectonic rifts in the dance world, it is once they are woven together by time and performance that we see how they establish an uneven, paradoxical, knotty ground for dance, one forever undermining the possibility of flow and of representation. My point is that not only can those two moments be reunited by historical hindsight, but that they have been inextricably bound to each other and distilled by contemporary European dance, as this dance restages, recasts, retells and reclaims some central aspects of both Judson's proposals and Pina Bausch's experiments in Wuppertal. This recasting, this retelling, this reclaiming is less a question of direct influence and formal resemblance than a matter of being unable to escape the incredible creative and iconoclastic forces embedded in those early radicalizations of what was understood as dance. Contemporary European choreography is thus predicated upon a rereading, a reinterpreting (and also upon creating a sort of self-conscious historical fantasy) of those two foundational moments in twentieth-century dance. For what those moments have founded is the impossibility for dance to stand by itself and to flow in a solitary space. After Judson and Bausch, dance could no longer be certain of where it stood, and what it stood for. We will see in a moment that this incertitude (and even distrust) with regard to dance's stance is fundamental for an understanding of the work being proposed currently in Europe.

What were the elements the Judson choreographers and Pina Bausch and her dancers explored that I believe inform current European practices? Starting with the Judson generation, I would like to invoke particularly the work and the words of dancer, choreographer and filmmaker Yvonne Rainer. Dance historian Sally Banes has characterized Rainer's *Trio A* (1966) as the "paradigmatic statement of the aesthetic goals of post-modern dance" (Banes 1987: 44). What compositionally makes *Trio A* paradigmatic is its explicit attempt to ground itself outside the usual parameters of theatrical dance and to draw explicitly from the visual arts its compositional integrity. Indeed, what Banes has called *Trio A*'s aesthetic "reductionism" (p. 44) parallels explicitly the aesthetic project of minimal art. Rainer's innovative view departed from her careful study and embracing of minimal art, and from her desire to bring dance into a deeper dialogue with the most experimental trends in visual arts at the time. This parallel between dance and minimal art initiated by Judson is instrumental for an understanding of the contemporary European dance scene. For this parallel illuminates the latter's contention with the theatrical space and with movement. It is between minimalism and a radical questioning of the possibilities of body and presence; between a certain distilling of elements and a reduction of movement and a deep emphasis on the insanities that form us that Rainer and Bausch can be seen not so much as direct influences on the current European proposals, but more as activators of possibilities that only now can be fully grasped in their performative and political implications for dance. Of the general characteristics of the contemporary European scene I briefly outlined above, I would consider that distrust of representation, and an insistence on the dancer's presence, are Bauschian legacies; a suspicion of virtuosity and the reduction of unessential props and scenic elements are Rainer's legacies; and the deep dialogue with the visual arts and with performance art, and a politics informed by a critique of visuality, are legacies from both choreographers (albeit each have dealt very differently with these elements).

By abiding to minimalism, one reduces the scale and the scope of movement to what philosopher José Gil (1996) has called a "microscopy of perception" – by working the microscopic, one has radically to rethink the space where dance has been taking place. The proscenium theatre, and even the black box, may no longer function as ideal optical architectures for a minimal dance. The work of Spanish choreographer La Ribot is illustrative of this remapping of the theatrical space for dance. In 1993, La Ribot set herself up to make one hundred solo pieces, performed by her, each lasting between thirty seconds and seven minutes. These pieces are known as *Piezas Distinguidas* (*Distinguished Pieces*). After a first series of thirteen distinguished pieces in 1993/94, and a second series

Mas Distinguidas (*More Distinguished*, 1997) all presented and choreographed for black box, its most recent development in 2000, titled *Still Distinguished*, takes place in the (white) space of an art gallery. The relationship to the audience changes radically, as well as the understanding and force of the body's presence and its use of movement. With La Ribot, three events take place at once that recast the place of dance – its displacement to a non-theatrical space (an art gallery); the investment in small perceptions, or a certain stillness; the disregard for any formal concerns on whether what is presented belongs, or may be easily identified with, the common understanding of what dance is. The question then is: what remains of the dance, or of a choreographic imagination, once its formal boundaries are put into crisis by the evacuation of movement, the displacing of the theatre building, and the sharing of the ground with the audience? In a recent essay on the work of La Ribot, Spanish art historian Jaime Salazar-Conde answers this question as follows: "Standing there [in the Gallery space with La Ribot], the only certainty is the weight of our body on the ground" (Salazar-Conde 2002). The ground serves as index of, and support for, co-presence – the bodies of the audience and of performer gain materiality and are bound to presence through an emphasis on their irreducible grounding. This emphasis on presence as that which acknowledges grounding as both matter and a historical act of caring is essential for contemporary European dance's strategies of representational distrust. It is only through this emphasis on the material conditions of presence that dance moves away from the illusion-machinery of theatre and steps into that "maniacally charged present" of performance (Phelan 1993: 148).

These aspects in La Ribot's work, born out of her use of notions from minimal and conceptual art, were already present in a foundational piece for the contemporary European dance scene: French choreographer's Jérôme Bel's group work *Jérôme Bel* (1995). *Jérôme Bel* challenges the grounding of dance by operating a thorough dismantling of the black box, a parody of its optical, acoustic, representational and spatial modernist presuppositions. In this extraordinary work, the black box is presented as already a ruin, a failed machine, dusty, dark, a terrain for naked bodies of dancers to explore, for fifty minutes, the absolute minimal requirements for dance to happen. In a radical shift from modern dance's "discovery" of dance's essence as movement,[4] *Jérôme Bel* indicates that dance's ontology and foundation lies somewhere else: in the unstable tension between presence and absence, light and shadow, the space between bare flesh and hidden flesh. In this work, the stage is presented as working space: not so charming, but dusty, rough, hopelessly waiting for the lighting design to operate its optical metamorphosis of delight, the eruption of the fourth wall, an eruption the piece constantly forbids. That empty and unattractive space is the ground of choreographic labor, bare of props and "theatrical" effects (a theatre without theatre). This ruinous space hosts four bodies, naked (a fifth performer, fully dressed, will arrive in the last five minutes of the piece). They arrive simultaneously in a space without lights or scenery, only to become visible within the somewhat limited space defined by the yellowish glow of a normal light bulb brought to the stage and held for the entire piece by an older female performer. The musical score is rendered by another woman who sings Stravinsky's *Sacre du Printemps*. This singing is not only a pun on history, on dance history's obsession with the modernist narrative of heroic ruptures and geniuses, but also a remarkable pun on representation, for the singer does not sing a proper transposition of the orchestral score for voice – she does the best she can to condense the massive sound of the orchestra in her body and release it the best she can through her mouth, belly, throat. If we choose so, we can follow the small dance her naked body engages in by simply standing and producing music. Choreography exists in the excruciatingly precise timing of gestures, on a chronometry of quiet and sparse moves, always invested towards the bare body, the incantation of a private puzzle being revealed to us.

Much is contained in a title that is also an autograph. The function of the name in this piece, of the name of its author as both signature and title, creates a tension regarding those naked and bare presences on stage. For this autographic title reframes the structure of our reading of those bodies' function, purpose and actions. Such reframing by the means of the autographic word creates a distancing between viewer and spectator. What is then this (historical) distancing? It is that of re-emphasizing the body as a site where history gets inscribed as a skin of discomfort and oddity. There is no reclaiming of the performative body as a democratic project but the unveiling of the body as a terrible inheritance, particularly that glamorized body of the dancer, deemed virtuous and perfect, but inhabited by regimentation and control. What I believe *Jérôme Bel* makes explicit is how much the ground on which one stands is filled with, and haunted by, so many absent presences. Stravinsky, Thomas Edison, Sting, Dior (all will have their names scribbled sometime during the piece), the five performers are and are not there. And, of course, haunted by Jérôme Bel, who does not perform, but whose absent-presence emerges as the signature of the event; and haunted by the ghosts of Judson, and of that other ghost hovering about this piece punning modernism, Vaslav Nijinsky. On and off the stage, the remnants of the past are made absolutely contemporary, through what Peggy Phelan calls performance's privileged relation to the invisible. It is not by chance that *Jérôme Bel* is set to the soundtrack of Stravinsky's *Sacre*: the ghost of the modernist scandal, of the modernist mad genius, Nijinsky, are inescapable, just as the naked bodies of performance art in the 1960s are also inescapable landmarks in the ground of dance. *Jérôme Bel* shows how the past is not that which vanishes at every second that passes, but rather that which presents itself in the present as a forceful absence, a set of references, signs, lines of forces, all traversing the body on stage, and defining the ground on where dance (all of us) stands. This understanding of the past as always already present, embodied, insurmountable, is a rather liberating proposition: it allows one to create outside the logic of reaction, outside the position of being permanently against. Such is the historical rearticulation, the attentive project, the shift from a theatrical dance to a performative one.

The choreographic web that Jérôme Bel creates in *Jérôme Bel* is so tight that the piece becomes a machine. The audience can perceive the many levels of regimentation those bodies obey, over-determined that they are by the name of the author. The choreographic autograph is as despairing and mysterious as it is humorous. In a more recent piece, *Shirtologie* (1997), Jérôme Bel explicitly points towards forms of regimentation by the means of the letter: in three separate occasions a dancer stands still, center stage, and proceeds to remove layer after layer of t-shirts. A narrative is weaved by the signs, numbers, words and images printed on the t-shirts. The discomfort of being already written is again patent; but so is the possibility of endless playing and wandering between the house of language and the ground of dance. Choreographing becomes a way of peeling away meaning by the careful manipulation of time. Choreography's ground becomes both bodies and objects, the body as object, verging abjection as it proposes stillness.

The intricate and intimate relationship between word, writing and action which this piece proposes, its quiet atmosphere, its demand for concentration (for both performer and audience), its relentless trust on detail and small perceptions takes us not only towards a certain minimalism but also points quite strongly to conceptual art. This is a very important pointing. For if minimal art is about reduction, distillation and economy, what typifies conceptual art since Marcel Duchamp is its profound engagement in challenging "the traditional status of the art object as unique, collectable or saleable" (Godfrey 1998: 4). That is, conceptual art is preoccupied less with formal variations than with challenging the notion of economy. Traditionally, dance enters economy by escaping its ephemerality through an investment and reliance on precise techniques defined also as signature of a choreographer's personal style (Humphrey technique, Graham technique, Cunningham technique). This practice generates both a system of recognition (the audience recognizes the hand of the choreographer, through its signature technique; the dancer recognizes the familiar vocabulary of the master) and of reproduction (each dancer is initiated in a specific technique that allows the choreography to enter into a fixed repertory and be transmitted along generations and across borders with a minimum of variation).

Contemporary European dance poses radical challenges to the choreographic art object precisely at the level of the possibility of its reproduction. Not only does this object not rely on technique (which is different from saying that it does not have one); it doesn't even concern itself with making technique the specific signature of a choreographer. Rather, it challenges absolutely the very "saleability" of the dance object by withdrawing quite often from it what should be its distinctive (market) trait: dance. The emergence of stillness as a staple in contemporary European choreography has many causes and implications, but its role as a resistance to the spectacular has to be seen not only as an aesthetic reduction (which would side it with minimalist concerns) but importantly as a political statement on the market value of the dance object – essentially a concern of conceptual art.

It is with this concern that the work of Portuguese choreographer Vera Mantero has been unfolding in extraordinarily unpredictable ways in the past decade. Mantero has been evenly dividing her work between solo pieces performed by herself and group works with a diversity of collaborators. It is a 1991 solo titled, after a line from Beckett's *Waiting for Godot* (but with the necessary gender adjustment), *Perhaps She Could Dance First and Think Afterwards*, that her approach to dance as impossibility was clearly articulated. Since then, Mantero has created three very important solos: *Olímpia* (1993), *The Dance of Existing* (1995) and *a mysterious Thing said e.e. cummings* (1996). It is perhaps the latter that is most widely known in Europe. Mantero had been commissioned to produce a twenty-minute piece for an evening of solo works inspired by the life and persona of Josephine Baker. Mantero's solo reflects a deep understanding of the dangerous trap being set up by the event: how does a white woman from the last European colonial empire, Portugal, dance "based" on Josephine Baker? After months of historical research, and only when Mantero was literally a few days from the opening night, did the answer to this central question for an ethics of post-colonial representation come to her clearly. She would diffuse representation to its most tangential presence, she would not dance, she would organize her body as intrinsically paradoxical, she would choreograph her piece by making it also into a poem. The result is an uncanny rendering of a body that performs itself as already hyper-theatrical: white face heavily made up as a cabaret dancer, a disrobed body "browned up", white hands, her legs ending in goat's hooves. During the solo her figure is made visible very slowly, first face then gradually torso and arms, finally the bestial feet. The goat hooves force Mantero's feet into *demi-pointe* and the physical labor of this piece is for Mantero to keep her balance. She wobbles constantly, and her wobbling indexes a ground too scarred and plundered for an image to remain peaceful. This impossible figure in this excruciating task, trying to stand and address an audience on a ground that refuses stability, has something to tell us: she carefully and quietly voices a repetitive text, a litany on the atrocious impossibility of being, on the atrocious non-vision of the gaze, on the tenderness and joy before the abyss. *a mysterious Thing said e.e. cummings* articulates the possibilities of a postcolonial intervention on the shattered, racialized bodies of dance's recent past. By radically displacing representation and embracing small perceptions, Mantero finds a way into those hollow grounds where the discarded bodies of history gather. She proposes a perceptual regime where what becomes apparent is less the grand gesture than the intricate mechanisms of social construction of the (in)significant and the (in)visible. These mechanisms allow the very possibility of language and economy, two major aspects in Mantero's work. It is no wonder that lately her work has been inspired directly by research on poetry; it is also no wonder that in two important moments in her career, Mantero turned down prestigious (and well-funded) commissions after she realized a few weeks into rehearsals that the work was not being honest, not arriving at a place of truth, nor that she had something clear to say at that time.

In her most recent group pieces, *The Fall of an Ego* (1997), *Poetry and Savagery* (1999), *A Being Here Full* (2001), we find a staging apparently closer to a more familiar theatrics than the one found in the works of Bel, La Ribot, or Le Roy. How, then, can one identify in Mantero's group pieces the moving away from theatrical dance towards a performative dance? I would say that this moving appears in these group works as a move away from representation and towards presence. What is absolutely extraordinary in Mantero's group work is how these pieces take as their starting point a plateau of being that immediately proposes a scenic state beyond any recognizable parameter. Mantero throws her audience and her performers immediately and without pity into a place where all is vividly potentially possible and potentially impossible. Objects, colors, wigs, machines, paint, words, inaction, sounds, symbols, voice, organs, plastic, nature, electronics, poetry, bodies, personalities are all thrown into such a state of upheaval that they literally become filled with a paradoxical tension: everything hovers between familiarity and the proper name, the unfamiliar and the nameless, form and formlessness. All that remains is a sort of state of recognition, the ground and duration – both invariably littered by the debris of existing. In her most recent work at the time of writing,[5] the set is entirely surrounded by breathing walls: soft surfaces that expand and contract rhythmically for the entire duration of the piece. This breathing motion of a surface that should remain hard and still subverts the dialectics of inside and outside (is the stage architecture or organ?) while at the same time reinforces the question of theatre as the riddle of presence. In this sense, Mantero's work distinguishes itself from explicit influences from minimal and conceptual art – but it certainly participates of the ethical and performative emphasis on the need to throw representation into a state of absolute crisis.

As contemporary European dance treads the wavering, plundered ground of choreography, one could then say that its major mode of operation is the one of reduction. A reduction of the expansive, of the spectacular, of the unessential – which is essentially a minimalist trait explored by Rainer and articulated in her essay "A Quasi Survey of Some 'Minimalist' Tendencies in the Quantitatively Minimal Dance Activity Midst the Plethora, or an Analysis of *Trio A*" (Rainer 1968). There is also an emphasis on the body in itself, in its bareness, in its superficial strength, in its massively complicated presence – which is an emphasis typical of Bausch's work. The collapsing of both is not a question of addition; for what one finds today is a distillation: the end result looks more like a subtraction. And what is being subtracted by the proposals from the European choreographers that concern this essay is the word "dance". Such displacing of what has been, until recently, unproblematically called "choreographing" can be considered as the result of an increasing contamination of dance by some of the main characteristics of performance art: the insistence on presence.

Notes

1 For a discussion of modernist ideology in modern and post-modern American dance see Manning 1988.

2 The opening sequence of Pina Bausch's film *The Lament of the Empress,* with a solitary woman dressed as a playboy bunny and stumbling across a field of mud on high heels, could be seen as an allegory of this ground which contemporary dance now negotiates. There is no striated linoleum set geometrically in a flat horizontal space.

3 See Manifesto for a European Performance Policy, http://www.meeting-one.info/manifesto.htm.

4 This "discovery" of the essence of dance as movement by modern dance shows how fragile is dance's relationship to what supposedly is its reason for being. John Martin in his classic *The Modern Dance* tells us of this discovery. The consequences are immediately apparent as well. Movement is what allows dance to withdraw itself within the walls of modernism: "This beginning [of modern dance] was the discovery of the actual substance of the dance, which it found to be movement . . . With this discovery the dance became for the first time an independent art . . . completely self-contained . . ." (Martin [1933] 1979: 6).

5 This work, premiered in June 2002, has as title the phonetic transcription of a few stanzas of a poem by Portuguese poet Ruy Belo. Mantero refuses to transcribe the title in cursive, thus prompting the spectator to an exercise of attention and experimentation with tongue, vocal cords, and air. I give you the translation of what I think the title of her piece might be: "What is the support that separates/and contains the two/worlds and undulates."

Bibliography

Banes, S. (1987) *Terpsichore in Sneakers*, Hanover: Wesleyan University Press.

Bentivoglio, L. (1994) *O Teatro de Pina Bausch*, Lisboa: Acarte, Fundação Gulbenkian.

De Belder, S. and Tachelet, K. (eds) (2001) *The Salt of the Earth. On Dance, Politics and Reality*, Brussels: Vlaams Theater Instituut.

Gil, J. (1996) *A Imagem Nua e as Pequenas Percepções*, Lisboa: Relógio d'Água.

Godfrey, T. (1998) *Conceptual Art*, London: Phaidon.

Lepecki, A. (1999) "Skin, Body and Presence in Contemporary European Choreography", *The Drama Review*, 164: 129–40.

Manning, S. (1988) "Modernist dogma and post-modern rhetoric, *The Drama Review*, 120: 32–9.

Martin, J. ([1933] 1979) *The Modern Dance*, New York, NY: Dance Horizons.

Phelan, P. (1993) *Unmarked: The Politics of Performance*, London and New York, NY: Routledge.

Ploebst, Helmut (2001) *No Wind No Word. New Choreography in the Society of the Spectacle*, K. Kaiser Verlag.

Rainer, Y. (1968) "A Quasi Survey of Some 'Minimalist' Tendencies in the Quantitatively Minimal Dance Activity Midst the Plethora, or an Analysis of *Trio A*", in G. Battcock (ed.) *Minimal Art*, New York, NY: E. P. Dutton.

Salazar-Conde, J. (2002) "On the ground", *Ballett International*, October: 60–3.

Smeets, Gabriel (2002) "Why all these questions?", The Mouson-Springdance/dialogue, Amsterdam: Theater Instituut Nederlands.

Index

Titles are given in italics, n indicates a reference to a note